A+ Exam Notes™: Core Module

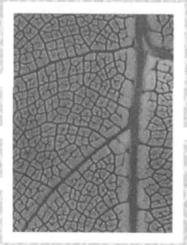

David Groth
Michael Jones

San Francisco • Paris • Düsseldorf • Soest

Associate Publisher: Guy Hart-Davis
Contracts and Licensing Manager: Kristine Plachy
Acquisitions & Developmental Editor: Neil Edde
Editor: Suzanne Goraj
Project Editor: Dann McDorman
Technical Editor: Jon Hansen
Book Designer: Bill Gibson
Graphic Illustrator: Tony Jonick
Electronic Publishing Specialist: Bill Gibson
Production Coordinator: Rebecca Rider
Indexer: Matthew Spence
Cover Designer: Design Site
Cover Illustrator/Photographer: Jack D. Myers

Screen reproductions produced with Collage Complete.

Collage Complete is a trademark of Inner Media Inc.

SYBEX is a registered trademark of SYBEX Inc.

Exam Notes is a trademark of SYBEX Inc.

TRADEMARKS: SYBEX has attempted throughout this book to distinguish proprietary trademarks from descriptive terms by following the capitalization style used by the manufacturer.

The author and publisher have made their best efforts to prepare this book, and the content is based upon final release software whenever possible. Portions of the manuscript may be based upon pre-release versions supplied by software manufacturer(s). The author and the publisher make no representation or warranties of any kind with regard to the completeness or accuracy of the contents herein and accept no liability of any kind including but not limited to performance, merchantability, fitness for any particular purpose, or any losses or damages of any kind caused or alleged to be caused directly or indirectly from this book.

Library of Congress Card Number: 98-86615
ISBN: 0-7821-2345-7

Manufactured in the United States of America

10 9 8 7 6 5 4 3 2

To Yeshua, who made it happen.

Acknowledgments

To my wife, Deborah, who worked the hardest on this joint venture: Deborah, your contributions to this book came in the form of love, support, and sacrifice. I love you!

The next mention goes to David Groth, who authored the *A+: Core Module Study Guide*, and his contributing writers, Christel Fritz and Patti Heisler. They have been my primary resource. Thanks, David and company.

Carl Harris, O friend and guru of computerdom, you gave me some oomph when I was just a Mac guy. I needed that.

Neil Edde, thanks for making that phone call in October of '97. (Can one man make a difference? Neil can.)

Thank you, mom and dad, for your unwavering support (and for watching the girls!).

To my editors, Suzanne Goraj and Jon Hansen: your friendly comments and helpful slash marks remind me of Solomon, who said that wounds from a friend are better than the kiss of an enemy. You both have long futures in this business.

Thanks also to Dann McDorman and the rest of the folks over at Sybex, without whom this book would be a vague idea, at most.

Table of Contents

Introduction

If you've purchased this book, then you must be in pursuit of your A+ certification. This is a great goal, and it is also a great career builder. Glance through any newspaper and you'll find employment opportunities for A+ certified computer professionals—these ads are there because finding qualified employees is a challenge in today's market. The certification means you know something about how computers and computer operating systems work, but more importantly, it means you have the ability, determination, and focus to learn—the greatest skills any employee can have!

What Is A+ Certification?

A+ is a certification program designed to quantify the level of critical thinking skills and general industry knowledge demanded of computer service technicians. It was developed by the Computer Technology Industry Association (CompTIA) to provide an industry-wide recognition of those service technicians who have attained this level of knowledge. A+ is comparable to programs such as Novell's Certified Novell Engineer (CNE), which certifies network professionals who deal with NetWare products, and Microsoft's Microsoft Certified Service Engineer (MCSE), which certifies network professionals who deal with Microsoft products. The theory behind these certifications is that service is best performed on these products by technicians whose knowledge of the products has been thoroughly tested and verified.

The A+ certification program was created to be a wide-ranging certification involving hardware and the most common operating systems (i.e., Windows/DOS). In any case, if any computer hardware or Windows/DOS service is needed, an A+ certified technician should be able to solve the problem.

What Is an AASC?

More service companies are becoming A+ Authorized Service Centers (AASCs). This means that over 50% of the technicians employed by that service center are A+ certified. At the time of the writing of this book, there are over 1,400 A+ Authorized Service Centers in the world. Customers and vendors are recognizing that AASCs employ the most-qualified service technicians. Because of this, an AASC will get more business than a non-authorized service center. And because more service centers want to reach the AASC level, they will give preference when hiring technicians to those who are A+ certified over those who are not.

Is This Book for You?

The A+ Exam Notes books were designed to be succinct, portable exam review guides that can be used either in conjunction with a more complete study program (book, CBT courseware, classroom/lab environment) or as an exam review for those who don't feel the need for more extensive test preparation. It isn't our goal to give the answers away, but rather to identify the topics on which you can expect to be tested and to provide sufficient coverage of those topics.

Perhaps you've been working with computer technologies for years now. The thought of paying lots of money for a specialized A+ exam preparation course probably doesn't sound too appealing. What can they teach you that you don't already know, right? Be careful, though. Many experienced computer professionals have walked confidently into test centers only to walk sheepishly out of them after failing an A+ exam. As they discovered, there are many computer-related technologies that people take for granted in the everyday world; when presented with detailed exam questions on these topics, their everyday knowledge can fail them. After you've finished reading through this book, you should have a clear idea of how your understanding of the technologies involved matches up with the expectations of the A+ test-makers at CompTIA.

Or perhaps you're relatively new to the world of computers, drawn to it by the promise of challenging work and higher salaries. You've just waded through an 800 page A+ study guide or taken a class at a local training center. Lots of information to keep track of, isn't there? Well, by organizing the Exam Notes books according to the official CompTIA A+ exam objectives, and by breaking up the information into concise, manageable pieces, we've created what we think is the handiest exam review guide available. Throw it in your briefcase and carry it to work with you. As you read through the book, you'll be able to quickly identify those areas you know best and those that require more in-depth review.

NOTE   The goal of the Exam Notes series is to help A+ candidates familiarize themselves with the subjects on which they can expect to be tested in the exams. For complete, in-depth coverage of the technologies and topics involved, we recommend the *A+: Core Module Study Guide, 2nd ed.* by David Groth (Sybex, 1998).

How Is This Book Organized?

As mentioned above, this book is organized according to the official exam objectives list prepared by CompTIA for the A+ Core Module exam. The chapters coincide with the broad objectives groupings, such as *Installation, Configuration, and Upgrading* or *Safety and Preventive Maintenance*.

Within each chapter, the individual exam objectives are addressed in turn. And in turn, the objectives sections are further divided according to the type of information presented.

Critical Information
This section presents the greatest level of detail on information that is relevant to the objective. This is the place to start if you're unfamiliar with or uncertain about the technical issues related to the objective.

Necessary Procedures

Here you'll find instructions for procedures that require a lab computer to complete. From installing operating systems to modifying configuration defaults, the information in these sections addresses the hands-on requirements for the A+ exams.

NOTE Not every objective has procedures associated with it. For such objectives, the Necessary Procedures section has been left out.

Exam Essentials

In this section, we've put together a concise list of each subject area's most crucial topics, those that you'll need to fully comprehend prior to taking the A+ exam. This section can help you identify the topics that might require more study on your part.

Key Terms and Concepts

Here we've compiled a mini-glossary of the most important terms and concepts related to the specific objective. You'll understand what all those technical words mean within the context of the related subject matter.

Sample Questions

For each objective, we've included a selection of questions similar to those you'll encounter on the actual A+ exam. Answers and explanations are provided so you can gain some insight into the test-taking process.

How to Get A+ Certified

A+ certification is available to anyone. You don't have to work for any particular company. It's not a secret society. It is, however, an elite group. In order to become A+ certified you must do two things:

- Pass the A+ Certification Core exam.

- Pass the A+ Certification Operating System Specialty exam (DOS/Windows).

These exams are administered by Sylvan Prometric and can be taken at any Sylvan Prometric Testing Center. Once you pass these exams, you will get a certificate in the mail from CompTIA saying that you have passed. To find the Sylvan Prometric training center nearest you, call (800) 755-EXAM (755-3926).

NOTE Sybex also publishes the *A+: DOS/Windows Study Guide, 2nd ed.,* by David Groth (Sybex, 1998), available now at bookstores worldwide.

To register for the tests, call Sylvan at (800) 77-MICRO (776-4276). To register, you must give them your name, social security number, mailing address and phone number, employer (if applicable), and credit card number to charge the test. Let them know on what date and at which Sylvan center you want to be tested.

NOTE For more information on the A+ program, visit the CompTIA Web site at `www.comptia.org`.

Tips for Taking the A+ Exams

Here are some general tips to keep in mind when you go to take your exam:

- Arrive early at the exam center so you can relax and review your study materials, particularly tables and lists of exam-related information.

- Read the questions carefully. Don't be tempted to jump to an early conclusion. Make sure you know *exactly* what the question is asking.

- Don't leave any unanswered questions. Unanswered questions are scored against you.

- When answering multiple-choice questions you're not sure about, use a process of elimination to get rid of the obviously incorrect questions first. This will improve your odds if you need to make an educated guess.

- Because the hard questions will eat up the most time, save them for last. You can move forward and backward through the exam.

How to Contact the Publisher

Sybex welcomes reader feedback on all of their titles. Visit the Sybex Web site at www.sybex.com for book updates and additional certification information. You'll also find online forms to submit comments or suggestions regarding this or any other Sybex book.

CHAPTER

1

Installation, Configuration,
and Upgrading

A+ Core Module Exam Objectives Covered in This Chapter:

▶ Identify basic terms, concepts, and functions of system modules, including how each module should work during normal operation. *(pages 3 – 16)*

▶ Identify basic procedures for adding and removing field replaceable modules. *(pages 17 – 33)*

▶ Identify available IRQs, DMAs, and I/O addresses and procedures for configuring them for device installation. *(pages 33 – 44)*

▶ Identify common peripheral ports, associated cabling, and their connectors. *(pages 44 – 51)*

▶ Identify proper procedures for installing and configuring IDE/EIDE devices. *(pages 51 – 59)*

▶ Identify proper procedures for installing and configuring SCSI devices. *(pages 59 – 68)*

▶ Identify proper procedures for installing and configuring peripheral devices. *(pages 68 – 77)*

▶ Recognize the functions and effective use of common hand tools. *(pages 78 – 86)*

▶ Identify concepts and procedures relating to BIOS. *(pages 86 – 89)*

▶ Identify hardware methods of system optimization and when to use them. *(pages 90 – 102)*

This chapter dissects the personal computer, identifies its various components, and attempts to explain those components as succinctly and precisely as possible. As a doctor must be intimately acquainted with human anatomy, so a computer technician must understand the physical and functional structure of a personal computer.

This chapter is also concerned with the installation and configuration of PC components. A PC is a complex machine. It could be described as a kind of "melting pot" of various technologies and products, manufactured by a host of companies in many different countries. This is a great advantage, and it gives the PC its versatility. However, the components don't always "melt" into a unified whole without the help of a technician. These different products, whether they are hard disks, modems, sound cards, or memory boards, must share one processor and one motherboard, and therefore must be made to work in harmony.

For this reason, configuration of the computer components is especially emphasized on the test, and nearly one-third of the exam questions pertain to the Chapter 1 objectives.

Identify basic terms, concepts, and functions of system modules, including how each module should work during normal operation.

The aim of this objective is simply to identify the primary components of a PC, explain how they function, and describe how they work together with the other parts of the computer. Subjects that are heavily emphasized on the test will be covered in more detail later in this chapter or other chapters of the book.

Critical Information

The system modules described in this section are either essential computer components or available on the market as optional equipment. Each has a distinct and very practical function.

System Board

The spine of the computer is the system board, otherwise known as the *motherboard*. This is the olive green or brown fiberglass sheet that is fixed to the bottom of the computer. Figure 1.1 shows a typical system board, as seen from above. All other computer components are attached to this sheet. On the system board you will find the CPU, underlying circuitry, expansion slots, video components, RAM slots, and a variety of other chips.

FIGURE 1.1: A typical system board

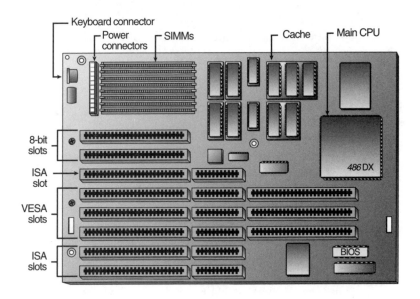

There are two major types of system boards: *integrated* and *non-integrated*.

- **Integrated system boards** are called that because most of the circuitry that would otherwise be installed as an expansion card is integrated into the motherboard circuitry. Although they are cheaper to produce, they are more expensive to repair; when one component breaks, the whole motherboard must be replaced.

- **Non-integrated system boards** have each major assembly installed in the computer as an expansion card. The major assemblies include items like video circuitry, disk controllers, and accessories. These boards are easily identified by the presence of such expansion cards.

Non-integrated system boards come in two forms: AT and ATX. An AT design includes a processor, memory, and expansion slots that are in line with each other. A modification of the AT design in which the components are compressed into a smaller area is called the *"baby" AT* configuration.

The ATX design has the processor and memory slots at right angles to the expansion cards. This puts the processor and memory in line with the fan output, allowing it to run cooler. Where the AT design has space for only one or two full-length expansion cards, all the slots in the ATX design contain space for full-length expansion cards. This results from the repositioned processor and memory slots.

Processor/CPU

The role of the CPU, or central processing unit, is to control and direct all activities of the computer using both external and internal buses.

SEE ALSO   For more information on the internal and external bus, see Chapter 4, "Motherboards/Processors/Memory."

The CPU is a processor chip consisting of an array of *millions* of transistors. CPUs are generally square in shape with transistors arranged in a pin grid array (PGA). Prior to 1981, chips were found in a rectangle with two rows of 20 pins known as a dual inline package (DIP). (See Figure 1.2.) There are still integrated circuits that use the DIP form factor. However, this form factor isn't used for PC CPUs anymore.

SEE ALSO   For detailed information on chips, transistors, and other hardware components, see the *A+ Core Module Study Guide, 2nd ed.* by David Groth (Sybex, 1998).

F I G U R E 1.2: DIP and PGA

DIP (Dual In-line Package)   PGA (Pin Grid Array)

An important measurement of CPU performance is clock speed, which is rated in megahertz (MHz). One megahertz is one million cycles per second. The original 8088 processor was rated at 4.77MHz; a modern Pentium processor may exceed 300MHz.

Memory

As the CPU of a computer processes data, it stores information in the computer's memory. The rule of thumb is, the more memory a computer has, the better it will operate. There are three major types of computer memory: DRAM, SRAM, and ROM.

- **DRAM** is dynamic random-access memory. When you expand memory on a computer, you are adding DRAM chips. Dynamic RAM requires a constant update signal or *refresh* signal to retain information.

- **SRAM** is static random-access memory. SRAM is faster and more expensive than DRAM, and doesn't require the refresh signal that DRAM does. It is often used for cache memory.

- **ROM** stands for read-only memory. It is called read-only because once information has been written to ROM, it can't be changed. ROM is normally used to store the BIOS software. The system ROM enables the computer to "pull itself up by its bootstraps," or "boot" (start the operating system).

Power Supply

The computer's components would not be able to operate without power. The device in the computer that provides this power is the power supply (Figure 1.3). A power supply converts 110-volt AC current into the four voltages that a computer needs to operate. These are +5 volts DC, –5 volts DC (ground), +12 volts DC, and –12 volts DC (ground). By the way, you may frequently see volts DC abbreviated as VDc.

FIGURE 1.3: A power supply

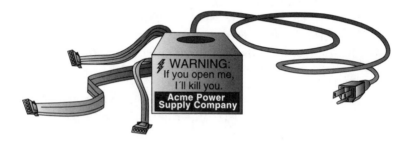

WARNING   Power supplies contain transformers and capacitors that carry LETHAL amounts of current. They are not meant to be serviced. DO NOT attempt to open them or do any work on them.

BIOS

BIOS stands for basic input/output system. The BIOS communicates between the computer and hardware devices. The BIOS is usually stored in ROM. It was created by IBM to act as a translator to run the same operating systems on different hardware platforms. When the operating system needs to access a piece of hardware, it now asks the BIOS, rather than just taking control of the hardware. The use of BIOS prevents programs from fighting over hardware. As long as the operating system uses the BIOS for its hardware requests, operating systems such as DOS can run on different hardware platforms. It creates a standard reference point for many different types of hardware.

CMOS

CMOS is an acronym for complementary metal-oxide semiconductor. It is a special PC memory chip that holds the BIOS configuration settings. CMOS memory is powered by a small battery so that the settings are retained when the computer is shut off. The BIOS will read information like which hard drive types are configured for this computer to use, what drive(s) it should search for boot sectors, and so on. Unlike the BIOS ROM, however, CMOS memory is usually NOT upgradeable.

Interfaces

Computers need ways of getting information in and getting information out. These ways are called *interfaces*. There are two major types of interfaces available on computers today: *parallel* and *serial*. They differ primarily in the speed of transfer and method of connection.

Parallel

The most popular type of interface available on computers today is the parallel interface. The parallel interface transfers data eight bits at a time over eight separate transmit wires inside a parallel cable (one bit per wire). Normal parallel interfaces use a DB-25 female connector on the computer to transfer data to peripherals. The most common use of the parallel interface is printer communication.

Serial

Almost every computer made since the original IBM PC has at least one serial port. They are easily identified because they have either a DB-9 male or DB-25 male port. Standard serial ports have a maximum data transmission speed of 57Kbps and a maximum cable length of 50 feet.

Storage Devices

A computer storage device holds the user data, as well as the files that the system needs in order to operate. The many different types of storage media differ in terms of their capacity (how much they can store), access time (how fast the computer can access the information), and physical type. The test has several questions pertaining to the PC's three major storage mediums, which are hard disk systems, floppy drives, and CD-ROM drives.

Hard Disk Systems

For permanent storage and quick access, a hard disk system is used (Figure 1.4). Hard disks reside inside the computer and can hold more information than other forms of storage. The hard disk system contains three critical components: the controller, the hard disk (hard drive), and the host adapter. The controller controls the drive. It understands how the drive operates and sends signals to the various motors in the disk and receives signals from the sensors inside the drive. The drive is the physical storage medium. Hard disk systems store information on small disks (between three and five inches in diameter) stacked together and placed in an enclosure. Finally, the host adapter is the translator, converting signals from the hard drive and controller to signals the computer can understand. Some hard disk technologies incorporate the controller and drive into one enclosure.

SEE ALSO   You will read more about installing the various hard disk types later in this chapter.

FIGURE 1.4: A hard disk system

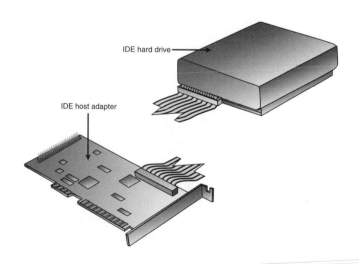

IDE hard drive

IDE host adapter

Floppy Drives

A floppy disk drive is a magnetic storage medium that uses a floppy diskette made of thin plastic encased in a protective casing. The floppy disk itself (or "floppy," as it is often called) enables the information to be transported from one computer to another very easily. The downside of a floppy disk drive is its limited storage capacity. Whereas a hard drive can hold thousands of megabytes of information, most floppy disks were designed to store only in the vicinity of one megabyte. Table 1.1 shows the five different floppy disk drives that you may run into, with five corresponding diskette sizes supported in PC systems. (Note that the drives that offer anything less than 1.2MB are increasingly rare, as most computers today do not carry the 5¼" size.)

T A B L E 1.1: Floppy Diskette Capacities

Floppy Drive Size	Number of Tracks	Capacity
5¼"	40	360KB
5¼"	80	1.2MB
3½"	80	720KB
3½"	80	1.44MB
3½"	80	2.88MB

CD-ROM Drives

CD-ROM stands for compact disk read-only memory. The compact disk is virtually the same as those used in audio CD players. The CD-ROM is used for long-term storage of data. It can hold about the same amount of data as a hard disk system, but CD-ROMs are read-only, meaning that once information is written to a CD, it can't be erased or changed. Also, it takes much longer to access data on a CD than on a hard drive. Why, then, is it so popular? Mainly because it makes a great software distribution medium. Programs are always getting larger and larger, requiring more and more disks to install them. So, instead of installing a program using 100 disks (a real possibility), you can use a single CD—because it can hold approximately 650 megabytes.

Input Devices

The most important input device of any computer system is the keyboard. It is the basic component used to enter information or data to the processor and storage device.

The other important input device is the mouse (or, generically, the *pointer device*, since many people use trackballs or touchpads instead of mice). The mouse changes the position of a pointer on the screen relative to the position of the mouse. It is used to select menu options and other items within graphical user interfaces (GUIs).

Other input devices include digitizing tablets, light pens, and touch screens, but there are no test questions pertaining to these devices, so they will not be covered here.

Output Devices

An output device gives the user a means to receive reports, communications, or the results of calculations. The most common output devices are printers, modems, and of course display systems (monitors). These devices are connected to ports in the back of the computer.

Monitor

Another important tool to use with computer systems is the monitor. A monitor converts computer signals into text and pictures and displays them on a TV-like screen. There are several different types of computer displays in use today, including the TV. All of them use either the same *cathode ray tube* (*CRT*) technology found in television sets (almost every desktop monitor uses this technology) or the *liquid crystal display* (*LCD*) technology found on all laptop and palmtop computers.

Printer

A printer is a device that converts signals from the computer into paper documents. Most printers are electromechanical devices that put either ink or toner on the paper to form the images. There are three main types of printers: dot-matrix, ink-jet, and laser.

Dot-Matrix Printer Dot-matrix printers are the oldest type of printer, as well as the simplest. This type of printer uses an array of pins to strike an inked ribbon, which in turn makes a pattern of dots on the paper. The patterns of dots ultimately form letters and images. The best dot-matrix printers are only "near letter quality" (letter quality is the quality found with a typewriter). Although they are relatively slow and very noisy, dot-matrix printers are easy to use and inexpensive.

Ink-Jet Printer Ink-jet printers spray the ink on the page instead of using an inked ribbon. The major advantages of ink-jet printers are their low cost, increased image quality, and ability to use colored ink and a variety of paper styles and sizes. However, they aren't very fast (though admittedly they are faster than dot-matrix), and the ink cartridges need to be frequently replaced.

Laser Printer The laser printer is the most sophisticated type of printer. A laser printer uses lasers, electric charges, and toner (a black carbon substance similar to the lead in a pencil) to create images on paper. Laser printers have the highest image quality and speed when compared to dot-matrix and ink-jet printers. Laser printers are the most expensive to purchase, and their consumables (like toner) are also more expensive than those used by other types of printers.

SEE ALSO For more information on printers, see Chapter 5.

Modem

Modems (MOdulator/DEModulators) are the devices that computers use to talk to one another over phone lines. They can be considered a type of output device because they move data out of the computer to another device. Modems work by converting digital signals (binary 1s and 0s) into analog signals (tones over a phone line), and vice versa. Modems are added to a computer either as an external device or as an expansion card installed inside the computer. Internal modems are usually less expensive than external modems, but external modems are easier to troubleshoot than internal modems because you can see the lights that indicate what is happening.

Exam Essentials

To understand the context of many of the test questions, you will need to know how the various components of a PC function as a whole. The exam essentials presented below reflect this emphasis.

Understand the purpose of the system board and its relationship to other components of the PC.   The system board (motherboard) is the backbone of the computer, to which all other components are attached.

Understand the function of the processor/CPU.   The processor is the heart of the computer; it performs critical computations and controls the internal functions of a PC.

Understand the purpose of the power supply.   The power supply converts 110 AC volts into the four voltages a PC needs to operate: +5 VDc, -5 VDc, +12 VDc, and -12 VDc.

Understand the differences between the three major types of memory.   Dynamic random-access memory (DRAM) is used for the main memory and requires a refresh signal to maintain its contents. Static random-access memory (SRAM) is often used for cache memory and does not require a refresh signal. Read-only memory (ROM) is non-programmable memory, used for permanent storage of information.

Understand the function of the different types of storage devices. A hard disk drive is the main storage device of a PC, and can store hundreds of megabytes of data. A floppy disk drive typically holds transportable disks of 1.44MB. A CD-ROM drive, though slow, is a high-capacity drive for transportable CD-ROMs, which have a data capacity of about 650MB.

Understand the function of the input/output devices. Input devices include the keyboard and mouse. Output devices include the monitor, printer, and modem. See the Critical Information section for more information.

Understand the two interfaces. The parallel interface is used primarily for printer connections. The serial interface is commonly used for mice and modems.

Understand the purpose of BIOS. The basic input/output system (BIOS) handles communication between the hardware devices in a PC. It also runs the power-on self test (POST), which tests PC hardware, every time you boot your computer.

Understand the purpose of CMOS. CMOS is a programmable memory chip that stores information for the BIOS regarding current hard disk drive configuration. This permits the computer to enter the boot phase and load the operating system.

Key Terms and Concepts

BIOS: Acronym for basic input/output system. In the PC, a set of instructions, stored in read-only memory (ROM), that prevents programs from contesting control of hardware.

Bus: An electronic pathway along which signals are sent from one part of a computer to another.

Cathode ray tube: Abbreviated CRT. A display device used in monitors and television sets. It consists of a glass vacuum tube that contains three electron guns (red, green, and blue) in a color display. Electron beams from these guns sweep rapidly across the inside of the CRT screen at a rate of between 43 and 87 times per second.

CD-ROM drive: A disk device that uses compact disk technology for information storage.

CMOS: A type of circuit used in the PC to store operating parameters, such as hard disk type, when the computer is shut off.

CPU: Acronym for centralized processing unit. A chip that controls and directs all the activities of the computer using both external and internal buses.

Floppy disk drive: A device used to read and write data to and from a floppy disk.

Gigabyte: Abbreviated GB. Usually 1,073,741,824 binary digits or bits of data.

GUI: Acronym for graphical user interface. A GUI is a user interface that allows users to select files, programs, or commands by pointing to a pictorial representation on the screen.

Hard disk drive: A storage device that uses a set of rotating, magnetically coated disks called platters to store data or programs.

Host adapter: A device that translates signals from the hard drive and controller into signals the computer bus can understand.

Kilobyte: Abbreviated KB. Usually 1,024 binary digits or bits of data.

Megabyte: Abbreviated MB. Usually 1,048,576 binary digits or bits of data.

Memory: The primary random-access memory installed in the computer.

Modem: Contraction of MOdulator/DEModulator. A device that allows a computer to transmit information over a telephone line.

Monitor: A video output device capable of displaying text and graphics, typically in color.

Mouse: A small movable input device with buttons. Movements of the mouse correspond to the on-screen movements of the mouse cursor or pointer. Pressing one of the buttons initiates an action or operation.

Power supply: The part of the computer that converts the power from a wall outlet into the lower voltages, typically 5 to 12 volts DC, required by the computer.

RAM: Acronym for random-access memory. The main system memory in a computer, used for the operating system, application programs, and data processing.

ROM: Acronym for read-only memory. A semiconductor-based memory system that does not lose its contents when power is switched off.

System board: Also known as the motherboard. The fiberglass sheet to which all other components of the computer are attached.

Transistor: A semiconductor component that acts like a switch, controlling the flow of an electric current.

Sample Questions

1. Which component contains all the circuitry necessary for all components or devices to communicate with each other?

   A. System board

   B. Adapter card

   C. Hard drive

   D. Expansion bus

   Answer: A. Every PC component must be connected directly or indirectly to the system board.

2. Clock speeds are measured in what?

   A. Ohms

   B. Volts

   C. Megahertz

   D. Milliseconds

   Answer: C.

Identify basic procedures for adding and removing field replaceable modules.

The addition and removal of field replaceable modules or units (FRUs) is procedural information, so the Necessary Procedures section contains the bulk of it. Because this information is mandatory for any PC technician, several test questions pertain to the "nuts and bolts" of device removal/installation.

Critical Information

When you choose an area to work on a computer, pick a workspace that is sturdy enough to support the weight of a computer and any peripherals you are adding to your system. The area must also be well lit, clean, and large enough to hold all the pieces and necessary tools.

A few prerequisites are common to the procedures for adding and removing FRUs—things you need to do before you move the computer to your work area. They are as follows:

1. Shut down any running programs and turn the computer off.

2. Remove all cables (*especially the power cable*) that are attached to the computer before you take it apart.

3. Make sure you have a written backup of the CMOS configuration settings, in case you remove or disconnect the battery.

WARNING That second step (removing all cables before disassembling) is at least as important as the first. If you disassemble the computer with it plugged in or turned on, you could get ELECTRO-CUTED! Additionally, components could be damaged if inserted or removed while power is applied.

---

4. Use electrostatic discharge (ESD) precautions. This includes wearing an antistatic wrist wrap.

SEE ALSO For more information on ESD, go to Chapter 3, "Safety and Preventive Maintenance."

---

5. Remove the screws on the back of the case. (Some systems use switch tabs in place of screws.)

6. Remove the case and set it aside.

Be careful to write down a diagram of the installed positions of any cables that you remove, so that they can be correctly reattached. You can also use a pen to make identifying marks on the cables. In addition, you should have some container for screws so they don't get lost (an egg carton works great for this).

TIP When reattaching ribbon connectors, a helpful rule to remember is the "pin 1" rule. One of the edge wires will be a darker color (usually red, possibly blue or brown). This wire needs to be attached to pin 1, which is usually stenciled in on a circuit board. If it's not stenciled in, checking the back of the circuit board will usually reveal a square solder pad behind pin 1. Attach the dark wire here.

Necessary Procedures

The Critical Information section contains important information that is preparatory for all of the following procedures.

Removing an Expansion Card

Expansion cards or *adapter cards* are circuit boards that fit into the bus slots at the back of a computer. Network cards, hard disk controllers, sound cards, internal modems, and video adapters are examples of expansion cards.

There are four major steps in removing expansion cards; they need to be followed in this order for it to be done correctly:

1. Shut off the power, use ESD precautions, and remove the case.

2. Remove any internal or external cables or connectors.

3. Remove any mounting screws that are holding the boards in place.

4. Grasp the board by the top edge with both hands and *gently* rock it front to back (*NOT* side to side). Figure 1.5 clarifies this procedure. If the expansion board doesn't come out easily, don't force it. You may damage it. Check to see that the board is not being obstructed.

5. Finally, once the board is out, place it in an antistatic bag to help prevent ESD damage while the board is out of the computer.

F I G U R E 1.5: Removing an expansion card

1. Remove any connectors (diagramming them first).
2. Remove the board's mounting screw.
3. Grasp the board along its top edge and rock it *gently* up and out.
4. Once the board is out of its slot, avoid touching the edge connector.

Rock gently front to back (not side to side)

Motherboard

Adding an Expansion Card

Mounting an expansion card means installing an expansion card into an expansion slot and securing it with a screw. Most expansion cards can be inserted in the same way.

1. Shut off the power, use ESD precautions, and remove the case.

2. If you are installing a new board, you must configure the board for installation.

SEE ALSO For more information on configuring a new expansion card, see the next section of this chapter, titled "Identify available IRQs, DMAs, and I/O addresses and procedures for configuring them for device installation."

---

3. Second, if the place you are installing the device has a *blank* (a piece of plastic or metal that covers the slot opening where the device is going to go), remove it.

4. Next, align the connector on the bottom of the card with the connector on the motherboard, and insert the card into its connector. You should feel a slight amount of resistance. Push the card firmly into place with an even pressure on the front and back of the card. Stop pushing when all of the card's connectors are making contact with the "fingers" in the expansion slot.

5. If it is a new expansion card, you must install the necessary software drivers.

Removing a Disk Drive

Most disk drives are installed in IBM-compatible computers with rails that are attached to the drives with screws. These rails allow the drive to be slid into the computer's drive bays like a drawer. To remove the drive, take the following steps:

1. Shut off the power, use ESD precautions, and remove the case.

2. Disconnect the power connector and the data connector (a hard disk drive may have two data connectors).

3. Remove the two mounting screws on the side of the drive (see Figure 1.6).

4. Slide out the drive.

FIGURE 1.6: Removing the hard drive

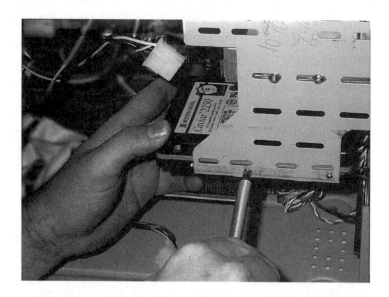

Some computers (like Compaqs, IBM PS/2s, and Hewlett-Packards) use a special drive carrier that holds the drive in place and can be easily removed without tools. Consult the computer's documentation to see exactly how to remove this type of drive.

Adding a Disk Drive

The installation of any fixed disk drive follows basically the same procedure:

1. Shut off the power, use ESD precautions, and remove the case.

2. If you are upgrading your disk drive system (IDE/EIDE or SCSI, for example), you may need to configure and install a new adapter card.

3. If the drive is a new disk drive, you must configure it (this may involve setting jumpers, configuring CMOS, setting SCSI device numbers, etc.).

4. Slide in the drive along the rails.

5. Screw in the mounting screws, at least one on each side.

6. Connect the drive cable to the drive and to the disk adapter (or motherboard if your motherboard has an integrated disk adapter). Remember to orient the cable so that the dark (usually red) wire in the drive cable is positioned towards pin 1.

7. Connect the data cables.

8. If the drive is a SCSI drive, you must terminate both ends of the SCSI bus.

The number of wires on an internal cable will help you know what type of storage device they attach to:

- floppy drives use 34-wire cables

- SCSI devices use 50-wire cables

- IDE/EIDE drives use 40-wire cables

SEE ALSO For more information on installing disk drives, see the two sections of this chapter on IDE/EIDE and SCSI drives.

WARNING A common technician's trick to remember how to connect floppy drives is to say "Point the red stripe towards the power cable." The problem is that this trick doesn't work with every brand of floppy drive. It could be considered a general "rule of thumb," but not a "rule to live by."

Removing the Power Supply

To remove the power supply, take the following steps:

1. Shut off the power, use ESD precautions, and remove the case.

2. Disconnect the power supply connectors from the internal devices. Grasp one connector at a time and wiggle it out of its receptacle. The system board and disk drives both use power connectors. Make sure all of them are removed, including (if they exist) the

cable and connector that run to a power switch at the front of the case. Figure 1.7 shows the Molex, Berg, and P8 and P9 power supply connectors.

FIGURE 1.7: Power supply connectors

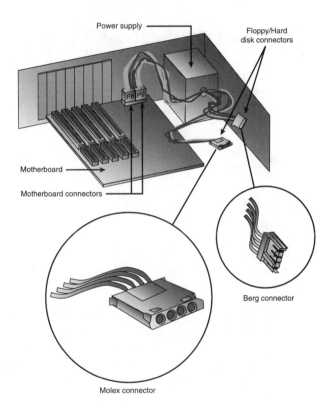

3. Remove the mounting hardware for the power supply. In most PCs, you can detach the power supply from the case by removing four screws (see Figure 1.8).

Some power supplies don't need to have screws removed; instead, they are installed on tracks or into slots in the case and only need to be slid out or lifted out.

F I G U R E 1.8: Removing power supply screws

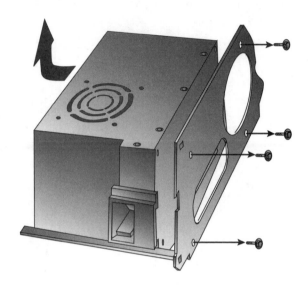

Adding the Power Supply

1. Seat the power supply in its case and install the four mounting screws (if necessary).

2. Connect the power connectors to each component (including the disk drives and motherboard) and make sure they are secure. When connecting the connectors labeled P8 and P9 to the motherboard, position the connectors at a backward tilt as shown in Figure 1.9, and then slip them down into position. This will allow them to slide past the locking tabs.

3. Connect the power switch connector to the power supply.

Removing the Processor/CPU

The processor chip comes in a square package, either a pin grid array (PGA) or a plastic leadless chip carrier (PLCC). PGA and PLCC extractors are designed to remove the two respective types of processors. The extractor can also be used for reinsertion of the component. You should not remove the CPU unless it needs to be replaced or upgraded.

F I G U R E 1.9: Connecting power supply connectors P8 and P9

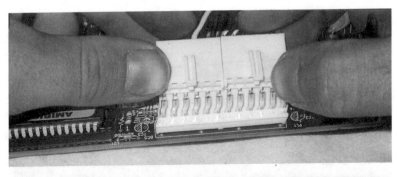

NOTE You can tell the difference between a PGA and a PLCC package by noting the arrangement of the pins. The two square sets of pins on a PGA are beneath it, while the pins on a PLCC protrude outward from its side and bend downward.

PGA packages are the most common, and they are fitted into two kinds of sockets: zero-insertion force (ZIF) or low-insertion force (LIF) sockets. ZIF sockets have a side lever or retaining bar holding the CPU in place, and are extremely simple to use. LIF sockets, on the other hand, are more complicated and require an extraction tool.

1. Shut off the power, take ESD precautions, and remove the case.

2. Take notes on how the processor is aligned in its socket. Usually one corner of the CPU will be notched. Write down which corner has the notch.

3. If the processor is in a ZIF socket, pull the retaining bar out of the way. (A screw holds the retaining bar in place.) Remove the processor.

4. If the processor is in a LIF socket, use the extractor tool to slowly work it out of its socket. Be careful not to dislodge the socket from the motherboard.

Some processors are surface-mounted, meaning they are soldered in. Do not try to remove a surface-mounted processor.

Adding a Processor/CPU

The most common type of processor upgrade is to replace an original CPU with an overdrive chip. You must be sure the new chip will fit into the motherboard's socket type.

SEE ALSO For more information on overdrive chips and sockets, see Chapter 4, "Motherboard/Processors/Memory."

---

1. Shut off the power, take ESD precautions, and remove the case.

2. Align the new chip correctly for placement. If the original chip had a notch in the corner, make sure the replacement chip is aligned so its notch also faces the same direction (e.g., front-right, front-left, etc.).

3. If the processor is going into a ZIF socket, simply set the chip in place, make sure the pin connections are correct, and pull down the retainer bar. Screw the retainer bar in place.

4. If the processor is going into a LIF socket, position the chip so the pins are properly aligned. Work the chip very slowly into its socket using the extractor tool. Use a firm, even pressure; do not force the chip or you may break its pins.

5. Attach a new heat sink/fan to the processor if necessary. The heat sink may be a separate component that attaches to the CPU using an adhesive back.

Removing SIMMs and DIMMs

Single inline memory modules (SIMMs) are small circuit boards that fit into parallel slots on the motherboard. A dual inline memory module (DIMM) looks like a SIMM, except it has memory chips on both sides of the circuit board.

1. Shut off the power, use ESD precautions, and remove the case.

2. Use your fingernails or a small screwdriver to *gently* push out the small tabs that hold the SIMM in place.

3. Rotate the SIMM forward. It will loosen up for easy removal.

Adding SIMMs and DIMMs

When purchasing new RAM memory for a computer, check to see whether the memory slots are 30-pin or 72-pin slots, and buy the appropriate type of memory boards (see Figure 1.10).

F I G U R E 1.10: Single inline memory modules (SIMMs)

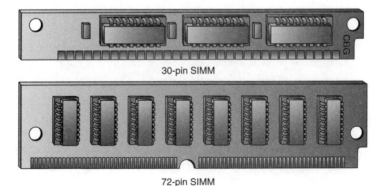

30-pin SIMM

72-pin SIMM

Most memory chips are 32-bit, and this is fine if you have a 32-bit processor. However, if you have a 64-bit processor (such as a Pentium) you must install SIMMs in pairs or change to a 64-bit DIMM installation.

1. Shut off the power, use ESD precautions, and remove the case.

2. Place the SIMM in the socket at a forward angle.

3. Push the SIMM into place. As the SIMM touches the tabs, apply a small outward pressure on the tabs to help the SIMM fit into its correct position.

4. If the SIMM does not snap into position, remove it and start over from step 2.

Removing the System Board (Motherboard)

The only time the system board should need to be removed is when it needs to be upgraded or replaced. Otherwise, you should leave the motherboard in the PC's case to prevent either physical or ESD damage.

The motherboard is held away from the metal case using plastic spacers and is secured and grounded using mounting screws. To remove the motherboard:

1. Shut off the power, use ESD precautions, and remove the case.

2. Remove all expansion cards.

3. Remove all connectors attached to the power supply, reset switch, and turbo button (if present).

4. Remove the screws holding the motherboard to the mounting brackets.

5. Slide the motherboard to the side to release the spacers from their mounting holes in the case (see Figure 1.11).

FIGURE 1.11: Removing the motherboard

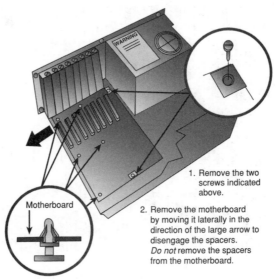

1. Remove the two screws indicated above.

2. Remove the motherboard by moving it laterally in the direction of the large arrow to disengage the spacers. *Do not* remove the spacers from the motherboard.

Motherboard

There are five spacers holding the motherboard off the case. A spacer is shown above, viewed from its side.

Adding the System Board

To install the system board, reverse the removal steps previously described. This involves positioning the board in the case and securing it with either screws or plastic circuit board fasteners.

Once the motherboard is secured in the case, you must connect the individual connectors that run to things like the reset switch and the turbo button (if present). Figure 1.12 details this step.

FIGURE 1.12: Reconnecting the cables

Removing Input/Output Devices

The input/output devices (monitor, keyboard, mouse, printer, modem, and other peripherals) are attached to the computer with cables that can be easily detached and reattached. Procedures for removing an input/output device are as follows:

1. Shut off the computer.

2. Shut off the device to be removed if it has an independent power source.

3. Remove the connecting cable.

Adding Input/Output Devices

1. Shut off the computer.

2. Attach the power cable to a power source (if necessary).

3. Attach the connecting cable.

4. Turn on the computer and its peripherals. (The computer will not boot unless the keyboard is already plugged in.)

SEE ALSO Detailed information on the port connections and cables is found later in this chapter.

NOTE Mice will either plug into an expansion card, the serial port, or a PS/2 mouse interface that is hardwired to the motherboard.

Exam Essentials

The emphasis on the test may be surprising in that it focuses on (apparently) minor details more than generic procedures for adding/removal FRUs. The following exam essentials reflect this.

Know what preparations to take before removing components from your computer. Preparations include recording CMOS settings, shutting off the power, removing the power cord, and taking ESD precautions such as using an antistatic wrist wrap.

Know how to recognize the internal cables of a PC. P8 and P9 connectors are used to power the motherboard. Ribbon cables with a varying number of wires are used to connect the disk drives. Berg and Molex connectors are used to provide power to the disk drives.

Understand the significance of pin connections. Pin 1 must be placed correctly when reconnecting cables to adapter cards or other devices. Often, this is made simple because the cables are designed to only fit one way. However, if this is not the case, match the red edge wire to pin 1.

Understand the basic procedures for installation of each FRU. See the Critical Information section for information specific to each component.

Key Terms and Concepts

Antistatic wrist wrap: A specially constructed strap worn as a preventive measure to guard against the damages of electrostatic discharge (ESD).

DIMM: Acronym for dual inline memory module. A memory module with memory chips on both sides of the circuit board.

ESD: Acronym for electrostatic discharge. The exchange of electrons that occurs when two objects of dissimilar charge come in contact with one another. It can be damaging to electronic components.

IDE: Acronym for integrated drive electronics. A hard disk technology with an integrated drive and controller card.

PGA: A type of integrated circuit (IC) chip that consists of pins connected in a square, flat package.

SCSI: Acronym for small computer system interface. A high-speed, system-level parallel interface used to connect a personal computer to several peripheral devices using just one port.

SIMM: Acronym for single inline memory module. A memory module with memory chips on one side of the circuit board. Primarily used for RAM memory on a PC.

Sample Questions

1. What device uses a 34-wire internal ribbon cable?

A. Floppy drive

B. SCSI device

C. IDE drive

D. EIDE drive

Answer: A. Floppy drives use a 34-wire cable, SCSI drives use a 50-wire cable, and IDE/EIDE drives use a 40-wire cable.

2. Before removing the computer case, you should:

    A. Record monitor settings.

    B. Disconnect the network cable.

    C. Shut down the computer.

    D. Disconnect the monitor.

Answer: C. You should never remove the case while the computer is running.

Identify available IRQs, DMAs, and I/O addresses and procedures for configuring them for device installation.

Interrupt request lines, direct memory access channels, and input/output addresses are configurable aspects of the communication between the devices inside a PC. Interrupt request lines or *IRQs* are used to signal that an event has taken place that requires the attention of the CPU. Input/output addresses or *I/O addresses* refer to the hardware communication lines that carry data between the CPU and the bus slots of the PC. Direct memory access channels or *DMA channels* allow a storage device or adapter card to send information directly into memory without passing through the CPU, which results in a faster data transfer rate.

Whenever a new component such as an internal modem or sound card is installed in a PC, its IRQs, I/O addresses, and DMA channels must be correctly configured, or the device will not function correctly. It is the most common problem when installing new circuit boards. For this reason, the test will include several questions pertaining to the determination and configuration of these resources.

Critical Information

At some point, every computer will require the installation of a new component, whether it's a new sound card, a memory upgrade, or the replacement of a failed device. If the component (typically an expansion card) requires an I/O address, an IRQ, or a DMA channel, a few general steps should be taken:

1. Determine available resources.

2. Configure the new component.

3. Install the component.

4. Install the software drivers.

5. Test the component.

Step 1: Determine Available Resources

If this is the first time a component has been installed in a given computer, you must determine if there are any available resources such as IRQs, DMA channels, and I/O addresses. Do not assign currently used resources to new components; it will result in hardware conflicts and often renders devices non-functional.

One way to determine available IRQs, DMA channels, and I/O addresses is to use a hardware configuration discovery utility. This type of program communicates with the PC's BIOS and hardware, and will display which IRQs, DMA channels, and I/O addresses are being used. The utility included with MS-DOS for this purpose is called the Microsoft Diagnostics (MSD or MSD.EXE). A Windows 95 computer displays available resources in the System properties sheets.

NOTE In addition to determining the configurations of these resources, there is also the obvious requirement for physical space— that is, in order to install a hard disk there must be an open disk bay; in order to install a PCI card, there must be an open PCI slot.

Interrupt Request Lines

PCs have 16 interrupts available. Common uses for these interrupts are shown in Table 1.2. When determining which interrupt to use, you must pick one that is not in use or it will create conflicts.

T A B L E 1.2: Common uses for IRQs in a PC

IRQ	Device	Notes
0	Timer	
1	Keyboard	
2	Wired to IRQ 9	Avoid this interrupt; usually used to enable interrupts 9-15
3	COM2	Can also be used for COM4
4	COM1	Can also be used for COM3
5	Available	Usually free unless configured for LPT2; often used for sound cards and network cards
6	Floppy disk controller	
7	LPT1	
8	Clock	
9	Wired to IRQ 2	Avoid this interrupt
10	Unused	Usually free
11	Unused	Usually free
12	Motherboard InPort	Used for built-in mouse port
13	Coprocessor	
14	Hard disk controller	
15	Unused	Usually free

Input/Output Addresses

Table 1.3 shows a list of some of the common memory addresses for different devices. The CPU needs a memory address to communicate with any peripheral device. The address ranges are in hexadecimal, a "base 16" numbering system (decimal is a base 10 system). In hexadecimal, after the numbers 0–9, A–F are used to represent numbers 10-15.

T A B L E 1.3: Common I/O Address

Address (Hex)	Component
00–0F	DMA Controller
20–21	Interrupt Controller
40–43	Timer
1F0–1F8	Hard disk controller
200–20F	Joystick controller
238–23B	Bus mouse
278–27F	LPT2
2E8–2EF	COM4 serial port
2F8–2FF	COM2 serial port
300–30F	Ethernet card
330–33F	MIDI port
378–37F	LPT1 port
3E8–3EF	COM3 serial port
3F0–3F7	Floppy disk controller
3F8–3FF	COM1 serial port

Direct Memory Access Channels

There are eight DMA channels on most PCs. They are used to transport blocks of data directly from RAM without passing through (and tying up) the CPU. Disk controllers, sound cards, and network cards may require a DMA channel.

Channels 4–7 are generally available. Channel 0 is used to refresh DRAM. Channel 1 is often used by the hard disk controller or a sound card. Channel 2 is usually the floppy disk controller.

TIP   In modern PCs, you can sometimes obtain faster data transfer rates by NOT using DMA. DMA is often slow because of the need to maintain backward compatibility with earlier PCs. Check your documentation to see if DMA can be disabled, then experiment.

Step 2: Configure the New Component

There are two essential steps in the configuration process:

1. Reading the instructions.

2. Setting the configuration of the component.

Reading the Instructions

When reading the instructions for a component, you should find out which IRQs, DMA channels, and I/O addresses a component will support. The key is to match a supported IRQ, DMA channel, or I/O address to an available resource on the PC.

The instructions for a component usually have diagrams that show where jumpers and DIP (dual inline package) switches, if present, are located. Jumpers and DIP switches have physical positions or *settings* that correspond to specific interrupts or memory addresses.

Jumpers consist of a row of pins and a small plastic cap with metal inserts. The cap can be moved by the user to cover different pairs of pins. The cap completes a circuit between those two pins, thus selecting one of the possible configuration options for that device.

DIP switches are very small rocker or sliding-type switches. Small imprinted numbers usually indicate the *on* position. Some DIP switches are marked by a "0" to indicate the *off* position. Different configuration options are selected depending on which switches are turned on.

Setting the Configuration

Setting the configuration of a component involves moving jumpers, moving DIP switches, running a software setup program, or allowing automatic configuration to take place via Plug-and-Play technology.

An example of a sound card I/O configuration table is shown in Table 1.4. In this example, Jumper J2 has five pairs of pins.

TABLE 1.4: Sample I/O Address Settings

I/O Address	Jumper these pins on jumper J2
220h (default)	1
240h	2
260h	3
280h	4
300h	5

If you knew that I/O address 220h is available on the PC, you would jumper pin 1 on jumper J2.

If the component you are installing is an identical replacement part, simply set the jumpers or DIP switches the same way as they were on the component you removed.

Most expansion cards, however, do not use DIP switches or jumpers, but use a software setup program instead. When you run the program, it will present menu choices for setting its IRQ, DMA channel, and I/O address.

An automatic configuration method is employed with Plug-and-Play technology. Plug-and-Play computers will automatically configure components using a special BIOS that checks the configuration of each expansion card at startup. If a change has occurred, the system will detect the change, and configure the card to the correct settings.

NOTE   The Plug-and-Play technology often doesn't work, and the BIOS will choose conflicting settings. This problem is exacerbated in that Plug-and-Play expansion cards cannot be manually configured. In cases of resource conflicts, the best solution is to free up the resources that the Plug-and-Play component is attempting to use. Experimentation may be necessary to determine these resources.

Step 3: Install the Component

Now that the component is configured, you can finally mount the device into the computer. Mounting the device usually means attaching it to the computer's case with some kind of fastener and attaching the device to an interface.

WARNING   Make sure the power is off and the power cord disconnected before installing any computer component. This will prevent possible electrocution and possible damage to the computer!

SEE ALSO   For more information on installing components, go to the section in this chapter titled "Identify basic procedures for adding and removing field replaceable modules."

Step 4: Install the Software Drivers

After the component is installed, you must install the software drivers so the operating system can communicate with its new hardware.

(This software will probably be on floppy disks in a white envelope.) Utility software, which allows the user to interact with the device, is also usually installed at this time.

Step 5: Test the Component

The component should be tested after installation. The simplest method of testing is through observation; does it do what it has been designed to do? If you installed a sound card, can you hear sounds when you play video games?

The other method of testing components is to run diagnostics that may have come with the device. These simple programs usually give their results in the form of pass/fail. If there are problems with the component, the diagnostics will report a test result of "fail."

SEE ALSO For more information on diagnostics, see Chapter 2, "Diagnosing and Troubleshooting."

Necessary Procedures

The procedures for this exam objective summarize the steps to be taken to configure and install new components (as detailed in the Critical Information section) and describe how to install device drivers for the components.

Configuring and Installing a New Component

1. Determine available resources (IRQs, DMA channels, I/O addresses).

2. Configure the new component.

3. Install the component.

4. Install the software drivers.

5. Test the component.

Installing Software Drivers in MS-DOS

The drivers for a new component are installed as follows:

1. Type **A:INSTALL** at the DOS prompt. (Sometimes **A:SETUP** is used in place of this command.)

2. Hit Enter.

Installing Software Drivers in Windows 95

The drivers for a Windows 95 computer are installed as follows:

1. Click on Start ➤ Run in the taskbar.

2. Type **A:SETUP** (or **A:INSTALL**) and hit Enter.

Exam Essentials

Because every computer will eventually require new components, the test heavily emphasizes the configuration of these components. These resources must be correctly configured or the component will not function properly.

Know how to identify switch and jumper settings. The documentation that comes with a new component will contain diagrams showing the resources that correspond to specific DIP switch and jumper settings.

Know the common uses for the fifteen IRQs. These IRQs are given in Table 1.2.

Know the common memory addresses for main components. These common memory addresses are given in Table 1.3.

Know which devices require a DMA channel. Sound cards, video cards, network adapter cards, and disk drive controllers are the devices that typically use DMA.

Know how to configure a new computer component. Components are configured with jumpers, DIP switches, software setup programs, or automatically through Plug-and-Play technology.

Understand the function of device drivers. Device drivers are software programs that communicate with and control the device for which they are designed. This can be an expansion card, monitor, keyboard, disk drive, etc.

Key Terms and Concepts

Device driver: A small program that allows a computer to communicate with and control a device, such as a monitor, keyboard, expansion card, or disk drive.

DIP switch: A small switch used to select the operating mode of a device, mounted as a dual inline package.

Direct memory access: Abbreviated DMA. A method of transferring information directly from a mass-storage device or adapter card into memory (or vice versa), without the information passing through the processor.

Input/output address: Abbreviated I/O address. Lines on a bus used to allow the CPU to send instructions to the devices installed on the bus slots.

Interrupt request line: Abbreviated IRQ. A hardware line that carries a signal from a device to the processor. A hardware interrupt signals that an event has taken place requiring the processor's attention.

Jumper: A row of pins and a movable small plastic and metal connector cap that completes a circuit, usually to select one option from a set of user-definable options.

Plug and Play: A standard from Compaq, Microsoft, Intel, and Phoenix that defines automatic techniques designed to make PC configuration simple and straightforward.

Sample Questions

1. What interrupt is used by the keyboard?

 A. 1

 B. 4

 C. 5

 D. 7

 Answer: A.

2. What is the default I/O address for COM2?

 A. 140 hex

 B. 2F8

 C. 3F8

 D. 280

 Answer: B.

3. Which device requires an interrupt?

 A. Master drive

 B. Internal cache

 C. Master controller

 D. Slave controller

 Answer: C. There is only one controller card—the master controller. Disk drives do not require a separate IRQ.

4. Which two items can use a DMA channel?

 A. Sound card and mouse

 B. Mouse and LAN board

 C. LAN board and hard disk drive

 D. Keyboard and hard disk drive

 Answer: C. Devices that move large blocks of data typically require access to a DMA channel. This includes sound cards, LAN boards, disk drives, and video cards.

5. What interrupts are usually available for a mouse and an internal modem?

   A. 2 and 9

   B. 3 and 4

   C. 7 and 10

   D. 5 and 7

   Answer: B. The mouse and an internal modem will require a serial port. Serial ports are named COM1 and COM2, and use IRQ 3 and 4.

Identify common peripheral ports, associated cabling, and their connectors.

T he peripheral ports of a computer are the physical connectors found outside the computer. Cables of various types are designed to plug into these ports and create a connection between the PC and the external devices that may be attached to it.

Because peripheral components need to be upgraded frequently, either to keep pace with technological change or simply to replace broken devices, an in-depth knowledge of the ports and their associated cabling is required on the test.

Critical Information

Numerous types of connectors can be found outside the computer. The most common type, the DB connectors, are typically designated with "DB-*n*," with the letter *n* being replaced by the number of connectors. DB connectors are usually shaped like a trapezoid, as you can see in the various end-on views in the following three-page figure (Figure 1.13A, B, C).

NOTE DB-*n* connectors are also known as D-shell or D-sub connectors. The terms may be used interchangeably.

Another type, the DIN-*n* connectors (again with the *n* being replaced by the number of connectors) are usually circular. DIN connectors are typically used for mice and keyboards.

F I G U R E 1.13A: Common PC connectors

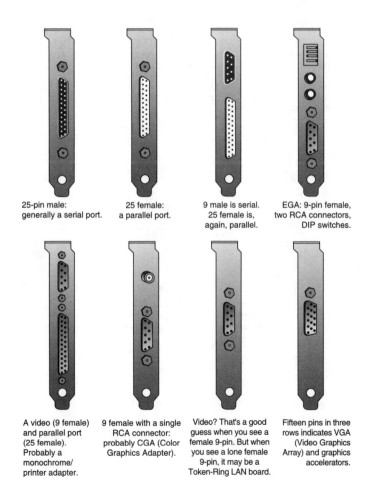

25-pin male: generally a serial port.

25 female: a parallel port.

9 male is serial. 25 female is, again, parallel.

EGA: 9-pin female, two RCA connectors, DIP switches.

A video (9 female) and parallel port (25 female). Probably a monochrome/ printer adapter.

9 female with a single RCA connector: probably CGA (Color Graphics Adapter).

Video? That's a good guess when you see a female 9-pin. But when you see a lone female 9-pin, it may be a Token-Ring LAN board.

Fifteen pins in three rows indicates VGA (Video Graphics Array) and graphics accelerators.

FIGURE 1.13B: Common PC connectors

A BNC connector helps give this away as an Ethernet LAN board. Here, the female 15-pin connector is for Thick Ethernet cable, not games.

A 10baseT Ethernet card has an RJ-45 connector with a few LEDs. Some combination Ethernet boards include BNC and 15-pin connectors, too.

Two RJ-11 phone jacks: an internal modem.

Joysticks and standard Ethernet (Thicknet) use 15-pin connectors. This may be a game card or an Ethernet LAN board.

Not all mice use a 9-pin serial connection; PS/2s use a round 6-pin mouse port.

A round port with nine holes identifies this as a bus mouse interface card.

F I G U R E 1.13C: Common PC connectors

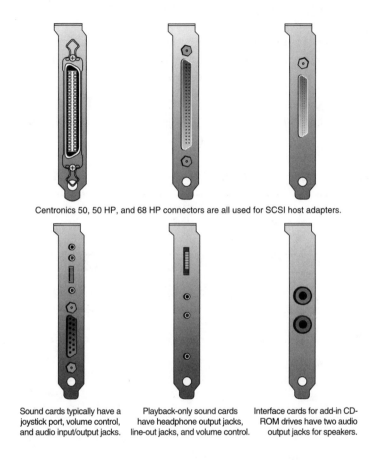

Centronics 50, 50 HP, and 68 HP connectors are all used for SCSI host adapters.

| Sound cards typically have a joystick port, volume control, and audio input/output jacks. | Playback-only sound cards have headphone output jacks, line-out jacks, and volume control. | Interface cards for add-in CD-ROM drives have two audio output jacks for speakers. |

For communications, there is another type, following the RJ-*n* specifications. These connectors are easy to identify—just look at the connectors on your telephone. The connector on the end of the cord that runs from the phone to the wall is an RJ-11 connector. The connector on the end of the cable that runs from your handset to your phone is the smaller, RJ-12 connector. 10baseT Ethernet cables use a larger RJ-45 connector.

The last major types of connectors are the Centronics and HP connectors. The 36-pin Centronics connector is used on your parallel printer cable (one end has a DB-25 connector, the other a 36-pin Centronics connector). SCSI interfaces use either Centronics or HP connectors. HP connectors can be recognized by two matching rows of pins (rather than two or three staggered rows of pins).

Connector identifications are often given with male or female designations—*DB-9 male*, for example. Table 1.5 indicates the common uses of various connectors.

T A B L E 1.5: PC Connectors

Connector	Number of Pins or Sockets	Male or Female	Common Applications
DB-9	9 pins	Male	Serial port
DB-9	9 sockets	Female	EGA/CGA video port (might also be a Token Ring adapter port)
DB-15	15 sockets	Female	If there are three rows of five, it's probably a VGA/SVGA video adapter.
			If it's one row of eight and one row of seven, it might be a network transceiver port or, more commonly, a joystick port.
DB-25	25 pins	Male	Serial port
DB-25	25 sockets	Female	Most often a parallel port. On Macintoshes, however, this type of connector is used for the external SCSI bus.
RJ-11	4 pins	Male	Telephone wall jack phone cord

T A B L E 1.5: PC Connectors *(continued)*

Connector	Number of Pins or Sockets	Male or Female	Common Applications
RJ-12	4 pins	Male	Telephone handset cord
RJ-45	8 pins	Male	10baseT Ethernet cable
Centronics 36	36 pins	Male	Parallel cable
Centronics 50	50 pins	Male	SCSI connector
DIN-6	6 sockets	Female	PS/2 mouse port
DIN-8	8 sockets	Female	Macintosh printer connector
DIN-9	9 sockets	Female	Bus mouse port

Exam Essentials

The test contains several questions on the subject of peripheral port connections. Ports may be shown by a visual representation, and you will be asked to describe what kind of port you're looking at.

Know what DB-*n* connectors look like and what they are used for. DB (or D-sub or D-shell) connectors can be serial or parallel ports, video ports, or VGA/SVGA adapter ports. Male DB ports are serial ports.

Know what RJ-*n* connectors look like and what they are used for. RJ-*n* connectors are used for telephone cords (used by a modem) or Ethernet ports.

Know what Centronics connectors look like and what they are used for. Centronics connectors are used for parallel ports or SCSI devices.

Know what DIN connectors look like and what they are used for. DIN connectors are used for mouse ports and keyboards.

Key Terms and Concepts

DB connector: Any of several types of cable connectors used for parallel or serial cables. The number following the letters DB (for data bus) indicates the number of pins that the connector usually has.

DIN-*n*:   A circular type of connector used with computers. (The *n* represents the number of connectors.)

Parallel port: An input/output port that manages information eight bits at a time, often used to connect a parallel printer.

RJ-11:   A commonly used modular telephone connector used on phone cords.

RJ-45:   A commonly used modular telephone connector used for data transmission over twisted-pair wiring, which can be used for networking.

Serial port: A computer input/output port that supports serial communications, in which information is processed one bit at a time.

Sample Questions

1. A male DB-9 connector indicates what type of port?

   A. Parallel

   B. RJ-11 or RJ-45

   C. Joystick port

   D. Serial

   Answer: D. Nine-pin male DB-9 ports are serial ports.

2. Which type of connector can be recognized by two matching rows of pin connections?

   A. PS/2

   B. HP connector

    C. BNC connector

    D. DIN connector

Answer: B. HP connectors, which are used for SCSI devices, have two matching rows of pins.

3. What type of port has a female DB-15 connector?

    A. VGA graphics port

    B. Serial port

    C. 10baseT network port

    D. Centronics port

Answer: A. Three rows of five pins on a DB-15 connector are usually VGA/SVGA video adapters.

Identify proper procedures for installing and configuring IDE/EIDE devices.

While the heart of a personal computer is the CPU, surrounded by a kind of hardwired system of veins and arteries, the heart of a user is in the data running through the system, contained permanently on its hard disk.

The most popular hard disk types are the Integrated Drive Electronics (IDE) and the Enhanced IDE (EIDE) disk drives. The major feature of an IDE/EIDE system is a controller card located right on the drive itself, using a relatively short cable to connect the drive/controller to the system. This has the benefits of decreasing signal loss (thus increasing reliability) and making the drive easier to install.

In addition, since the controller is integrated into the same assembly as the drive, the only board that needs to be installed in the computer is an adapter that converts signals between the motherboard and the drive/controller. The board is normally called a pass-through or paddle board.

NOTE The paddle board is often, incorrectly, called a controller. This is incorrect because the paddle board is often integrated with a floppy controller, two serial ports, a game port, and a parallel port. (In fact, this combination is normally called a multifunction interface board.) With some of today's systems, the IDE adapter is integrated into the motherboard.

Critical Information

IDE drives, in addition to being relatively simple to install, also can support drives of up to 528MB. Enhanced IDE (EIDE), a new technology developed in the last few years, can support drives of several gigabytes. These newer drives have data transfer rates greater than 10Mbps.

The main limitation to IDE is that it supports only two drives (or four if you're using EIDE). In order to add more drives, you must use a different technology, like SCSI.

Master/Slave Jumpers

One situation that does complicate matters is when you have two or more drives in an IDE/EIDE system. Because an IDE drive has the controller mounted on the drive, you need to establish which controller will be active. You do this by setting the first drive to be the *master* and the others to be *slaves*. The master is the drive whose controller is used by the other drives (the slaves).

The master/slave setting is actually accomplished by jumpering a set of pins. There are several different configurations of these pins, so check your documentation to determine which method your drive uses. Generally, none of the jumpers should be set if there is only one drive in the system.

WARNING If you have two drives in your system and both are set to *master*, or both are set to *slave*, neither drive will work. In the first case (two masters), they will be fighting each other for control of the disks. In the latter case (two slaves), the disks won't know where to get their instructions from.

In addition to setting the master/slave jumper, you may encounter a jumper on older drives that enables logical block addressing (LBA). LBA is used to bypass the 1024-cylinder limit that DOS imposes. In order for a DOS or Windows machine to access a drive above 504MB, LBA must be enabled.

Drive Geometry and CMOS

A hard disk consists of a number of *platters*, stacked together and mounted through their centers on a small rod. Each side of a hard disk platter requires a read/write head to transfer data to and from the disk. Each platter is divided into usable sections called cylinders and sectors, as illustrated in Figure 1.14.

Once you have the cable installed and the drives configured as either master or slave, you must tell the computer that the drives exist and what their drive geometry is. Drive geometry refers to the total number of cylinders, heads, and sectors. The documentation for a drive will show this information.

SEE ALSO For more information on disk drive geometry, see *A+ Core Module Study Guide, 2nd ed.* (Sybex, 1998).

You tell the computer about its disk drive geometry by entering the BIOS's CMOS setup program (or the disk-based BIOS setup program for older computers). This setup program modifies the configuration information for that computer.

FIGURE 1.14: Hard drive geometry

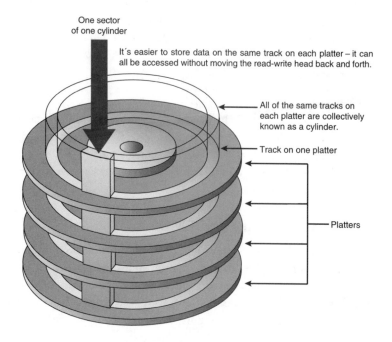

One sector
of one cylinder

It´s easier to store data on the same track on each platter – it can all be accessed without moving the read-write head back and forth.

All of the same tracks on each platter are collectively known as a cylinder.

Track on one platter

Platters

The CMOS setup program is accessed by a special key or key combination at startup. Some BIOSes use Del, Esc, or one of the function keys; others use Ctrl+Alt+Esc. It should be noted that some of the newer BIOSes will auto-detect the type of drive installed in the system and automatically configure these parameters. (This type of system requires only an acceptance of these parameters and a reboot.)

Once you enter the setup program, go to the "Fixed Disk" area and enter the appropriate numbers for the number of cylinders, heads, and sectors that the drives have. You then save these values and reboot the machine. At this point the system should recognize that there is at least one drive in the system.

After it is installed, you can then format the drive. As any drive you purchase is already low-level formatted, you only need to perform a high-level format for the operating system you have chosen. Then, finally, you can install your operating system of choice.

WARNING YOU DO NOT LOW-LEVEL FORMAT IDE (or SCSI) DRIVES. IDE drives are low-level formatted at the factory and should never be redone. The manufacturers use a special utility to perform this delicate procedure. Performing a low-level format on an IDE or SCSI drive will render your drive unreliable, at the least. At the worst, it will make the drive completely useless.

Necessary Procedures

This section translates the preceding Critical Information section into an easy-to-follow step-by-step procedure.

Installing and Configuring One or More IDE/EIDE Devices

1. Configure and install the host adapter.

2. Obtain configuration information for the drive(s).

3. Jumper the drives appropriately for a single drive, or to designate master and slave drives (see Figure 1.15).

4. Install the drive(s).

5. Connect the cables, as illustrated in Figure 1.16.

NOTE If you need a ribbon cable with three connectors (for installing a second drive, as shown in Figure 1.16), you may have to go to your local electronics supplier to find the cable.

6. Configure CMOS to make it "see" the new drive(s).

7. Partition and then format the drive(s).

FIGURE 1.15: Master/slave jumpers

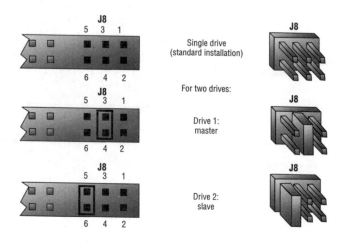

FIGURE 1.16: IDE cable installation

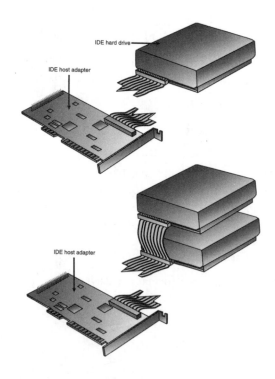

Exam Essentials

As hard disks contain the most valuable part of a computer (the user's data), there are numerous questions on the test about hard disk drives, and several of these pertain to IDE drives.

Know how many devices an IDE/EIDE system can support. An IDE system supports two devices, while an EIDE system can support four devices.

Know the significance of the master/slave designations and how to change them. Master/slave designations must be used in an IDE system with multiple drives. The master drive is the drive whose controller will manage the multiple drives.

Know the purpose of logical block addressing. Logical block addressing (LBA) is used to allow DOS and Windows to use drives over 504MB.

Understand drive geometry. Drive geometry consists of the number of cylinders, heads, and sectors that are on a hard disk. The heads are used for the reading and writing of data. Cylinders and sectors are used by the operating system for disk organization.

Understand the purpose and use of the CMOS setup program. The CMOS setup program is entered by pressing a key or key combination at startup. Within CMOS, the number of cylinders, heads, and sectors can be entered into the computer. This allows the PC to communicate with its hard disk.

Key Terms and Concepts

Cylinders: A collection of all the disk tracks which occupy the same concentric position on a hard disk.

Hard disk controller: An expansion board that contains the necessary circuitry to control and coordinate a hard disk drive.

Heads: The electromagnetic device used to read and write to and from magnetic media such as hard and floppy disks and compact disks.

High level format: The process of initializing a hard disk so that it can be used to store information. This can only be performed after a low-level format has been completed.

IDE: Acronym for Integrated Drive Electronics. A hard disk technology with an integrated drive and controller card.

Low-level format: The process that creates the tracks and sectors on a blank hard disk or floppy disk, sometimes called the physical format. Most hard disks are already low-level formatted at the factory.

Sector: The smallest unit of storage on a disk, usually 512 bytes.

Track: A concentric collection of sectors (shaped like a ring) on a hard disk or floppy disk.

Sample Questions

1. What does the CMOS setup program allow you to do?

   A. Address disks of larger than 504MB.

   B. Use sector translation.

   C. Enter in drive geometry information.

   D. Maintain a variable number of sectors per track.

   Answer: C. Using the CMOS setup program allows the PC to communicate with the hard disk drive.

2. An EIDE system supports how many devices per channel?

   A. 7

   B. 2

   C. 3

   D. 4

   Answer: D. IDE supports two devices. EIDE, however, supports four devices.

3. How would you designate a drive as a slave drive in an IDE system?

   A. Upgrade BIOS.

   B. IDE systems don't use slave drives.

   C. Set a jumper.

   D. Change CMOS settings.

   Answer: C. Master/slave designations, which are necessary when you have two or more disk drives, are set with a jumper.

Identify proper procedures for installing and configuring SCSI devices.

The small computer systems interface (SCSI) is a type of subsystem that is both highly flexible and robust. The range of devices that can use SCSI technology includes hard disk drives, scanners, tape drives, and CD-ROM drives. This is why it's so flexible. Conversely, it's probably the most complex. In this section we'll discuss the different types of SCSI, and configuration and installation issues.

Critical Information

SCSI (pronounced "scuzzy") is a technology developed and standardized by the American National Standards Institute (ANSI). The standard specifies a universal, parallel, system-level interface for connecting up to eight devices (including the controller) on a single shared cable (called the *SCSI bus*). One of the many benefits of SCSI is that it is a very fast, flexible interface. You can buy a SCSI disk and install it in a Mac, a PC, or virtually any computer if a SCSI host adapter exists for it. SCSI systems are also known for their speed. At its introduction, SCSI supported a throughput of 5MBps (five to ten times faster than previous buses).

Types of SCSI

Table 1.6 describes the different types of SCSI implementations. SCSI-1, the earliest version, uses Centronics 50 or DB-25 female connectors, whereas the later versions of SCSI use a higher density connector. Despite the change in connectors, later implementations maintain backward compatibility with SCSI-1. SCSI-3 is in the proposal stage, and is not yet available.

T A B L E 1.6: Types of SCSI

Type:	Bus Width:	Data Transfer Rate:
SCSI-1	8-bit	5MBps
Fast SCSI-2	8-bit	10MBps
Wide SCSI-2	16-bit	10MBps
Fast-Wide SCSI-2	16-bit	20MBps
SCSI-3	16-bit	20MBps

Switch and Jumper Settings

SCSI works by assigning a unique device number (often called a SCSI "address") to each device on the SCSI bus. These numbers are configured either through jumpers or rotary switches. When the computer needs to send data to the device, it sends a signal on the wire "addressed" to that number. The device then responds with a signal that contains the computer's device number and the data itself.

This information is sent back to the SCSI adapter, which operates somewhat like a controller and somewhat like a paddle board.

The SCSI device number can be assigned by jumper (with internal devices), or with a rotary switch (on external devices). This number can be any number from 0 to 7 on the 8-bit bus of SCSI-1 and SCSI-2, as long as no other device is using that ID. Higher numbers are given higher priority. The adapter is usually preset to ID 7 (on an 8-bit bus), giving it the highest priority, and it should be left that way.

Every device can be set to any existing number as long as it's not in use. However, there are some recommendations for other devices that are commonly accepted by the PC community. Remember that these are guidelines, not rules.

- Generally speaking, give slower devices higher priority so they can access the bus whenever they need it.
- Set the bootable (or first) hard disk to ID 0.
- Set the CD-ROM to ID 3.

Cabling

SCSI devices can be either internal or external to the computer, and the adapter typically contains connectors for both. If devices are internal, they use a 50-pin ribbon cable (similar to the 40-pin IDE drive cable). If the devices are external, they use a thick, shielded cable with Centronics 50 or female DB-25 connectors on it.

The order in which other devices are connected to the adapter is unimportant. Figure 1.17 shows external devices cabled in a fashion known as *daisy-chaining*. Up to seven devices plus the SCSI host adapter are allowed on an 8-bit SCSI bus.

FIGURE 1.17: A "daisy chain"

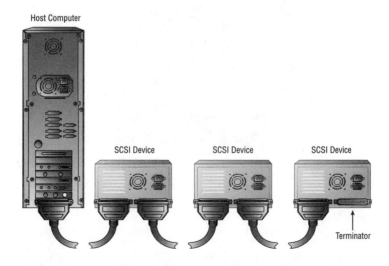

Termination

A device called a *terminator* (technically a terminating resistor pack) must be installed at both ends of the bus to keep the signals "on the bus." There are two different methods of termination, depending on the physical setup of your system.

1. The first situation is where you have internal devices only or external devices only (Figures 1.18 and 1.19). You install the terminating resistors on the adapter and on the last device in the chain only. All other terminating resistors are removed.

NOTE Some devices and adapters don't use terminating resistor packs, but instead use a jumper or DIP switch to activate or deactivate SCSI termination on that device. (Where do you find out what type your device uses? In the documentation, of course.)

FIGURE 1.18: Cabling internal SCSI devices only

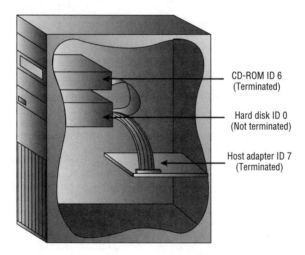

CD-ROM ID 6
(Terminated)

Hard disk ID 0
(Not terminated)

Host adapter ID 7
(Terminated)

FIGURE 1.19: Cabling external SCSI devices only

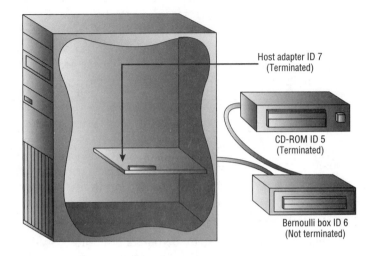

2. The other situation is where you have both internal and external SCSI devices (Figure 1.20). In this case, you terminate the last device on each chain, leaving the adapter *unterminated*.

FIGURE 1.20: Cabling internal and external SCSI devices together

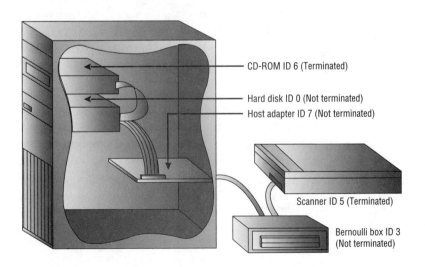

NOTE Even though the third technique described above is the technically correct way to install termination for the hybrid situation some adapter cards (for instance, Adaptec AHA-1542s) still need to have terminators installed. If you set up both internal and external devices and none of them work, you might have one of these adapters. Try enabling termination on it to see if that fixes the problem.

NOTE Many SCSI devices have built-in terminators that engage automatically when they are needed.

Communicating with the PC

Unlike an IDE/EIDE system, if you are installing a SCSI hard disk, you don't have to modify the PC's CMOS settings. As a matter of fact, because SCSI devices are intelligent, you tell the PC that there is NO DISK INSTALLED and let the adapter handle the controlling of the devices.

You must use one of the following methods of getting the PC to recognize the SCSI devices:

- If the device is going to be bootable (a hard disk), then you must set the card to be "BIOS enabled," meaning that the card has its own BIOS extension that will allow the PC to recognize the device without a software driver. The adapter must be configured to use a memory area in reserved memory for its BIOS.

- If you are booting from some other, non-SCSI device, you must load a software driver for the adapter into the operating system. This method is commonly used when the only SCSI device attached to the computer is a scanner or CD-ROM drive.

TIP Generally speaking, it's a bad idea to mix SCSI with any other disk technology. The only way you can make mixing work is to have the SCSI disks be secondary storage devices. It will degrade the performance of your system, however, since the boot files will be located on the first hard disk (the non-SCSI one). It will not work to have it the other way around (SCSI first, other disks second), because in that situation their BIOSes will conflict as to who is the "boss."

Necessary Procedures

Installing SCSI devices is rather complex, but you still follow the same basic steps as mentioned with the other types of drives. This section translates the preceding Critical Information section into an easy-to-follow step-by-step procedure.

Installing and Configuring a SCSI Device

1. Install and configure the SCSI host adapter, if necessary (motherboards often come with built-in SCSI support or a SCSI adapter preinstalled).

2. Assign a unique ID to each SCSI device.

3. Mount any internal SCSI devices inside the PC.

4. Plug in external SCSI devices.

5. Attach cables to SCSI devices and host adapter.

6. Terminate both ends of the SCSI bus.

WARNING Remember the note about low-level formatting IDE and SCSI drives—DON'T DO IT!

TIP If there are problems, double-check the termination and ID numbers. If everything looks correct, try changing ID numbers one at a time. SCSI addressing is one of those areas that is a "voodoo" art. Some things that should work don't, and some things that shouldn't work do.

Exam Essentials

Because SCSI is a fast, versatile, and popular hard disk system, there are several test questions pertaining to the SCSI subsystem.

Understand SCSI device numbers. SCSI devices must each have a unique device number, usually a number from 0 to 7. The adapter is usually preset to ID 7, allowing for seven other devices to be used on a SCSI bus.

Know the features of the different types of SCSI. SCSI-1 and Fast SCSI-2 feature an 8-bit bus with device numbers ranging from 0-7. Wide SCSI-2, Fast-Wide SCSI-2, and SCSI-3 feature a 16-bit bus with device numbers ranging from 0-15.

Know the types of SCSI connectors. SCSI-1 uses Centronics 50 or DB-25 connectors; SCSI-2 uses a 50-pin HP connector; SCSI-3 uses a 68-pin HP connector.

Know how to set up SCSI cabling. Internal and external SCSI cabling is set up in a daisy-chain fashion.

Understand SCSI termination. Both ends of the SCSI bus must be terminated.

Know how to enable the PC to communicate with SCSI devices. The BIOS on the SCSI adapter must be enabled if you have a bootable SCSI drive. Otherwise, a device driver must be loaded into the operating system.

Key Terms and Concepts

SCSI: Acronym for small computer system interface. A high-speed, system-level parallel interface used to connect a personal computer to several peripheral devices using just one port.

SCSI-1:   1986 definition of an 8-bit interface with a maximum data transfer rate of 5 megabytes per second.

SCSI-2:   1994 definition of the interface that broadened the 8-bit bus to include a 16- or 32-bit data bus (in three available configurations known as Fast, Wide, and Fast-Wide SCSI), doubling the data transfer rate to 10 or 20 megabytes per second.

SCSI-3:   Proposed definition of the interface that will increase the number of connected peripherals from 7 to 16, increase cable lengths, and add support for a serial interface and for a fiber optic interface. Data transfer rates are at least 20 megabytes per second.

SCSI adapter: A device that is used to manage all the devices on the SCSI bus as well as to send and retrieve data from the devices.

SCSI bus: Another name for the SCSI interface and communications protocol.

SCSI terminator: A device used to terminate the SCSI interface to prevent signals echoing on the bus.

Sample Questions

1. What SCSI ID is possible for SCSI-3?

   A. 14

   B. 33

   C. 110

   D. 220

   Answer: A. The SCSI-3 implementation supports up to 32 devices, which are given a device number from 0 to 31.

2. How do you terminate a SCSI system with both external and internal devices?

  A. Leave the adapter unterminated; terminate the last external device and the last internal device.

  B. Terminate the adapter and both ends of the bus.

  C. Terminate all external SCSI devices.

  D. Terminate only internal SCSI devices.

  Answer: **A.** The first and last device in the SCSI bus should be terminated. No other devices in the bus should be terminated.

3. How do you enable the PC to communicate with a bootable SCSI disk drive?

  A. Configure CMOS.

  B. Tell the BIOS there is no hard disk installed.

  C. Enable the BIOS on the SCSI adapter card.

  D. Load SCSI drivers.

  Answer: **C.** Although you must tell the BIOS there is no disk installed in the system, communication will only take place after the BIOS is enabled. SCSI drivers are required for a non-bootable SCSI drive.

Identify proper procedures for installing and configuring peripheral devices.

Three of the more common (and complicated) peripheral devices external to the PC are monitors, modems, and printers. Because printers are the subject of Chapter 5, the bulk of this objective section is about monitors and modems.

A monitor is the user interface that allows you to see not only what you're doing, but also the results of the computer's computations.

Modems have also become a fixture in the present age of e-mail and Internet communications. Both of these technologies are described in detail in this section; a PC technician must know how they work, how to install them, and how to configure them. These devices are the subject of several test questions.

Critical Information

Configuration of monitors and modems requires an understanding of display system and modem technology.

Monitor/Video Card

A monitor and video card work together to form a computer display system. Most display systems work the same way. First, the computer sends a signal to a device called the *video adapter*—an expansion board installed in an expansion bus slot—telling it to display a particular graphic or character. The adapter then *renders* the character for the display—that is, it converts that single instruction into several instructions that tell the display device how to draw the graphic—and sends the instructions to the display device. The primary differences after that are what type of video adapter (monochrome, EGA/CGA, VGA, or SuperVGA) and what type of display (CRT or LCD) you are using.

Video Technologies

The four major types of video technologies— monochrome, EGA/CGA, VGA, and SuperVGA (SVGA)—differ in two major areas: the largest resolution they support and the maximum number of colors in their palettes. Resolution depends on how many picture units (called *pixels*) are used to draw the screen. The more pixels, the sharper the image. The resolution is given as a report of the screen's dimensions, indicating how many pixels across and down are used to draw the screen. For example, a resolution of 1024×768 means 1024 pixels across and 768 pixels down were used to draw the pixel "grid." The video technology in this example would have used 786,432 (1024×768=786,432) pixels to draw the screen. Table 1.7 summarizes some of these differences between video adapters.

TABLE 1.7: Video Display Adapter Comparison

Name	Resolutions	Colors
Monochrome Display Adapter (MDA)	720×350	mono (text only)
Hercules Graphics Card (HGC)	720×350	mono (text and graphics)
Color Graphics Adapter (CGA)	320×200 640×200	4 2
Enhanced Graphics Adapter (EGA)	640×350	16
Video Graphics Adapter (VGA)	640×480 320×200	16 256
Super VGA (SVGA)	800×600 1024×768	256 16
Extended Graphics Array (XGA)	800×600 1024×768	65,536 256

SEE ALSO For more information on video technologies, see *A+ Core Module Study Guide, 2nd ed.* (Sybex, 1998).

Monitor Characteristics

There are two ways of measuring a monitor's quality of image: dot pitch and refresh (scan) rate. A monitor's *dot pitch* is the shortest distance between two dots of the same color on the monitor. Usually given in fractions of a millimeter (mm), it tells how sharp the picture is. The lower the number, the closer together the pixels are and, thus, the sharper the image. An average dot pitch is 0.28mm. Anything smaller than 0.28mm is considered superior.

A monitor's *refresh rate* (technically called the *vertical scan frequency*) specifies how many times in one second the scanning beam of electrons redraws the screen. The phosphors coating the inside of a CRT monitor only stay bright for a fraction of a second, so they must constantly be hit with electrons to stay lit. Given in draws per second, or Hertz, this rate specifies how much energy is being put into keeping the screen lit. The standard refresh rate is 60Hz for VGA. However, some monitors have a refresh rate of 72Hz, which is much easier on the eyes (less flicker is perceived).

You must use a video card that supports the type of monitor you are using. For example, you can't use a CGA monitor on a VGA adapter.

NOTE   To use a 72Hz monitor, your video card must also support the 72Hz refresh rate. Most video cards sold today support this faster 72Hz refresh rate, but are configured as 60Hz out of the box. If you intend to use the 72Hz rate, you must configure the card to do so. Check the documentation that came with the card for details on how to do this.

Monitors are either of the cathode ray tube (CRT) variety, like a standard television set, or a liquid crystal display (LCD). LCD screens are used in laptop computers because they are lightweight and consume relatively little power. These computer screens can be further categorized as *active matrix* or *passive matrix* LCD screens. Active matrix screens have a superior image quality, but will only last about two hours on battery power.

Modem

Modems are devices used by computers to communicate over long distances. The word "modem" is actually a partial acronym; it stands for MOdulator/DEModulator. It got this name from the way it works. When a computer wants to send data, it uses a digital signal (fluctuations in voltage, representing 1s and 0s). The problem is that these signals can attenuate (decrease in strength) over long distances, with the result that the data can become undecipherable. Modems convert digital signals into analog signals by using variations of tones to represent 1s and 0s (this is the MOdulation). The modem then sends these sounds over a phone line. At the other end, the tones are converted back into 1s and 0s (this is the DEModulation). Using two modems and a phone line, you transmit digital data through an analog medium.

The only downside to modems is that this process is relatively inefficient. Because modem communications are so sporadic, they use
asynchronous communications, which have their overhead of start
and stop bits. Also, today's phone lines are limited to a maximum
throughput of 56Kbps.

NOTE The most confusing terms used to describe modem speed
are *bits-per-second* (or *bps*) and *baud*. Actually, it's a very easy distinction. The bps value of a modem is how much data is being transmitted
in one second. Baud refers to how many signal (tone) changes are happening in one second. Through a process known as encoding, several
bits can be transmitted using only a few signal changes. Modern phone
lines are limited to 9600 baud. If you increase the baud rate any higher,
the modem on the other end starts to have difficulty distinguishing the
individual tonal changes. However, with modern encoding techniques,
it is possible to get up to 56 kilobits-per-second (Kbps) transmitted with
9600 baud.

There are two types of modems: internal and external. There are
advantages and disadvantages to each. Internal modems are installed
as expansion cards inside a computer. External modems have their
own power supplies and connect to an external COM port with an
RS-232 cable.

Internal modems are usually smaller and cheaper than their external
counterparts. However, they are more difficult to configure. You need
to configure them to use an unused COM port. Table 1.8 lists the IRQ
and I/O port addresses of the standard COM ports installed.

T A B L E 1.8: Standard COM Port and IRQ Addresses

COM Port	IRQ Address	I/O address
COM1	4	3F8–3FF
COM2	3	2F8–2FF

T A B L E 1.8:   Standard COM Port and IRQ Addresses *(continued)*

COM Port	IRQ Address	I/O address
COM3	4	3E8–3EF
COM4	3	2E8–2EF

An internal modem with a serial port adds a third COM port to the system. This may introduce an interrupt conflict. Check the documentation to see if the modem will support a non-standard interrupt. If it does, try using it and test the modem with your communication software. If you have problems, you may have to disable one of the COM ports.

External modems use an existing serial port, so they don't have the configuration problem with IRQs and I/O addresses. You need to make sure you're using an RS-232 cable to connect the modem to the serial port. The cable must be less than 25 feet in length.

TIP   If you're configuring the modem on an older computer, make sure the serial port is using a 16-bit UART (model 16450 or 16550). The UART (Universal Asynchronous Receiver-Transmitter) is the chip that manages the serial data that's moving in and out through the serial port. To find out what UART you have, run MSD in DOS mode, select the COM port option, and read the last entry line. If the UART chip is an 8550, you should replace the chip to increase your data throughput.

Necessary Procedures

Basic procedures for installing and configuring external modems and monitors are described here.

Installing and Configuring a Monitor

1. Configure and install the display adapter. Configuration will include setting IRQs, I/O addresses, and running installation software. Install the adapter card as you would any other expansion card.

2. Plug in the monitor power cord.

3. Attach the monitor to the adapter port on the PC using a connecting cable.

4. Turn on the monitor's power switch. Turn on the PC.

5. Configure monitor resolution and color palette. On a Windows 95 computer, you configure resolution and color in the Display properties sheet in the Control Panel.

6. Set the refresh to the highest rate possible. Consult your documentation to find the highest possible rate and for procedures on how to set it.

SEE ALSO   For more information on ports and cabling, go to the section of this chapter titled "Identify common peripheral ports, associated cabling, and their connectors."

Installing and Configuring a Modem

1. If you have an internal modem, install it and configure it as you would any other expansion card. You must also plug it into a phone jack using a standard RJ-11 phone cord.

2. If you have an external modem, plug in the power cord and connect it to the PC (usually an RS-232 cable attached to the serial port). Then plug it into a phone jack.

3. Install modem communication software. (The Modems properties sheet in the Windows 95 Control Panel contains a valuable diagnostics tool with which you can test your setup.)

SEE ALSO For information on configuration and installation of expansion cards, go to the section of this chapter titled "Identify available IRQ's, DMA's, and I/O addresses and procedures for configuring them for device installation.

Exam Essentials

The exam is more concerned with some details of monitor and modem technologies, and less concerned with procedural knowledge. You'll do better if you concentrate on the details of video and modem technology. The exam essentials reflect this.

Know the types of video technologies and their basic characteristics. Video technologies include monochrome, EGA/CGA, VGA, and SVGA, all with different resolutions and color palettes.

Know what a CRT and an LCD are. Cathode ray tube (CRT) monitors use the same technology as television sets. Liquid crystal display (LCD) is a different technology used in laptop computers.

Know the main characteristics of a CRT monitor. The main characteristics of a CRT monitor are its vertical scan frequency (refresh rate) and its dot pitch.

Understand how to install and configure a monitor. Before installing a monitor, you must install and configure the display adapter. The monitor must be plugged into the display adapter port and a power source. Configure resolution and color palette after turning on the computer.

Understand how to install a modem. Internal modems are installed like any expansion card and require an unused COM port, while external modems are hooked up using one of the serial ports and the RS-232 standard interface.

Key Terms and Concepts

Analog: Describes any device that represents changing values by a continuously variable physical property such as voltage in a circuit, fluid pressure, liquid level, and so on.

Asynchronous: Describes a type of communication that adds special signaling bits to each end of the data.

CRT: Acronym for cathode ray tube. A display device used in monitors and television sets.

Digital: Describes any device that represents values in the form of binary digits.

Dot pitch: In a monitor, the vertical distance between the centers of like-colored phosphors on the screen of a color monitor, measured in millimeters (mm). As the dot pitch becomes smaller, finer details appear on the screen.

EGA/CGA: Acronym for Enhanced Graphics Adapter/Color Graphics Adapter. A video technology that provides a resolution of 640×350 pixels, and can use 16 colors out of its palette of 64 at any given time.

LCD monitor: A monitor that uses liquid crystal display technology.

Monochrome monitor: A monitor that can display text and graphics in one color only.

Pixel: Contraction of "picture element." The smallest element that display technology can use to create text or graphics.

Refresh rate: In a monitor, the rate at which the phosphors that create the image on the screen are recharged.

RS-232: In asynchronous transmissions, a standard interface that defines the specific lines, timing, and signal characteristics used between the computer and a peripheral device.

SuperVGA: Abbreviated SVGA. An enhancement to the Video Graphics Array video standard.

> **VGA:**   Acronym for Video Graphics Array. VGA supports resolutions of 640×480 pixels, and can display 256 colors out of its palette of 262,114 at any given time.

Sample Questions

1. A SVGA adapter using a standard configuration would have what resolution?

   A. 640×480

   B. 1024×640

   C. 640×350

   D. 800×600

   Answer: D. A SVGA adapter has either 800×600 resolution or 1024×768.

2. What is another name for vertical scan frequency?

   A. Dot pitch

   B. Hertz

   C. Refresh rate

   D. CRT

   Answer: C. The refresh rate specifies how many times in one second the scanning beam of electrons redraws the screen.

3. Modems use what type of cable?

   A. Null modem cable

   B. Centronics

   C. DIN

   D. RS-232

   Answer: D. RS-232 is a standard interface for serial communications. This standard defines specific lines, timing, and signal characteristics.

Recognize the functions and effective use of common hand tools.

Behind every great technician is an even greater set of tools. A technician's troubleshooting skills can get him or her only so far. Once they've exhausted their intellectual resources, they must turn to additional troubleshooting tools. And once the problem has been identified, yet a different set of tools needs to be used—to fix the problem.

There are two major types of tools: hardware and software. This objective has to do with knowledge of the common hardware tools. Most of the questions on the test about this material involve the use of, and measurements taken with, a multimeter; the other information is included for background and reference information. Although—who knows?—maybe you'll get the Land of Oz version of the A+ test, and there will be lots of questions on the Phillips screwdriver. It could happen...

Critical Information

Hardware tools are those tools that are "hard," meaning you can touch them, as opposed to software tools, which cannot be touched. There are several different kinds of hardware tools used in PC service today.

Screwdrivers

The tool that can most often be found in a technician's toolkit is a set of screwdrivers. Most of the larger components in today's computers are mounted in the case with screws. If these components need to be removed, you must have the correct type of screwdriver available. There are three major types: flat blade, Phillips, and Torx.

Flat Blade Screwdrivers

The first type is often called a flat blade screwdriver or flathead screwdriver, though most people simply refer to it as a "standard" screwdriver. The type of screw that this screwdriver is designed to remove is not used much anymore (primarily because the screw head was easily damaged).

Phillips Screwdrivers

The most commonly used type of screwdriver for computers today is the Phillips driver. This screwdriver has two crossing blades that taper to a common point. Phillips-head screws are used because they have more surfaces to turn against and thus a reduced risk of being damaged. More than 90% of the screws in most computers today will be Phillips-head screws.

NOTE   Phillips screwdrivers come in different sizes that are given in numbers. The most common size is a #2 Phillips. It is important to have a few different size screwdrivers available. If the wrong size is used (for example, a Phillips driver that is too pointed or too small), it can damage the head of the screw.

Torx Screwdriver

The last important type of screwdriver is used for working with those maddening little screws that are found on Compaq and Apple computers; it is the Torx screwdriver. This driver has a star-shaped blade. The Torx type of screw has the most surfaces to turn against and therefore has the greatest resistance to screw-head damage.

The sizes of Torx drivers are given with the designation T-*xx*, where the *xx* is replaced with a number from 1 through 20. The most common sizes are T-10 and T-15, though for some notebook computers you will need to have much smaller Torx drivers on hand.

TIP   Several screwdrivers are available with changeable tips, like bits for a drill. The advantage is that these screwdrivers can easily change from a flat blade to a Phillips to a Torx just by changing the bits in the driver. The bits are usually stored in the handle of this type of screwdriver.

WARNING Although it may seem convenient, don't use a multiple-bit driver that is magnetized. Magnetism and computers don't make good friends. The magnetism can induce currents in conductors and burn out components without the technician's knowledge. It could also erase magnetic disk storage media.

IC Pullers

When removing integrated circuits (ICs) from their mounting sockets, use a specialized tool called a *chip puller* (Figure 1.21). This tool is usually made of spring steel and is shaped like the letter U. It has fingers at the ends of the "U" that are designed to be slipped between the chip and socket. All the technician has to do is pull up on the tool, and it will exert equal force on the different sides of the IC, thus removing the chip.

WARNING BE CAREFUL WHEN USING AN IC PULLER. It is possible to remove the socket as well as the chip if you pull hard enough. You may also damage the motherboard permanently. A potentially safer option is to use a flat blade screwdriver. Use the driver to pry up one side of the chip a bit, switch to the other side and do the same. Continue switching sides in this manner until you work the IC out of its socket.

FIGURE 1.21: An IC puller

Multimeters

Another hardware device is the multimeter. It gets its name from the fact that it is a combination of several different kinds of testing meters, including an ohmmeter, ammeter, and voltmeter. In trained hands, it can help detect the correct operation or failure of several different types of components.

The multimeter consists of either a digital or analog display, two probes, and a function selector switch. This rotary switch selects not only the function being tested but also the range that the meter is set to. If you're measuring a battery using an older meter, you may have to set the range selector manually (to a range close to, but no greater than, 1.5 volts). Newer meters, especially the digital ones, will automatically set their ranges appropriately.

WARNING   NEVER connect a non-auto-ranging meter to an AC power outlet to measure voltage. This action will most surely result in permanent damage to the meter mechanism, the meter itself, or both.

When measuring circuits, it is very important to have the meter hooked up correctly so that the readings are accurate. Each type of measurement may require that the meter be connected in a different way. The following paragraphs will detail the most commonly used functions of the multimeter, and how to make measurements correctly with them.

Measuring Resistance with a Multimeter

The measurement of resistance is the most common measurement used in troubleshooting components. Measured in ohms, resistance is most often represented by the Greek symbol omega (Ω). A measurement of infinite resistance indicates that electricity cannot flow from one probe to the other. If a multimeter is used to measure the resistance in a segment of wire and the result is an infinite reading, there is a very good chance that the wire has a break in it somewhere between the probes.

To measure resistance, the multimeter must first be set to measure ohms. This is done either through a button on the front, or through the selector dial. (Assume for the rest of this book that newer, auto-ranging multimeters are being used.) Then the component to be measured must be connected properly between the probes (see the following Warning and Figure 1.22). The meter will then display the resistance value of the component being measured.

WARNING   DO NOT test resistance on components while they are mounted on a circuit board! The multimeter applies a current to the component being tested. That current may also flow to other components on that board, thus damaging them.

F I G U R E 1.22: Connecting a multimeter to measure resistance

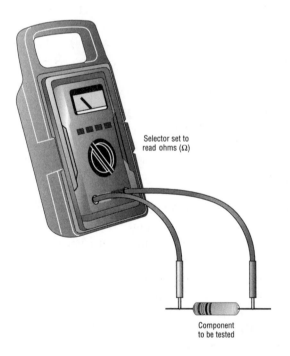

Selector set to read ohms (Ω)

Component to be tested

Measuring Voltage with a Multimeter

There is a similar procedure to follow when measuring voltage, but with two major differences. First, when measuring voltage, you must be sure you connect the probes to the power source correctly: with DC voltage, the + must connect to the positive side and the – to the negative. (The position doesn't matter with AC voltage.) Second, you must change the selector to VDc (volts DC) or VAc (volts AC), whichever is appropriate, to tell the meter what you are measuring. (See Figure 1.23.) It should be noted that these settings protect the meter from overload. If you plug a meter into a power supply while it's still set to measure resistance, it may blow the meter.

If you must set the voltage range manually and you do not know the voltage of the device you want to test, set the multimeter at its highest level and work your way downward.

FIGURE 1.23: Connecting a multimeter to measure voltage

Selector set to
read DC or
AC volts

Black probe (-)

Red probe (+)

Connect directly
to terminals
of power source

Battery

Measuring Current with a Multimeter

The final measurement that is commonly made is that of current, in amperes (amps). Again, the procedure is similar to those used for the other measurements. A major difference here is that when you connect a multimeter to measure the current that a circuit is drawing, you must connect the multimeter in series with the circuit being measured. Figure 1.24 illustrates the proper connection of a multimeter to measure current.

FIGURE 1.24: Connecting a multimeter to measure current

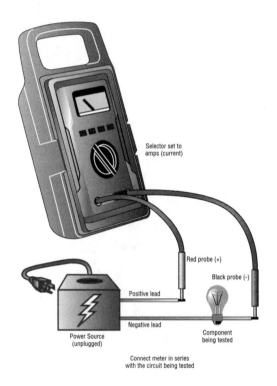

Exam Essentials

Of the common hand tools, the multimeter is the one that draws the most attention on the test. There may be several questions about measuring resistance, voltage, or current.

Know how to measure resistance with the multimeter. Resistance is measured in ohms represented by the Greek symbol omega (Ω). A measure of infinite resistance in a wire indicates a break.

Know how to measure voltage with the multimeter. When measuring voltage, you must set the meter to read volts DC (VDc) or volts AC (VAc). When measuring volts DC, you must connect the + to the positive side, and the – to the negative side.

Know how to measure current with the multimeter. Current is measured in amperes. You must connect the multimeter in series with the circuit being measured.

Key Terms and Concepts

Ampere: A unit of electrical current.

IC puller: A "U"-shaped tool used for pulling integrated circuit chips.

Integrated circuit: Abbreviated IC; also known as a chip. A small semiconductor circuit that contains many electronic components.

Multimeter: An electronic device used to measure and test ohms, amperes, and volts.

Ohm: A unit of electrical resistance.

Torx screwdriver: A type of screwdriver with a star-shaped blade.

Volt: A unit of electrical potential.

Sample Questions

1. If you set the multimeter to measure resistance in order to test the power supply, you might get what result?

   A. A high resistance

   B. A blown meter

   C. A reading of 2100 Ω

   D. A reading of 21000 Ω

   Answer: B. The multimeter must be set to measure voltage when testing a battery or the power supply.

2. A measurement of current gives its result in what?

   A. Amperes

   B. Ohms

   C. Volts

   D. Resistance

   Answer: A.

Identify concepts and procedures relating to BIOS.

Sometimes, hardware vendors will want to include new types of hardware the processor was never designed to talk to. In that case, a BIOS upgrade may have to be performed. BIOS stands for basic input/output system, and is the software the PC uses to communicate with its devices. You may be forced to upgrade BIOS if you are fixing one of the early-generation PCs.

Critical Information

A BIOS upgrade is required if you want to install a hard drive and the current (early-generation) BIOS does not permit you the option of entering in the number of cylinders, heads, and sectors (i.e., it doesn't have a user-definable drive type). Some other BIOS features include:

- Automatic detection of IDE drives. This BIOS does not require any configuration of CMOS for the hard disk.

- Option to enable/disable the processor/cache

- Bus speeds that can be altered through the setup program

- Plug-and-Play technology

- Password protection

The BIOS software is contained on a programmable ROM (PROM) or an electrically-erasable programmable ROM (EEPROM) chip. The type of chip determines how you must carry out the upgrade (see the following section). A PROM chip must be replaced, whereas an EEPROM chip can actually be reprogrammed.

Necessary Procedures

A BIOS upgrade is the process by which the BIOS software is upgraded to a newer version. There are two ways of doing this: upgrading the PROM or "flashing" the EEPROM.

Upgrading the PROM

1. Shut off the power.

2. Remove the BIOS chip from the motherboard.

3. Replace it with the new BIOS chip containing the new version of the software.

Flashing the BIOS

Flashing the BIOS involves using a special piece of software to upload the new BIOS software to the BIOS EEPROM. This software can be downloaded from the BIOS manufacturer or ordered through the mail. Consult the software documentation for specific procedures. Once the flashing is complete, the computer is rebooted and the new BIOS is functional.

WARNING   NEVER TURN OFF A COMPUTER DURING A BIOS FLASH UPGRADE! The computer won't come back up because it doesn't have the software to boot itself. Wait for the flash to complete, then reboot the computer (many times the software used to flash the BIOS EEPROM will do this for you automatically).

Exam Essentials

Though not emphasized, there will be one or two questions about BIOS upgrades.

Know how to upgrade the BIOS.   BIOS is upgraded by replacing the BIOS ROM. An EEPROM BIOS can be upgraded by a process known as "flashing" the EEPROM.

Know what occasions may necessitate a BIOS upgrade.   The most common situation in which a BIOS upgrade is required is if you want to install a new, high-capacity hard drive and the current BIOS does not give the option of setting a user-definable drive type.

Key Terms and Concepts

BIOS: Acronym for basic input/output system, pronounced "bye-os." In the PC, a set of instructions stored in ROM that prevents programs from contesting control of hardware.

EEPROM: Acronym for electrically erasable programmable read-only memory, pronounced "ee-ee-prom" or "double-ee-prom." A memory chip that maintains its contents without electrical power, and whose contents can be erased and reprogrammed.

PROM: Acronym for programmable read-only memory. A memory chip that maintains its contents without electrical power, and whose contents can be programmed only once and cannot be erased.

Sample Questions

1. What should you do when you upgrade BIOS?

   A. Replace the ROM.

   B. Delete the BIOS software.

   C. Reprogram the new BIOS.

   D. Reinstall your operating system.

   Answer: A. The BIOS is contained in a ROM that can be upgraded by replacing it or by flashing the EEPROM.

2. A BIOS upgrade is usually needed when replacing what component in an early-generation PC?

   A. Keyboard

   B. Hard disk

   C. CMOS battery

   D. Monitor

   Answer: B. An early-generation BIOS may be unable to see a drive of more than 340 or 504 MB.

Identify hardware methods of system optimization and when to use them.

Running down to the electronics store to upgrade your system isn't always the best thing to do when you need to increase the capabilities of your computer. Depending on your specific need, optimizing the equipment you have may save you time and money. Several test questions relate directly to optimizing memory, hard drives, and the CPU cache memory.

Critical Information

This section details how you can maximize your current system resources by optimizing memory for use by DOS programs, partitioning hard disks for more efficient use of storage space, and using cache memory to reduce the time required to access frequently used data.

Memory Optimization

With the number of DOS applications that exist, the need for a technician to know how to optimize memory continues to be important. In general, your DOS-based PCs will run best with the most possible *conventional memory* available. Conventional memory is the first 640K of RAM memory. When people talk about memory optimization, they usually mean making as much conventional memory available as possible.

NOTE Be aware that the term "conventional memory" often refers to the first 1024K (1MB) of memory. However, when discussing memory optimization, the term includes only the first 640K.

Most programs written for DOS are designed to work within this first 640K. Memory optimization involves loading portions of DOS or complete DOS programs into areas of memory called *upper memory* and the *high memory area* (or HMA) instead of conventional memory. The different areas of memory are shown in Figure 1.25.

FIGURE 1.25: The complete MS-DOS memory map

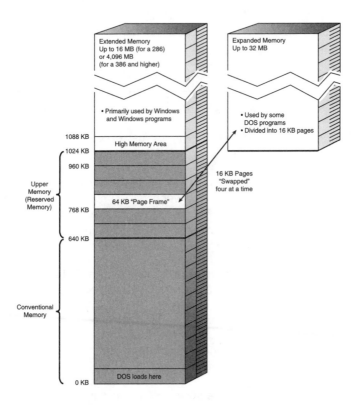

Memory above 1MB is inaccessible to DOS. This type of memory is called *extended memory*, and is accessed by invoking HIMEM.SYS, the extended memory driver.

Before you optimize memory, you must first make the determination whether or not memory optimization is needed. For DOS systems, you use the MEM.EXE program. This program allows you to determine how memory is being utilized within DOS.

The available options for use with MEM are described in Table 1.9. If you execute the command with the /C switch, the MEM command shows how much of each type of memory is installed, as shown in Table 1.10.

T A B L E 1.9: MEM.EXE Command-Line Options

Option	Description
/?	The *help switch*. It gives basic information on the syntax of the **MEM** command and its usage. It shows all the switches listed in this table and their usage.
/C	The *classify switch*. When executed, gives an output similar to the one following this table.
/D	The *debug switch*. It details the usage of the first 640KB of memory (conventional memory). This switch is helpful in finding out the memory addresses of the various programs that are loaded. (Remember that MEM itself is also a program and should be listed.)
/F	The *free memory switch*. Shows all the free memory blocks in the first 640KB and their starting addresses. Also useful in optimizing memory.
/M *<module>*	The *module switch*. Shows the starting addresses of the data, program, and free memory allocated to the module you specify.
/P	The *pause switch*. When used in conjunction with the other switches, /P displays the output of the command one page at a time. When a page is displayed, the display will pause until a key is pressed. The same effect can be accomplished by piping the command's results into the MORE command (i.e., using **MEM** *<option>* | **MORE**).

TABLE 1.10: A report from the MEM /C command

Modules using memory below 1 MB:

Name	Total		Conventional		Upper Memory	
SYSTEM	48,880	(48K)	10,592	(10K)	38,288	(37K)
HIMEM	1,168	(1K)	1,168	(1K)	0	(0K)
EMM386	4,320	(4K)	4,320	(4K)	0	(0K)
WIN	3,696	(4K)	3,696	(4K)	0	(0K)
--------	288	(0K)	288	(0K)	0	(0K)
vmm32	102,064	(100K)	448	(0K)	101,616	(99K)
COMMAND	7,456	(7K)	7,456	(7K)	0	(0K)
IBMIDECD	10,848	(11K)	0	(0K)	10,848	(11K)
IFSHLP	2,864	(3K)	0	(0K)	2,864	(3K)
DOSKEY	4,688	(5K)	0	(0K)	4,688	(5K)
Free	627,120	(612K)	627,120	(612K)	0	(0K)

Memory Summary:

Type of Memory	Total	Used	Free
Conventional	655,360	28,240	627,120
Upper	158,304	158,304	0
Reserved	393,216	393,216	0
Extended (XMS)	32,347,552	95,648	32,251,904
Total memory	33,554,432	675,408	32,879,024
Total under 1 MB	813,664	186,544	627,120

Largest executable program size   627,104   (612K)
Largest free upper memory block   0   (0K)
MS-DOS is resident in the high memory area.

Some key lines to look at in the MEM /C report are:

- The "Upper Memory" column on the right, showing which programs loaded into upper memory

- The "Upper" row in the Memory Summary at the bottom. If 0K is shown in the Total Memory, you must make sure the device driver for using upper memory (EMM386.EXE) has been invoked in the CONFIG.SYS file. Additionally, the DOS=UMB must also be present.

- The last output line indicating that MS-DOS is resident in the high memory area. If this last line is missing, either of two commands may be absent from or wrongly configured in CONFIG.SYS: Device=HIMEM.SYS (the extended memory device driver) or DOS=HIGH (which actually loads DOS into the HMA).

SEE ALSO   For more information on memory optimization, see *A+ Core Module Study Guide, 2nd ed.* (Sybex, 1998).

Partitioning a Hard Disk

Whenever you set up a drive, you must create a partition in order to use it. For Windows and DOS, you must create what is called a *primary partition* from which the computer will boot. You also have the option of creating an *extended partition*, which can be further partitioned into one or more *logical drives*.

Partitioning a disk and creating an extended partition is an effective means of optimizing storage space on the hard disk of a DOS- or Windows-based computer. These systems use a file system called the file allocation table (FAT).

TIP   Partitioning a hard disk is also useful if you wish to have the option of running different operating systems, such as Windows 95 and Windows NT, from your hard disk.

A FAT-based system stores files in units called *clusters*, which range from 2K to 64K in size. Each of these clusters can contain one file at most. If the file does not completely fill the cluster, any extra space is wasted. The size of these clusters depends upon the size of the logical drive that contains them. Table 1.11 describes the various cluster sizes.

TABLE 1.11: Logical Drive Size and Corresponding Cluster Sizes

Drive Size	Cluster Size (in K)
16–127MB	2
128–255MB	4
256–511MB	8
512MB–1GB	16
1GB–2GB	32
2GB–4GB	64

The drive cluster size becomes significant when there is a large number of relatively small files. If you have a 1.2GB drive, its clusters will be 32K in size. A 7K file on this drive will use an entire 32K cluster, wasting 25K in storage space. If you have 40 such files, you've wasted 25K x 40—1 megabyte!

The issue of whether or not to create additional logical drives through partitioning depends on the value placed on storage space. If purchasing additional hard disk drives is undesirable (it usually is!), partitioning is recommended. This is especially advisable if you create large numbers of relatively small files. Files created by a word processing program are typically smaller than graphics files, databases, and program files, which often take up large chunks of storage space.

What size should you make the drives if you do decide to create smaller partitions? No right answer exists. In the case of a 1.2GB drive, it would be advantageous to divide the drive into, say, a 900MB and 300MB drive. This gives you cluster sizes of 16K and 8K, respectively, and you could plan to store your personal files on the smaller drive.

NOTE This discussion of cluster sizes assumes a 16-bit FAT. Windows 95 OEM Service Release 2 and Windows 98 use a 32-bit FAT, which has smaller cluster sizes. In the 32-bit FAT, a 2GB drive requires only 4KB clusters. This is far more efficient than the 32KB clusters required by the 16-bit FAT.

Be careful not to create more drives than you would find convenient. Potential headaches include:

- greater difficulty remembering where to find files

- more effort required to back up or copy multiple drives

- lack of large blocks of free space in which to put new programs

Cache Memory

When a CPU goes to get either its program instructions or data, it always has to get them from main memory. However, in some systems there is a small amount of very fast SRAM memory (called *cache memory*) between the processor and main memory that is used to store the most frequently accessed information. Since it's faster than main memory and contains the most frequently used information, cache memory will increase the performance of any system.

There are two types of cache memory: on-chip (internal) and off-chip (external). Internal cache memory is found on Intel Pentium, Pentium Pro, and Pentium II processors, as well as on other manufacturers' chips. The original Pentium contains two 8KB-on-chip caches, one for program instructions and the other for data. External cache memory is typically either a SIMM of SRAM or a separate expansion board that installs in a special processor-direct bus.

TIP To get the most out of cache memory, if you have the option of installing an external cache card onto your motherboard, do it. It can give you as much as a 25% boost in speed.

Necessary Procedures

This section translates the preceding Critical Information section into easy-to-follow procedures.

Optimizing Memory

To optimize memory in a DOS-based PC, you must alter the CONFIG.SYS file. To see how your system is configured, open the CONFIG.SYS file. If DOS is installed with its default installation, you will have the CONFIG .SYS file shown here:

```
DEVICE=C:\DOS\HIMEM.SYS
Files=40
Stacks=9,256
SHELL=C:\DOS\COMMAND.COM /E:1024
```

To optimize your CONFIG.SYS file, take the following steps (the order of the steps is unimportant):

- Add the DOS=HIGH line to the CONFIG.SYS file. This has the effect of moving DOS to the HMA, thus freeing up the first 64KB block of conventional memory.

- Add DEVICE=C:\DOS\EMM386.EXE in your CONFIG.SYS file so that DOS can manage the UMBs (blocks of memory in the upper memory region). Be sure the DOS=HIGH command has also been added to CONFIG.SYS. If you have other device drivers in CONFIG.SYS, change DEVICE= commands in CONFIG.SYS to DEVICEHIGH= to force programs or drivers into the upper memory area. (Some device drivers, such as HIMEM.SYS or EMM386.EXE, will not function in the UMA. You may have to experiment.)

- Make sure the larger programs load first by listing them in order from largest to smallest in the CONFIG.SYS and AUTOEXEC.BAT files. (This only matters if they are going into UMBs.)

- If you have drivers loaded from the AUTOEXEC.BAT, you use the LOADHIGH <drivername> (or LH, for short) to load that driver or program into a UMB.

- Additionally, you should check to see if you have a program that uses expanded memory. If you don't, you can place the NOEMS line after C:\DOS\EMM386.EXE in the CONFIG.SYS. This frees up the 64KB area being used by the expanded memory page frame so it can be used for UMBs.

A CONFIG.SYS revised according to these directives is shown here:

```
DEVICE=C:\DOS\HIMEM.SYS
DEVICE=C:\DOS\EMM386.EXE NOEMS
Files=40
Stacks=9,256
DOS=HIGH,UMB
SHELL=C:\DOS\COMMAND.COM /E:1024
```

TIP   The most memory-efficient line in CONFIG.SYS for the EMM386 .EXE invocation is "DEVICE=EMM386.EXE NOEMS I=B000-B7FF I=E000-EFFF." The effect of the I=range switch is to make available areas of upper memory normally used by specific system ROMs and video RAM. The address ranges are given in hexadecimal.

Using Memory Optimization Utilities

Microsoft and IBM included intelligent memory optimization utilities with their ÐOS operating systems (starting with version 6 of each one). The programs are MEMMAKER (by Microsoft) and RAM-BOOST (by IBM). To run MEMMAKER, simply type in its name at the C:\ prompt MEMMAKER.

NOTE   For more information regarding RAMBOOST or MEM-MAKER, please refer to the respective user manuals.

MEMMAKER does have limitations. For example, it forgets to include the DOS=HIGH statement in CONFIG.SYS, which costs the system 64KB of conventional memory. Nor is it capable of altering the loading order of TSRs. So, while it's good at general optimization, MEMMAKER can't beat an intuitive technician with a good grasp of memory theory.

Partitioning a Hard Disk

The only built-in method of partitioning a hard disk on a DOS- or Windows-based system (this includes DOS, Windows 3.*x*, Windows 95/98, and Windows NT) is to use the FDISK command:

1. Boot or reboot the computer into MS-DOS mode.

2. At the command line, type **fdisk**. The FDISK main menu appears.

3. Select option 1, Create DOS Partition or Logical DOS Drive. Another menu appears.

4. Select option 1, Create Primary DOS Partition.

5. A screen appears, asking if you wish to create a primary partition of the maximum available size. Press "N" and Enter.

6. Punch in the size of the primary partition and hit Enter. Your primary partition will be designated as the C: drive.

7. Press Esc to continue. This returns you to the main FDISK menu.

8. Press 2 to set the C: drive as the active (bootable) partition.

9. You are prompted to tell FDISK how many partitions you wish to make active. Punch in "1" and Enter.

10. FDISK now gives you the maximum available size for an extended partition. Do not change this number. Hit Enter. A new menu appears.

11. Enter the size of the logical drive you want to create. If you don't use all the available space, FDISK will allow you to create multiple logical drives.

12. When you've used up all available space, press Esc three times. The system will reboot, completing the process.

Exam Essentials

Several questions on the test will include references to memory optimization, partition terminology, and cache memory.

Understand the structure of the DOS memory map. The first 1MB of memory consists of conventional memory and upper memory. Extended memory includes all memory above 1MB, the first 64K of which is termed the high memory area.

Understand how to optimize conventional memory. Optimizing memory involves invoking the memory management device drivers (HIMEM.SYS and EMM386.EXE) and altering some of the commands in the CONFIG.SYS file.

Understand the terminology related to partitioning. Partitioning a disk involves creating a primary partition from which the operating system will load into memory. An extended partition can also be created that will consist of one or more logical drives.

Understand the function and usefulness of cache memory. Cache memory is very fast memory used to store frequently accessed data. The CPU cache may be an internal cache or may be located in an expansion board in a processor-direct bus on the motherboard.

Key Terms and Concepts

Cache memory: A relatively small section of very fast memory (often static RAM) reserved for the temporary storage of the data or instructions likely to be needed next by the processor.

Cluster: The smallest unit of hard disk space that DOS can allocate to a file, consisting of one or more contiguous sectors.

Conventional memory: Normally the first 640K of memory accessible by DOS in a PC.

Extended DOS partition: A further optional division of a hard disk, after the primary DOS partition, that functions as one or more logical drives.

Extended memory: Memory beyond 1MB on computers using the Intel 80386 and later processors.

File allocation table: Abbreviated FAT. A table maintained by the DOS operating system that lists all the clusters available on a disk.

High memory area: Abbreviated HMA. The first 64K of extended memory above 1024K (1MB).

Logical drive: The internal division of an extended partition into one or more units.

Primary DOS partition: The portion of the hard disk that contains the operating system.

Upper memory blocks: Abbreviated UMBs. The unused blocks of memory between 640K and 1024K in a DOS computer. It was originally reserved for system and video use, but portions of this memory are available to other programs.

Sample Questions

1. If you want to speed up access time for frequently used memory addresses, you should do what?

    A. Add RAM.

    B. Replace your hard disk.

    C. Upgrade cache memory.

    D. Use pipelining.

    Answer: C. The cache is used for storing frequently accessed data and is the fastest type of memory. Therefore, upgrading the cache would be the best choice in this situation.

2. What is the name of the extended memory device driver used to access memory above 1MB?

   A. EMM386.EXE

   B. HIMEM.SYS

   C. DOS=HIGH

   D. vmm32

   Answer: B. HIMEM.SYS is used to allow DOS to load itself into the HMA, the lowest portion of extended memory. It also allows Windows to load into other areas of extended memory.

CHAPTER

2

Diagnosing and
Troubleshooting

A+ Core Module Exam Objectives Covered in This Chapter:

▶ **Identify common symptoms and problems associated with each module and how to troubleshoot and isolate the problems.** *(pages 104 – 125)*

▶ **Identify basic troubleshooting procedures and good practices for eliciting problem symptoms from customers.** *(pages 125 – 132)*

Diagnosis and troubleshooting describe the process of identifying a computer problem and fixing it. These problems range from poorly-trained users who aren't sure how their software works to power failures.

Until you've had the opportunity to troubleshoot several computers with several different types of customers, the only way to gain the troubleshooting skills you will rely on as a certified technician is to learn what has worked for others. This chapter provides an organized summary of tips that a few professional technicians have gleaned over the years. Many of these tips are common knowledge, and the exam contains many questions that are answered in this chapter.

Identify common symptoms and problems associated with each module and how to troubleshoot and isolate the problems.

One of the keys to hardware troubleshooting is to understand the common problems that come up with the various modules. These common problems usually have simple solutions. Knowing these problems along with their respective solutions will make you a more efficient troubleshooter. Hardware troubleshooting is heavily emphasized on the test.

Critical Information

As a prelude to specific hardware problems, this section first describes the power-on self test (POST), which automatically runs every time you turn on your computer, and the bootstrap loader. Knowledge of both is crucial to solving some of the hardware problems you may run into.

POST Audible/Visual Error Codes

This item isn't a hardware problem, but a hardware troubleshooting aid. Every computer has a diagnostic program built into its BIOS called the power-on self test, or POST. When you turn on the computer it very quickly executes this set of diagnostics:

1. **The processor is tested.** POST runs checks on the CPU. If the tests fail, the system stops, usually with no error message.

2. **The ROMs are checked.** POST computes a checksum for the BIOS ROMs. If the checksums do not match, the system halts with no error message.

3. **The DMA controller is tested.** Again, if there are problems, the system halts.

4. **The interrupt controller is checked.** If there is a problem with this component, the system will give an audible error message of a long beep, then a short beep, and then the system will stop.

5. **The system timing chip is tested.** This is not the chip that tells time, but rather the chip that provides timing signals for the bus and processor. If this chip fails, the system will (unfortunately) give the same message as it does with an interrupt controller problem—a long beep and a short beep—and then halt.

6. **The video card is checked.** At this point, the system runs the diagnostics for the video card. If the card fails the test, the system issues one long beep and two short beeps and halts. If it is successful, the video ROM BIOS is copied into RAM and you will usually see a message about the type of video card that the computer is using.

7. **Expansion boards are initialized.** During this part of the POST routine, any expansion boards that need to can initialize and copy their ROMs into upper memory.

8. **RAM is counted and tested.** The system tests and counts all RAM that's installed in the machine by writing a bit to each bit of memory. If a 1 is written and read back successfully, the counter increments. A failure during this portion of the POST will generate a "201–Memory Error" message on the screen. (Here's a free tip for you: Any POST error numbers starting with 2 are memory-related errors.)

9. **The keyboard is tested.** The keyboard controller is contacted and signals are sent to detect the presence of a keyboard. Checks for stuck keys are also made. If this test fails, a "301–Keyboard Failure" error is generated, along with a short beep. Some systems may halt, others may not. (Some systems also ask you to press <F1> ...which is kind of silly if the keyboard isn't working.)

10. **Test floppy drives.** The floppy disk adapter is contacted and asked to activate the drive motors of any floppy disk drives, in order (A:, then B:). If there are problems, a "601–Floppy Disk" error is generated.

11. **Check resources and boot the computer.** The POST routine queries any remaining devices (LPT ports, serial ports, etc.), makes a short beep, and then queries the disk drives looking for the master boot record (MBR), or the DOS boot record (DBR) in the case of a floppy. It will pass control of the system to the MBR or DBR as soon as they are loaded. If the POST cannot find the MBR, the system will typically freeze and not display a message.

The POST routines are a great tool for troubleshooting. In the event of an error, the POST issues an audible error beep code, then attempts to display the error code on the upper left corner of the screen, providing an English description of the problem (i.e., a visual error code). Some BIOS POST routines may actually give suggestions for how to fix the problem. Tables 2.1 and 2.2 summarize the common POST beep and error codes, respectively, most often seen on computers today.

T A B L E 2.1: Common POST Beep Codes

Beep Code	Problem
No beep, system dead	Power supply bad, system not plugged in, or power not turned on
Continuous beeps	Power supply bad or not plugged into motherboard correctly, or keyboard stuck
Repeating short beep	Power supply may be bad
1 short beep, nothing on screen	Video card failure
1 short beep, video present, but system won't boot	Bad floppy drive, cable, or controller
2 short beeps	Configuration error (on most PS/2 systems)
1 long, 1 short	System board bad
1 long, 2 short	Video card failure

T A B L E 2.2: Common POST Error Codes

Error Code	Problem
1**	Any number starting with 1 usually indicates a system board problem.
161	CMOS battery failure
164	Memory size error. Always happens after memory has been added. Running the BIOS setup program will allow the system to recognize the memory and the error should go away.
2**	Any number starting with 2 usually indicates a memory-related problem.
201	Memory test failed. One or more portions of RAM were found to be bad. Any numbers following this error code may indicate which RAM chip is bad. See the computer's documentation for information on interpreting those codes.

T A B L E 2.2: Common POST Error Codes *(continued)*

Error Code	Problem
3**	Any error number starting with 3 usually indicates a problem with the keyboard. Problems include a missing or malfunctioning keyboard, as well as stuck keys.
301	Keyboard error. Usually means that a keyboard is missing or malfunctioning, or that a key has been pressed too long during startup (are you resting your hand on the keyboard? is something leaning against one of the keys?). Also happens if a key remains depressed during the POST keyboard test.
4**	Monochrome video problems
5**	Color video problems
6**	Floppy disk system problems
601	Floppy disk error. Either the floppy adapter or the floppy drive failed. Check to see that the floppy cable isn't on upside down and that the power to the floppy drive(s) is hooked up correctly.
17**	Hard disk problems. The hard disk geometry might not be set correctly, or the disk adapter can't communicate with the hard disk.
1780	Drive 0 (C:) drive failure. The C: drive or controller isn't functioning. The disk might not be configured, or the adapter might be incorrectly installed.
1781	Drive 1 (D:) drive failure. The D: drive or controller isn't functioning. The disk might not be configured, or the adapter might be installed incorrectly.

The Bootstrap Loader

Knowing some facts about the booting process is helpful in solving problems that may occur during the loading phase of the operating system.

In the last phase of the POST, booting occurs as the BIOS looks for and loads the MBR. The MBR consists of 512 bytes located on cylinder 0, head 0, sector 1 of the hard disk. It contains information on how the drive is divided into partitions, and it will run its Partition Table program designed to locate a bootable partition. If there is a problem with the MBR, most likely the system will freeze and will not display any error messages. If the MBR is functioning properly but cannot locate a bootable partition, it will display this message:

```
Missing Operating System
```

If there is a problem with the MBR, it will need to be replaced with a fresh copy. The MBR can be backed up with a Utilities program such as DiskEdit, or by using the DEBUG command in DOS 6.

The job of the Master Boot Record is to load the first sector of the primary partition into memory and pass control to whatever program is residing there—the DBR, in this case.

The DBR then looks for the two hidden system files, IO.SYS and MSDOS.SYS. If it can't find them in the root directory, it will display the message:

```
Non-System disk or disk error
Replace and strike any key when ready
```

In this case, a bootable floppy disk containing the DOS system files may be required to boot the system. Once loaded, IO.SYS takes over from the DBR.

Motherboard Problems

The motherboard (or system board) functions are tested, for the most part, by the POST routines. The 1** errors and beep codes during startup indicate the biggest problems. Very few motherboard problems occur that don't show up in the POST.

BIOS Problems

The BIOS software can develop problems related to the configuration settings contained on the CMOS chip. A problem here is indicated when the system constantly loses its clock. The time will reset to 12:00 on 12/01/83, for example. At the same time, you may start seeing "1780–Hard Disk Failure" problems. When you try to reset the time, it will set correctly. But as soon as you turn off the computer and turn it back on, the time has been lost.

These symptoms indicate that the system CMOS is losing the time, date, and hard disk settings (as well as several other system settings). The CMOS is able to keep this information when the system is shut off because there is a small battery powering this memory. Because it is a battery, it will eventually lose power and go dead.

When the CMOS battery is replaced, the system settings must be reset. But they will be retained when the power is shut off. Some people immediately think "system board problem" when the answer is a cheap little battery and ten minutes of labor. Because of the simplicity of this repair, most service professionals replace these batteries as a courtesy service for their customers. Consider it an "outpatient" repair.

Other problems may occur with the BIOS software that are caused by BIOS incompatibility with DOS or Windows 3.*x*. In these cases, replacing or "flashing" the BIOS may be necessary.

TIP   Because the BIOS settings can eventually be lost when the CMOS battery finally loses its charge, we encourage all technicians (and PC owners in general) to record their BIOS settings (on paper, or save them to a floppy) so that they may be reset if you have to replace the CMOS battery. The BIOS settings are available from the computer's Setup program, which is accessible by a special key or key combination during startup. Some computers use the Delete key, one of the function keys, or Esc; others use Ctrl+Alt+Esc.

Hard Disk System Problems

Hard disk system problems usually stem from one of three causes:

- The adapter is bad or misconfigured.

- The adapter or disk is connected incorrectly.

- The disk is bad.

The first and second cause are easy to identify, because in either case the symptom will be obvious: the drive won't work. Check the adapter and disk connections. If they're OK, then the problem is usually a bad or misconfigured disk adapter.

However, if the problem is a bad disk drive, the symptoms aren't as obvious. As long as the BIOS POST tests can communicate with the disk drive, they are usually satisfied. But the POST tests may not uncover the following problems:

- You're permitted to save information to the disk, but when you try to read it back you get errors.

- The computer boots more slowly than it used to (this may happen because the disk drive can't read the boot information successfully every time).

Bad disk drives could be the cause of the problems in both of these examples, but neither problem would be indicated by a POST test.

In some cases, reformatting the drive can solve the problems described in the preceding paragraph. In other cases, reformatting only brings the drive back to life for a short while. The bottom line is, read and write problems usually indicate that the drive is "going south" and should be replaced soon. Never expect a "Band-Aid" type of repair like reformatting to cover a major trauma problem like disk failure.

WARNING   NEVER LOW-LEVEL FORMAT IDE OR SCSI DRIVES! (A low-level format is the process that creates the tracks and sectors on a blank hard disk or floppy disk, sometimes called the physical format.) They are low-level formatted at the factory and you may cause problems by using low-level utilities on these types of drives.

Floppy Disk Drive Problems

Troubleshooting the floppy drive is relatively simple. Check the obvious things like a disconnected floppy cable, unplugged power cord, or disk not inserted properly. A common problem that comes up immediately after installation is a drive light that refuses to go out. This is caused by having the floppy drive cable upside down on one side.

The type and size of the floppy drive must be set correctly in the CMOS setup. If this information is wrong, most computers will detect that the wrong drive type is selected and will give an error during bootup.

Another problem you can troubleshoot is sporadic read/write problems. More often than not, these are caused by a dirty drive. If this is the problem, it can be fixed with a floppy-disk head-cleaning kit. Another cause might be a bad floppy disk. Floppies have a finite number of uses in them and they *can* go bad. In 5¼" drives, read/write problems may also be caused by bad alignment. Replacing the drive is the most economical option in this case.

Modem Problems

The biggest set of peripheral problems are those related to modem communications. If a modem is malfunctioning, first make sure there is not an IRQ conflict. IRQ conflicts are a very common trouble source with modems. Other problems include the following:

- The modem won't dial.
- The modem keeps hanging up in the middle of a communication session.
- The modem spits out strange characters to your terminal screen.

If the modem won't dial, the problem usually has to do with *initialization commands*. These are the commands sent to the modem by the communications program to prepare it for communication. These commands tell it things like how many rings to wait before answering, how long to wait after the last keystroke was detected before disconnecting, and at what speed to communicate.

The set of modem initialization commands are known as the Hayes command set, based on the original Hayes line of modems. It is also known as the AT command set, since each Hayes modem command starts with the letters "AT" (presumably calling the modem to ATtention).

Each AT command does something different. The letters "AT" by themselves (when issued as a command) will ask the modem if it's ready to receive commands. If the modem returns "ok," that means it is ready to communicate. If you receive "error," it means there is an internal modem problem that may need to be resolved before communication can take place.

TIP The Modems properties sheet in the Windows 95 Control Panel contains a valuable diagnostics tool with which you can test your setup.

Table 2.3 lists a few of the more common AT commands, their functions, and the problems that they can solve. These commands can be sent to the modem by opening a terminal program such as HyperTerminal (supplied with Windows 95), WINTERM.EXE, or ProCOMM and typing them in. All commands should return "ok" if they were successful.

T A B L E 2.3: Common "AT" Commands

Command	Function	Usage
AT	Tells the modem that what follows the letters "AT" is a command that should be interpreted	Used to precede most commands
ATDT *nnnnnnn*	Dials the number *nnnnnnn* as a tone-dialed number	Used to dial the number of another modem if the phone line is set up for tone dialing

T A B L E 2.3: Common "AT" Commands *(continued)*

Command	Function	Usage
ATDP *nnnnnnn*	Dials the number *nnnnnnn* as a pulse-dialed number	Used to dial the number of another modem if the phone line is set up for rotary dialing
ATA	Answers an incoming call manually	Places the line off-hook and starts to negotiate communication with the modem on the other end
ATH0 (or +++ and then ATH0)	Tells modem to hang up immediately	Places the line on-hook and stops communication. (Note: The "0" in this command is a zero, not a letter.)
AT&F	Resets modem to factory default settings	This setting works as the initialization string when others don't. If you have problems with modems hanging up in the middle of a session, or failing to establish connections, use this string by itself to initialize the modem.
ATZ	Resets modem to power-up defaults	Almost as good as AT&F, but may not work if power-up defaults have been changed with S-registers
ATS0=*n*	Waits *n* rings before answering a call	Sets the default number of rings that the modem will detect before taking the modem off-hook and negotiating a connection. (Note: The "0" in this command is a zero, not a letter.)
ATS6=*n*	Waits *n* seconds for a dial tone before dialing	If the phone line is slow to give a dial tone, you may have to set this register to a number higher than 2.

TABLE 2.3: Common "AT" Commands *(continued)*

Command	Function	Usage
	Pauses briefly	When placed in a string of AT commands, the comma will cause a pause to occur. Used to separate the number for an outside line (many businesses use 9 to connect to an outside line) and the real phone number (e.g.: 9,555-1234).
*70 or 1170	Turns off call waiting	The "click" you hear when you have call waiting (a feature offered by the phone company) will interrupt modem communication and cause the connection to be lost. To disable call waiting for a modem call, place these commands in the dialing string like so: ***70,555-1234**. Call waiting will resume after the call is hung up.
CONNECT	Displayed when a successful connection has been made	You may have to wait some time before this message is displayed. If this message is not displayed, it means the modem couldn't negotiate a connection with the modem on the other end of the line, due possibly to line noise.
BUSY	Displayed when the number dialed is busy	If displayed, some programs will wait a certain amount of time and try again to dial.
RING	Displayed when the modem has detected a ringing line	When someone is calling your modem, the modem will display this in the communications program. You would type **ATA** to answer the call.

NOTE If you can't type anything, you either don't have the right COM port selected for the modem or you have half-duplex mode enabled. To address this problem, you must enter **ATF1**, then press Enter. The modem should return the message "ok" and you will now be able to see your commands.

If two computers can connect but both receive garbage to their screens, there's a good chance that the computers aren't agreeing on the communications settings. Settings like data bits, parity, stop bits, local echo, and compression must all agree for communication to take place. The most common settings are as follows:

- data bits = 8 or 7
- stop bits = 1
- parity = none, even, or odd
- local echo = on or off
- compression = yes or no

These settings are configured through software and can be easily changed.

Display System Problems

There are two types of video problems: No video and bad video. No video means that there is no image on the screen when the computer is powered up. Bad video means that the quality is substandard for the type of display system being used.

No Video

Any number of things can cause a blank screen. The first two are the most common: Either the power is off or the contrast or brightness is turned down. It's surprising how many people get stuck on that first one. Dials or buttons at the base of the monitor control the screen contrast and brightness.

If they really did check the power as well as the brightness and contrast settings, then it's either a bad video card or a blown monitor. The only effective way to quickly determine which one it is is to turn on the computer and monitor, then touch the monitor screen. The high voltage used to charge the monitor will leave a static charge on a working monitor, and it's a charge that can be felt. If there's no charge, there's a good chance the flyback transformer has blown and the monitor needs to be repaired. If there is a charge, suspect the video card or cable.

TIP This charge drains away fairly quickly after power-up, so this test only works immediately after power-up. Also, it's not a conclusive test, but it gives a good indication.

Bad Video

You may have seen a monitor that has a bad data cable. This is the monitor nobody wants because everything has a blue (or red, or green) tint to it and it gives everyone a headache. This monitor could also have a bad gun, but more often than not, the problem goes away if you wiggle the cable (indicating a bad cable). Check for bent pins on a bad cable; if someone tried to force the connection, they may have inadvertently bent the pins.

You also may have seen monitors that are out of adjustment. Their pictures don't fill the screen (size adjustment), or the images "roll" (vertical or horizontal hold), or they are distorted (angle and pincushion adjustments). Use the dials or buttons at the base of the monitor to fix the problem.

The earth generates a very strong magnetic field. This magnetic field can eventually cause swirls and fuzziness in high-quality monitors. To solve this problem, these monitors have a built-in feature known as the "degauss" feature. This feature removes the effects of the magnetic field by creating a stronger magnetic field with opposite polarity that gradually fades to a field of zero. A special degauss button activates it. The image will shake momentarily during the degauss cycle, then return to normal.

TIP The degauss feature should not be used every day. Once a month is usually sufficient if you are having color or clarity problems that get worse with time. You would only have to degauss every day if you lived in a place where high magnetic fields are a problem. If that's the situation you find yourself in, you might need to purchase a special, heavily shielded monitor.

Dislodged Chips and Cards

The inside of your computer is a fairly harsh environment. The temperature inside the case of some Pentium computers is well over 100°F! When you turn your computer on, it heats up. Turn it off, it cools down. After several hundred cycles of this, some components can't handle the stress and start to move out of their sockets. This phenomenon is known as "chip creep" and can really be frustrating.

Chip creep can affect any socketed device, including integrated circuits, RAM chips, and expansion cards. The solution to chip creep is simple. Open the case and reseat the devices. It's surprising how often this is the solution to "phantom" problems of all sorts.

Input Devices

The mouse and the keyboard typically do not have many problems. When they do, it is usually caused by the accumulation of dust and dirt.

SEE ALSO For information on cleaning the mouse and keyboard, go to Chapter 3, "Safety and Preventive Maintenance."

Memory Errors

Very rarely does anything go wrong with the memory in a PC. However, you need to have background knowledge of *possible* memory problems in case they do occur.

It is very easy to tell when a memory error occurs, because a computer malfunctions seriously with bad memory. With a memory error, the computer will do one of two things. If the computer is already running, it will report the error and stop the program. If the error occurs during the POST memory countup, the computer will not start at all.

There are two types of memory problems: soft errors and hard errors. Soft errors occur once and disappear after the computer is rebooted. They are usually caused by power fluctuations or single bit errors. The symptoms are typically unexplained problems with software, and are not reproducible. If these errors increase in frequency, it usually indicates a hard memory error is about to occur.

Hard memory errors are related to a hardware failure and *are* reproducible. When a hard memory error occurs, the computer might issue either a "Parity Error" or a "201–BIOS Error" or, at startup, issue a series of beeps. For example, if you are using AMI BIOS, and the computer issues one long and three short beeps on startup (other BIOSes will use different beep codes), you have a hardware-related memory error.

To solve a hard memory error, you must replace some memory chips. Since most computers have more than one memory chip, you must determine which chip(s) or SIMM(s) need to be replaced. One way to do this is to systematically replace one chip at a time until the memory error goes away. An easier alternative is to simply replace all the memory at once.

TIP Some BIOSes have beep or error codes that indicate which chip has failed. In those cases, use the manual that comes with the motherboard to determine which chip is causing the error (assuming there is a manual available).

Device Driver Problems

Device driver problems are software problems. If you suspect you may be having a software problem, boot the computer "clean."

In DOS/Windows computers, a clean boot means starting the computer with no software drivers loading. If the computer functions normally after a clean boot, then the problem is usually software-related, although it could be a hardware problem that manifests when the device driver enables the device.

Booting Clean in DOS

The way to perform a clean boot is to press the F5 key (or the Shift key) while your machine is booting up. The keystroke must occur after the message comes up that says:

```
Starting MS-DOS...
```

If this solves the problem, you are facing a device driver problem; you will need to find out which driver is to blame. You can do this by performing an *interactive boot*: reboot and press F8 when the "Starting MS-DOS" message appears.

In an interactive boot, each command in the CONFIG.SYS file will be displayed one at a time during bootup, followed by a [Y, N] query, as in the following example:

```
DEVICE=C:\HIMEM.SYS [Y,N]?
```

Here, DOS is requesting that you tell it whether you want this command line processed or ignored. After you respond, it will bring up the next command in your CONFIG.SYS file. By using a series of reboots, you can narrow down the problem to a specific command line. Start with the device driver commands, as these are most likely the cause of the problem. When you have answered Y or N to each query, another question will appear:

```
Process Autoexec.bat [Y,N]?
```

Unlike CONFIG.SYS, individualized control of the commands in AUTOEXEC.BAT is not available. DOS will either process the entire file or skip it altogether.

NOTE Another way to boot clean is to start the computer with a bootable floppy disk in the disk drive. The creation of a bootable floppy is very simple. Insert a blank 1.44MB or 720KB diskette into your floppy drive and type the following at a DOS prompt: **FORMAT A: /S**. The /S parameter instructs DOS to include the DOS system files on the floppy after formatting it. Make the disk while your system is operational; then save it for use as an emergency boot disk.

Booting Clean in Windows 95

A clean boot in Windows 95 is very similar to DOS. Press the F8 function key right after the text message appears:

```
Starting Windows 95...
```

The Windows 95 Startup menu will appear, providing a number of options such as those listed here:

```
1. Normal
2. Logged (\BOOTLOG.TXT)
3. Safe mode
4. Safe mode with network support
5. Step-by-step confirmation
6. Command prompt only
7. Safe mode command prompt only
```

Other options may appear in the Startup menu if you have a compressed drive or originally installed Windows 95 over an older version of DOS.

Option 3, *Safe mode*, is the one you'll want to try first. This will load Windows with a basic VGA video driver and no networking drivers, and will skip the CONFIG.SYS and AUTOEXEC.BAT files.

If this is successful, you can find out the source of the problem by process of elimination. From the Windows 95 Startup menu, select option number 5, *Step-by-step confirmation*. This option allows you to prevent specific drivers from loading, just as you would in DOS by using REM statements. Select a different driver or command to skip during each reboot until you've isolated the problem.

NOTE   You can create a Windows 95 bootable disk by double-clicking the Add/Remove Programs icon in the Control Panel. Select the Startup Disk tab and follow the directions. You can use this disk for a clean boot.

SEE ALSO For more information on troubleshooting, see *A+ Core Module Study Guide, 2nd ed.* (Sybex, 1998).

Power Supply

If you turn on your computer and nothing happens at all, the power supply becomes immediately suspect. Make sure the cables are properly seated, including the cable that attaches to the motherboard. The fan gets power first when you turn on the computer, so check it first. If the fan doesn't do anything, the power supply isn't getting any power and it needs to be replaced.

Additionally, some of the POST audible codes point to a problem with the power supply. Continuous beeps or a repeating short beep may indicate that either the keyboard is stuck or the power supply is bad.

Table 2.4 shows what voltages a power supply should produce. If you have questions about the power supply, test the yellow, blue, and red wires against the black grounding wires.

TABLE 2.4: Power Supply Output

Wire	Voltage Rating	Acceptable Output (volts)
Yellow	+12	+8.6–+12.4
Yellow	-5	-4.5–5.4
Blue	-12	-8.6–12.4
Red	+5	+2.4–+4.2

Exam Essentials

Technicians are paid to keep the machinery operational. Because the test designers know this, issues related to error messages and troubleshooting are heavily emphasized.

Understand what the POST can tell you, and what it can't.
Familiarize yourself with the 11-point POST summary at the beginning of the chapter to help you remember POST details.

Know how to fix problems with the BIOS software. The most common problem with BIOS is a low CMOS battery. In this case, the CMOS settings should be recorded and the battery replaced.

Know the signs of a failing hard disk. Difficulty in reading/writing information to and from disk or sporadic difficulty in booting may indicate a failing hard disk.

Understand the boot sequence. The POST loads the MBR and passes over control of the bootstrap. The MBR loads the DBR, which allows DOS to load. Problems in these phases will result in specific error messages.

Know the basic set of modem AT commands. A list of these commands is found in Table 2.3. Some of these commands are used in troubleshooting modem communications.

Know the difference between hard and soft memory errors. Soft memory errors are not reproducible, and are often solved with a reboot. Hard memory errors, by contrast, *are* reproducible, and may require replacement of a SIMM.

Know the signs of a failed power supply, including proper voltage levels. When you turn on the power and your computer does nothing at all, the power supply is likely to be the problem. Several POST error codes also point to the power supply.

Key Terms and Concepts

Clean boot: Refers to loading the operating system without its device drivers. This technique is a common troubleshooting tool for checking software.

DBR: Acronym for DOS boot record. A small program contained in the first sector of the primary partition, designed to find and load the DOS operating system.

HyperTerminal: A Windows program that can be used in modem communications and that recognizes the common AT command set.

MBR: Acronym for master boot record. A small program that will find and load the first sector of a DOS-bootable partition into memory. This sector will contain the DOS boot record.

Pincushion distortion: A type of distortion that usually occurs at the edges of a video screen where the sides of an image seem to bow inward.

POST: Acronym for power-on self test. A set of diagnostic programs, loaded automatically from ROM BIOS during startup, designed to ensure that major system components are present and operating.

Sample Questions

1. What command is used to begin a modem communication?

   A. AT&F

   B. ATM0

   C. ATZ

   D. ATDT

   Answer: D. ATDT followed by a phone number will dial up another modem, if the phone line is set up for tone dialing.

2. If you test a 12-volt power supply, and it reads 7 volts, what should you do?

   A. Replace the power supply.

   B. Repair the power supply.

   C. Do nothing; a slight fluctuation is okay.

   D. Test the current.

   Answer: A. Acceptable voltage in this case is between +8.5 and +12.6 volts.

3. What will a POST audible/visual error code indicate?

   A. Problem with the MBR

   B. Problem with a device driver in `CONFIG.SYS`

   C. Parity error

   D. Soft memory error

   Answer: C. A parity error is a hard memory error, which the POST checks.

4. The MBR is located where?

   A. Cylinder 0, head 0, sector 0

   B. The first sector of cylinder 0

   C. The first sector of cylinder 1

   D. Cylinder 0, head 1, sector 1

   Answer: B. The master boot record (MBR) containing partition information is located on cylinder 0, head 0, sector 1 of the hard disk.

Identify basic troubleshooting procedures and good practices for eliciting problem symptoms from customers.

Just like every artist has their own style, every technician has their own way to troubleshoot. Although an "industry standard" troubleshooting procedure does not exist, the 10 steps described here include some of the most frequently used troubleshooting methods.

The designers of the exam are very interested in whether a reputed computer technician is able to apply ordered and effective troubleshooting methods such as these, and they test accordingly.

Critical Information

These ten troubleshooting steps work best if you try them in order. If any step you're on doesn't narrow the problem down, you move on to the next one.

Step 1: Define the Problem

If you can't define a problem, you can't solve it. You can define the problem by asking questions of the user. Here are a few questions to ask the user to aid in determining exactly what the problem *is*:

- **Can you show me the problem?** This question allows the user to show you exactly where and when they experience the problem.

- **How often does this happen?** This question establishes whether this problem is a one-time occurrence (usually indicating a "soft" memory error or the like) that can be solved with a reboot, or whether the problem has a specific sequence of events that cause it to happen (usually indicating a more serious problem that may require software reinstallation or hardware replacement).

- **Were any error messages displayed?** Even a cryptic error message may yield some clues to the nature of the problem.

- **Has any new software been installed recently?** New software can mean incompatibility problems with existing problems. This is especially true for Windows programs. A new Windows program can overwrite a required DLL file with a newer version of the same name, which an older program may not find useful.

- **What applications were you using/working with at the time?** They may be using buggy or corrupted software that is responsible for the problem. A fresh installation of the application may be necessary.

- **Have any other changes been made to the computer recently?** If the answer is "Yes," ask if they can remember approximately when the change was made. Then ask them approximately when the problem started. If the two dates seem related, there's a good chance that the problem is related to the change. If it's a new hardware component, check to see that the hardware component was installed correctly.

Step 2: Check the Simple Stuff First

This step is the one that most experienced technicians overlook. Often, computer problems have a very simple cause. Some examples are:

- **Is it plugged in?** And on *both ends?* Cables must be plugged in on both ends in order to function correctly. Cables can be easily tripped over and inadvertently pulled from their sockets.

- **Is it turned on?** This one seems the most obvious, but we've all fallen victim to it at one point or another. Computers and their peripherals must be turned on in order to function. Most have power switches that have LEDs that glow when the power is turned on.

- **Is the system ready?** Computers must be ready before they can be used. "Ready" means that the system is ready to accept commands from the user. An indication that a computer is ready is when the operating system screens come up and the computer presents you with a menu or a command prompt. If that computer uses a graphical interface, the computer is ready when the mouse pointer appears. Printers are ready when the "On Line" or "Ready" light on the front panel is lit.

- **Are any of the chips or cables loose?** You can solve some of the strangest problems (random hang-ups or errors) by opening the case and pressing down on (reseating) each socketed chip. This remedies the "chip creep" problem mentioned earlier in the book. In addition, you should also reseat any cables and clean edge connectors to make sure that they are making good contact.

Step 3: Check to See If It's User Error

One of the more common errors that technicians run into is the user error. An indication that a problem is due to user error is when a user says they can't perform some very common computer task—e.g., "I can't print," "I can't save my file," "I can't run my favorite application," etc. As soon you hear these words, you should start asking questions to determine whether it is a user error or a computer problem (i.e., hardware or software). A good question to ask following their statement of the problem would be "Were you *ever* able to perform that task?" If they answer no to this question, it means they are probably doing the procedure wrong—user error. If they answer yes, you must move on to another set of questions.

TIP This doesn't mean you should assume "the user is always wrong." An attitude like that can come across on the phone, and in person, as arrogance.

Step 4: Restart the Computer

Restarting the computer after powering off clears the memory and gives the computer a clean slate. It is amazing how often this can solve a problem. Rebooting without powering off will often (but not always) produce the same effect.

Step 5: Determine If the Problem Is Hardware- or Software-Related

This step is an important one because it determines what part of the computer you should focus your troubleshooting skills on. Each part requires different skills and different tools.

To determine if a problem is hardware- or software-related, you could do a few things to narrow the problem down. For instance, does the problem manifest itself when you use a particular piece of hardware (a modem, for example)? If it does, the problem is more than likely hardware-related.

This step relies on personal experience more than any of the other steps do. You will without a doubt run into many strange software problems, which may even require reinstallation of the software or the entire operating system.

Step 6: If the Problem Is Software-Related, Boot "Clean"

If you are experiencing software problems, a common trouble-shooting technique with DOS-based computers is to boot clean. This means starting the computer without loading its device drivers by using the F5 or F8 function key at startup. In Windows 95, pressing F8 at startup will allow you to boot the computer in Safe mode.

SEE ALSO   For more information on clean boots, see the previous section of this chapter on device driver problems.

Step 7: If the Problem Is Hardware-Related, Determine Which Component Is Failing

Hardware problems are pretty easy to figure out. If the modem doesn't work, and you know it isn't a software problem, then swap the modem.

With some of the newer computers, several components are integrated onto the motherboard. If you troubleshoot the computer and find a hardware component to be bad, there's a good chance that the bad component (for example, the parallel port circuitry) is integrated into the motherboard and the whole motherboard must be replaced. An expensive proposition, to be sure.

Step 8: Check Service Information Sources

The service manuals are your "instructions" for troubleshooting and service information. Almost every computer and peripheral made today has a set of service documentation in the form of books, service CD-ROMs, and Web sites. The use of Web sites for this purpose seems to be growing in popularity as more and more service centers get connections to the Internet.

Step 9: If It Ain't Broke...Change It Back

When you troubleshoot, make one change at a time. If the change doesn't solve the problem, return the setting to its original state before trying something else.

Step 10: Ask for Help

If you don't know the answer, ask one of your fellow technicians. They may have run across the problem you are having and know the solution.

This solution does involve a little humility. You must first admit that you don't know the answer. It is said that the beginning of wisdom is "I don't know." If you ask questions, you will get answers, and you will learn from the answers. Making mistakes is valuable as well, as long as you learn from them.

TIP If you have no fellow technicians, get on the Internet and check out the technical chat rooms. See *A+ Core Module Study Guide*, Appendix C, for a list of Web sites that offer technical support and advice; some of them have chat rooms.

Exam Essentials

Several questions on the test pertain to general procedures that are effective in troubleshooting.

Know how to elicit information from a user when facing a computer problem. Asking specific questions such as "Can you show me the problem?" will help define the problem.

Know the simple problems common to a non-functional device. The simple solutions include devices that aren't plugged in, connections that are loose, and devices that are not turned on.

Know how to determine if the problem is user error. Find out how much experience the user has with the computer and with any application that isn't working.

Know how to determine a hardware vs. a software problem.   A combination of clean boots and troubleshooting experience will help you to isolate which component (or which device driver) is failing. If necessary, you can test a piece of hardware by swapping it.

Know the value of rebooting.   Rebooting the computer is helpful in solving "soft memory" errors.

Key Terms and Concepts

DLL: Acronym for dynamic link library. A program module that contains executable code and data that can be used by application programs in performing a task.

LED: Acronym for light-emitting diode. A small semiconductor device that emits light as current flows through it. Often used to show device activity.

Soft memory error: Errors that are usually caused by power fluctuations or single bit errors, and are usually solved by rebooting.

Sample Questions

1. If a user is experiencing a computer malfunction and is trying to describe it by saying that a certain application doesn't work, you should:

   A. Ask him to move from his seat so you can examine his computer more closely.

   B. Ask some questions to help define the problem.

   C. Reinstall the application.

   D. Suggest the user call the Tech Support department.

   Answer: B. The first step in troubleshooting is to define the problem.

2. A computer is experiencing random reboots and "phantom" problems that disappear after reboot. What should you do?

    A. Tell the customer that it's normal for the computer to do that.

    B. Replace the motherboard.

    C. Boot clean.

    D. Open the cover and reseat all cards and chips.

    Answer: D. Although rebooting may provide a momentary fix, it will not solve the problem. You should reseat all cards, chips, and cables.

CHAPTER

3

Safety and Preventive
Maintenance

A+ Core Module Exam Objectives Covered in This Chapter:

▶ Identify the purpose of various types of preventive maintenance products and procedures, and when to use/perform them. *(pages 135 – 139)*

▶ Identify procedures and devices for protecting against environmental hazards. *(pages 140 – 145)*

▶ Identify the potential hazards and proper safety procedures relating to lasers and high-voltage equipment. *(pages 145 – 148)*

▶ Identify items that require special disposal procedures that comply with environmental guidelines. *(pages 149 – 152)*

▶ Identify ESD (Electrostatic Discharge) precautions and procedures, including the use of ESD protection devices. *(pages 152 – 158)*

Besides needing to know how to take apart, repair, and reassemble a computer, you also need to know how to carry out these tasks *safely*. Be careful when you go to open the computer; there are many hazards that you may or may not already be aware of, and any one of them could ultimately harm you or the components of the PC.

As a provider of a hands-on service (repairing, maintaining, or upgrading someone's computer), it is important for you to be aware that computers, display monitors, and printers can be dangerous if not handled properly. A computer or a peripheral may contain lasers and high-voltage and high-temperature equipment. It may also contain hazardous chemicals that are dangerous to the environment and must be properly discarded when their usefulness has passed.

Conversely, the "environment" in which it is placed can also be dangerous to the computer's functioning. Because a computer is a sensitive (and expensive) piece of machinery, this chapter also explores environmental threats to the computer. These threats range from simple dirt that clogs a keyboard to the voltage irregularities emanating from a wall socket, and also include the most common danger to a PC: the hurried technician who strays inside its case, carrying chip-destroying static electricity in his fingertips, like a wizard with a handful of lightning bolts. All these issues are reflected by numerous questions you will encounter on the test.

Identify the purpose of various types of preventive maintenance products and procedures, and when to use/perform them.

Dirt or dust in a component may actually mimic more serious hardware problems. For this reason, a computer technician needs to know how to properly maintain computer components, what products to use in maintenance procedures, and what problems indicate that cleaning is required. However, only a few questions on the test pertain to cleaning and maintenance.

Critical Information

Dust is the cause of many common problems that afflict a PC. Dust may cause certain devices to malfunction, and can even contribute to the death of a PC due to overheating. In addition to dust, water, carbonic acid, and human skin oil contain corrosive acids that can also damage computer components.

Specific problems caused by dirty components and tips for cleaning the components are included here.

Keyboards

Usually, keyboard problems are environmental. They get dirty and the keys start to stick. A spilled soft drink will work its way into the plungers under the key caps and, instead of drying, turns into a sticky, syrupy substance that doesn't easily wash away.

To clean a keyboard, it's best to use the keyboard cleaner sold by electronics supply stores. This cleaner foams up quickly and doesn't leave a residue behind. Spray it liberally on the keyboard and keys. Work the cleaner in between the keys with a stiff toothbrush. Blow the excess away with a strong blast of compressed air. Repeat until the keyboard functions properly. If you do have to clean a keyboard that has had a soft drink spilled on it, remove the key caps before you perform the cleaning procedure. That makes it easier to reach the sticky plungers.

To clean the key caps on a keyboard, spray keyboard cleaner on a soft, lint-free cloth and rub it briskly onto the surface of each key.

For environments which contains an extreme amount of dust or dirt, fitted plastic coverings should be placed over keyboards. A product designed for this purpose that is widely available on the market is Safeskin.

NOTE Another way to clean a keyboard is to soak it in water! This can be especially effective immediately after spilling something on it such as a soft drink. However, make sure the keyboard is completely dry before you plug it back in.

Mouse/Trackball Problems

Dirt and dust stick to the mouse (or trackball) rollers and interfere with movement of the mouse pointer on the screen.

To clean the mouse, turn the mouse upside down and remove the ball by rotating the retaining ring counterclockwise. Flip the mouse right side up and the ball will drop out. Flip the mouse back over and locate the two rollers. To clean the "gunk" from the rollers, try using a small eyeglass screwdriver. If the gunk won't come loose, soak the deposits with a little isopropyl alcohol to loosen them. After cleaning the rollers, the mouse performance will be improved.

Floppy Disk Drive

Sporadic read/write problems in a floppy disk drive are often caused by dirt and dust. These devices are prone to dust infiltration because they are open to the air. If this is the problem, it can be fixed with a floppy-disk head-cleaning kit.

Displays

Glass cleaner can be used to remove dust from a CRT monitor screen. However, an LCD requires special treatment. In order to maintain optimal image quality on an LCD, the coating on the screen must be cleaned often. The best way to clean the LCD lens coating is to wipe it off occasionally with a damp cloth. This will ensure that the images stay crisp and clear.

Input devices

Touch screens, drawing tablets, and scanners are some of the other input devices that require special cleaning procedures.

Touch Screens

Cleaning touch screens is usually just as easy as cleaning a regular monitor. With optical touch screens, the monitor *is*, in fact, a regular monitor. It can be cleaned with glass cleaner. However, if the screen has a capacitive coating (made of plastic), the glass cleaner may damage it. Instead, use a cloth dampened with water to clean the dirt, dust, and fingerprints from the capacitive coating screen.

Drawing Tablet

To clean a drawing tablet, wipe the rubberized surface with a damp cloth (no detergents!). If there is a tough stain that the water won't remove, use a cloth dampened with denatured alcohol. After removing the stain, follow with a water-dampened cloth to remove any residue.

Scanner

A dirty scanner bed (the big sheet of glass between the scanning CCD [charge-coupled device] and the item being scanned) can cause image quality problems. Fingerprints show up as dark smudges in the scanned image. Since the scanner bed is simply glass, you can clean it with glass cleaner.

Circuit Boards

Use connector cleaner and a lint-free cloth to clean the edge connectors on a circuit board. Dirty edge connectors can contribute to "phantom" problems that may show up during computer operation.

Use a can of compressed air to clean dust from circuit boards. If there is a lot of dust, have a vacuum ready to handle the dust spray or you'll just be moving dust instead of removing it.

Case

To clean the case of a PC, you can use a water-dampened cloth. Add a few drops of ammonia if necessary. Make sure you remove any dust buildup from the air-intake grill.

Extreme Environmental Conditions

A high concentration of dust or dirt may be present in some work environments and may require special treatment. One solution for excessive dust is to use a power supply with a replaceable filter in the back. If there is a large amount of dirt, purchase plastic keyboard coverings to keep keyboards clean.

Exam Essentials

Though not emphasized on the test, there will be one or two questions pertaining to basic physical maintenance of computer components.

Know what cleaning agents to use on different components.
Some components require special cleaning agents, while a water-dampened cloth or glass cleaner can be used in other cases. See the Critical Information section for more details.

Know what problems dirty components may cause. Dirt in keyboards, mice, circuit boards, and other devices may cause specific problems such as stuck keys, malfunctions, and overheating. See the Critical Information section for more details.

Key Terms and Concepts

Charge-coupled device: Abbreviated CCD. A device that allows light to be converted into electrical pulses.

Edge connector: A form of connector consisting of a row of etched contacts along the edge of a printed circuit board that is inserted into an expansion slot in the computer.

Safeskin: A brand of plastic keyboard covers used to protect a keyboard from dirt and dust.

Sample Questions

1. You should use what to clean edge connectors?

A. Water and light detergent

B. A damp cloth

C. Connector cleaner

D. Isopropyl alcohol

Answer: C. Only specially designed liquids should be used to clean edge connectors.

2. Dirty mouse rollers are likely to cause what problem?

A. A dirty mouse pad

B. A bug in the mouse driver

C. A "sticking" or "jerking" mouse pointer

D. A "phantom" mouse pointer

Answer: C. Dirty rollers will often interfere with mouse movement.

Identify procedures and devices for protecting against environmental hazards.

The power available through an AC outlet is not always predictable or safe, at least from a computer's perspective. This may be the fault of the power company, the building electrician, a lightning storm—or it could even be your own fault. Power problems (usually described as *noise*) fall into three categories: too much voltage (overvoltage, spikes, and surges), too little voltage (undervoltage), or no voltage. Overvoltage can destroy chips suddenly or slowly over time. Undervoltage will cause the power supply to compensate, generating heat. This heat can also damage computer components. This section outlines some of these potential problems and what you can do about them.

Critical Information

Miswiring or power fluctuations may cause the following problems in a PC:

- "freezing up"
- soft memory errors
- lost data
- damaged IC chips

To protect against or solve these problems, make sure of the following:

1. The PC is not sharing power with a power-hungry device.

2. All devices are properly grounded.

3. Protection against power surges, spikes, and improper voltage is in place.

4. The outlets are correctly wired.

A circuit wiring tester will tell you if there's a wiring problem with an outlet. There are three wires in an AC outlet: green, white, and dark (usually black). The green should be wired to the cylinder (ground wire), the white should be attached to the small prong (return wire), and the dark wire should be attached to the large prong ("hot" wire). It is unusual, but possible, for these wires to be switched around.

Copiers, laser printers, air conditioners, refrigerators, space heaters, and coffee makers are examples of devices that draw excessive power. Unless special precautions are taken, it is *very important* that these devices not share an unprotected power line with a PC. You should use a power conditioner or get another circuit to the box.

A common ground is also important and will reduce communication errors between devices. It is also safer. Put devices on a common ground by attaching them to a single power plug strip. (This may not work with a laser printer, as indicated previously.)

Protection against surges, spikes, and improper voltage is accomplished by using a power protection device such as an uninterruptible power supply or surge protector. Surges are especially common after blackouts. Low-voltage brownouts result from the power company's attempts to meet energy demands, usually during heat waves or in the summer. Detailed information on protection devices is included here.

Uninterruptible Power Supply

An uninterruptible power supply (UPS) is a backup power supply that runs continuously. It receives power directly from the outlet, and provides power to the PC. If there is a power surge, the UPS takes the hit, and does not pass it on to the PC. If there is a power failure, the UPS will continue to power the computer, allowing time for a proper shutdown of the system.

A UPS can produce current in square waves or sine waves; the better and more expensive variety produce sine waves. Square waves can appear as electromagnetic interference (EMI) to a PC, and printers don't always handle square waves very well either. If your budget allows, invest your money in a sine-wave UPS.

Standby Power Supplies

A standby power supply (SPS) provides protection against undervoltage. If a power drop occurs, SPS battery power engages and takes over from the outlet. The important factor to consider in using an SPS is its *switching time*. Switching time refers to the time it takes to switch power to its batteries in the event of a power drop. A switching time of 4 milliseconds (ms) or less is adequate.

Unlike a UPS, an SPS provides no protection against power surges.

Surge Suppressers

A surge suppresser is designed to detect a large surge, and redirect it from the PC out to the electric ground. Power plug strips and surge suppressers are typically combined into one device.

A suppresser is designed to allow a specific amount of volts to pass. If the voltage exceeds this limit, it triggers the suppression.

While a suppresser may be better than nothing, it only works once in the event of a big surge, and often there is no way to know if it has already been "torched." The light on it is supposed to tell you if it's good or not. If the light goes out, you definitely need to replace it. However, smaller surges can destroy the suppresser without killing the light, leaving a dead suppresser that appears to be working. This is a severe limitation, and the best alternative to a surge suppressor is a power conditioner.

Power Conditioners

Power conditioners provide the same kind of protection as do surge suppressers, only much improved. They use an isolation transformer to provide superior protection against surges and spikes. You can also tell when they fail; they simply stop providing power. A power conditioner also provides protection against undervoltage by boosting power during brownouts.

Power conditioners provide a level of protection between a surge suppresser and a UPS, and they are priced accordingly.

SEE ALSO For more information on power systems and environmental hazards, see *A+ Core Module Study Guide, 2nd ed.,* by David Groth (Sybex, 1998).

Exam Essentials

Environmental hazards will be the subject of several of the test questions.

Know what signs may indicate power problems. Signs of power problems include "freeze-ups," data loss, soft memory errors, and damaged chips.

Know the safety measures that can be taken to avoid power problems. Safety measures include proper wiring, moving laser printers or other power-hungry machinery to separate lines, proper grounding, and use of power protection devices.

Know the difference between the various power protection devices. An SPS protects against power drops; a surge protector protects against power surges; and a UPS protects against both types of problems. A power conditioner provides protection against surges, and limited protection during power drops.

Key Terms and Concepts

Power conditioner: A device that uses an isolation transformer to protect against power surges, and also boosts power during brownouts.

Power spike: A brief (under 1 ms) but sudden increase in line voltage.

Power supply: A part of the computer that converts the power from a wall outlet into the lower voltages, typically 5 to 12 volts DC, required by the computer.

Power surge: A sudden increase in line voltage, usually lasting 1 ms to several seconds.

SPS: Acronym for standby power supply. A backup power source used in the event of a power drop.

Switching time: The time, rated in milliseconds, that it takes to switch power from the socket to the SPS in the event of a power drop.

UPS: Acronym for uninterruptible power supply. An alternative power source, usually a set of batteries, used to power a computer system if the normal power service is interrupted.

Sample Questions

1. If you want to protect your system against sudden power drops, you should do what?

   A. Use a battery backup system.

   B. Use a surge suppresser.

   C. Back up your data weekly.

   D. Use a power strip.

   Answer: **A.** Using a battery backup system is the best answer. While answer C (backing up your data) is a must, it does not protect against possible hardware damage due to power drops.

2. After a blackout, there is possible danger of what?

   A. EMI

   B. ESD

   C. A power surge

   D. Undervoltage

   Answer: **C.** A power surge takes place when power is restored after a blackout.

3. Grounding is important for what reason?

A. It prevents EMI.

B. It prevents damage from lightning.

C. It prevents ESD.

D. It is an effective safety precaution.

Answer: D. Grounding reduces communication errors and reduces the risk of electric shock.

Identify the potential hazards and proper safety procedures relating to lasers and high-voltage equipment.

A skilled computer technician must be aware of on-the-job health hazards. The greatest health risks in repairing computers come from high voltage capacitors and from lasers, which can cause electrocution, burns, and blindness. This objective describes the risks associated with these components and discusses how to avoid injury.

Critical Information

The power supply, printer, and monitor represent the greatest potential physical hazards to a computer technician. The dangers and precautions associated with these components are described here.

Power Supply

Do not take the issue of safety and electricity lightly. If you were to remove the power supply from its case (and don't get us wrong, we don't recommend it), you would be taking a great risk. The current flowing through the power supply normally follows a complete circuit; when your body breaks that circuit, your body becomes a part of the circuit.

The two biggest dangers with power supplies are burning yourself and electrocuting yourself. These usually go hand in hand. If you touch a bare wire that is carrying current, you may get electrocuted. If a large amount of current passes through your body, it can cause your heart to stop, your muscles to seize, and your brain to stop functioning. In short, it can kill you. If there is a large enough current passing through the wire (and you), you can get severe burns as well. Electricity always finds the best path to ground. And, since we are basically bags of salt water (an excellent conductor of electricity), electricity will use us as a conductor if we are grounded.

Although it is possible to work on a power supply, it is NOT recommended. Power supplies contain several capacitors which can hold LETHAL charges *long after they have been unplugged!* It is extremely dangerous to open the case of a power supply. A power supply should simply be replaced when it malfunctions.

Printer

The laser mechanism within a laser printer is protected by an enclosure, and is designed to function only with the lid closed. Make sure you do not circumvent this design in order to observe the printer at work. The laser beam it generates is dangerous to your eyes and can cause blindness.

In addition to danger from lasers, printers represent a number of potential hazards to the unwary repair technician. Keep in mind these facts and guidelines:

- When handling a toner cartridge from a laser printer or page printer, do not shake or turn the cartridge upside down. You will find yourself spending more time cleaning the printer and the surrounding area than you would have spent fixing the printer.

- Do not put any objects into the feeding system as the printer is running, in an attempt to clear the path.

- Laser printers contain a halogen heating lamp that heats the fusing roller to 350°F; it will burn you if you touch it!

- If it's an ink-jet, do not try to blow in the ink cartridge to clear a clogged opening. That is, unless you like the taste of ink.

- Some parts of a laser printer (like the EP cartridge) will be damaged if touched. Your skin produces oils and has a small surface layer of dead skin cells. These substances can collect on the delicate surface of the EP cartridge and cause malfunctions. Bottom line: Keep your fingers out of places they don't belong!

Monitor

Other than the power supply, one of the most dangerous components to try to repair is the monitor, or CRT. In fact, we recommend that you NOT try to repair monitors. To avoid the extremely hazardous environment contained inside the monitor—it can retain a high voltage charge for hours after it's been turned off—take it to a certified monitor technician or television repair shop. The repair shop or certified technician will know and understand the proper procedures to discharge the monitor, which involves attaching a resistor to the flyback transformer's charging capacitor to release the high-voltage electrical charge that builds up during use. They will also be able to determine whether the monitor can be repaired or whether it needs to be replaced. Remember, the monitor works in its own extremely protective environment (the monitor case), and may not respond well to your desire to try to open it.

Exam Essentials

You will probably encounter one question on the test related to the potential dangers of lasers and high voltage equipment.

Know what devices present a risk of electrocution. Power supplies and CRT monitors contain capacitors which present a risk of electrocution. These devices should not be opened up.

Know what devices present a risk of blindness due to lasers. Printers contain lasers which can cause blindness.

Key Terms and Concepts

Capacitor: An electrical component, normally found in power supplies and timing circuits, used to store electrical charges.

Laser printer: A high-resolution non-impact printer that uses a variation of the electromagnetic process used in photocopying machines to print text and graphics onto paper.

Sample Questions

1. A CRT presents a potential risk of what?

   A. Blindness

   B. Electrocution

   C. EMI

   D. ESD

   Answer: B

2. Which component presents a risk of electric shock?

   A. Capacitor

   B. Transistor

   C. Transformer

   D. Diode

   Answer: A. Capacitors retain a potentially lethal charge several hours after being turned off.

Identify items that require special disposal procedures that comply with environmental guidelines.

Old computers often end up in storage rooms, apparently awaiting the day on which they will again be called into service—or recycled. Alas, their waiting will be in vain. Most computers are obsolete as soon as you buy them. Moreover, if they have not been used recently, their components will more than likely never be used again.

The reason that recycling is usually not an option is because most computers contain small amounts of hazardous substances. Some countries are exploring the option of recycling electrical machines, but most have still not enacted appropriate measures to enforce their proper disposal. Proper (and legal) disposal of computer parts is the subject of this objective.

Critical Information

Monitor screens, batteries, and wiring are some of the computer components containing chemicals that require special disposal. Here are several resources for information on how to dispose of computer components:

- Check with the Environmental Protection Agency (EPA) or the manufacturer to see if what you are disposing of has a Material Safety Data Sheet (an MSDS). These sheets contain information about the toxicity of a product and whether or not it can be disposed of in the trash. It also contains "lethal dose" information.

- Contact the EPA for a list of local or regional waste disposal sites that will accept used computer equipment.

- Check out the Internet for possible waste disposal sites. Table 3.1 gives a few Web sites that deal with disposal of used computer equipment.

T A B L E 3.1: Computer Recycling Web Sites

Site Name	Web Address
Computer Recycle Center	`http://www.recycles.com/`
Re-Compute	`http://www.re-compute.com`
Re-PC	`http://www.repc.com/`

However, before resorting to one of the disposal options above, consider these alternatives:

- Disassemble the machine and reuse the parts that are good.

- Check with the manufacturer. Some manufacturers will take back outdated equipment for parts (and may even pay you for them).

- Check out businesses that can melt the components down for the lead or gold plating.

- Check with local nonprofit or education organizations interested in using the equipment.

In addition to hardware recycling, there are also businesses that offer to recycle consumables, like ink cartridges or printer ribbons. However, this isn't always the best way to keep up with the recycle agenda. Why not? Well, recycled ink cartridges may clog, the ink quality is not as good, and the small circuit board on the cartridge may be damaged. Similarly, recycled toner cartridges don't always operate properly after refilling.

You should, however, make a special effort to recycle *batteries*. Batteries contain several chemicals that are harmful to the environment and won't degrade safely. Batteries should not be thrown away, but rather recycled according to your local laws. Check with your local authorities to find out how batteries should be recycled.

Exam Essentials

Because protecting the environment from hazardous material is an important issue, the test will contain several questions on this subject.

Know which items require special disposal. Some of the items that require special disposal are batteries, monitors, and products which contain wiring.

Know how to find out whether an item requires special disposal. Check with the EPA or contact the product's manufacturer and request an MSDS. This will indicate whether special disposal is required.

Key Terms and Concepts

EPA: Acronym for Environmental Protection Agency. A division of the federal government that handles environmental safety issues.

MSDS: Acronym for Material Safety Data Sheet. A document that contains information about the toxicity of a product and whether or not it can be disposed of in the trash.

Sample Questions

1. When you discard a power supply, you should do what?

   A. Put it in a trash can.

   B. Drop it off at Goodwill.

   C. Read the label.

   D. Find out if it has an MSDS.

   Answer: D. If an MSDS for a component exists, it will indicate special disposal requirements.

2. Which of the following items does NOT require special disposal?

   A. A CRT

   B. A battery

   C. A circuit board

   D. A floppy disk

   Answer: D

Identify ESD (Electrostatic Discharge) precautions and procedures, including the use of ESD protection devices.

The major cause of damage to a PC is *electrostatic discharge* (ESD). ESD is the "shock" you feel after walking across a carpet and touching someone's hand. ESD is caused by static electricity transferring from one charged item (perhaps a person) to another item that is sensitive to the charge. It is very important to understand what causes ESD, the damage it can do, and the methods used to prevent ESD from occurring.

Because the chips inside a PC are most vulnerable to ESD damage, a computer technician is often to blame when it happens. For this reason, the subject of ESD comes up in several questions on the exam.

Critical Information

The static electricity that you generate every day creates ESD. Static electricity is electricity at rest, which is also termed electrostatic *charge*. Electrostatic *dis*charge occurs when the electrostatic charge transfers from one charged entity to another that is sensitive to that charge.

Facts about ESD

ESD can occur at many different levels, causing different degrees of damage. Here are some important facts about electricity and ESD:

- Computer components use 3 to 5 volts.
- If you can *see* a shock, it contains around 20,000 volts.
- A "carpet shock" can generate charges up to 30,000 volts.
- Humans can only feel charges that are greater than 2,500 volts.
- Just shifting in a chair can generate 200 volts.
- A discharge as low as *30 volts* can destroy a computer device.

What this means is that *you can destroy a device without ever feeling a shock*. If you were to damage a computer component in this fashion, you might just assume that the component was bad from the factory, instead of suspecting the real cause. ESD damages are responsible for a large number of supposedly "DOA" (dead on arrival) components (components that in all probability worked fine before you touched them), and for many "no problems found" incident calls.

ESD is a result of natural processes, and therefore cannot be eliminated entirely. However, it is controllable. The first step to controlling ESD is to determine what materials can create the charge. There are three basic characteristics of materials that can generate static electricity:

- insulative
- static dissipative
- conductive

Insulative material does not allow the flow of electrons; thus it presents a high electrical resistance. Examples of insulative materials include mica and rubber. *Static dissipative* material allows the transfer of electrons to ground or other conductive objects. This material has a lower electrical resistance. An example of a static dissipative material would be the antistatic spray that is available for monitors. *Conductive* material allows a charge to flow through it easily; thus it presents a low electrical resistance. Metals are an example of a conductive material.

Environmental factors of dust and moisture contribute to ESD. If dust is allowed to build up, it is able to hold an electrical charge. If a room is dry, which is often the case in the winter months, this dryness will increase the ability of materials to hold a charge. The humidity level should be set to between 50% and 70% to prevent dryness from occurring.

Damage caused by ESD

ESD can occur at many different levels, and it causes the same overvoltage problems described earlier in this chapter. At the very least, an ESD shock can reboot the computer. In the worst case, it can destroy components. Damage can be either *direct* or *latent*:

- Direct damage occurs immediately. This kind of damage is usually completely destructive. A component directly damaged is no longer usable and will need to be replaced.

- Latent damage doesn't happen immediately, but rather occurs over time. In this case, you will see intermittent errors followed by eventual failure of the component. This is more dangerous than direct damage in a way, because you will continue to use a latently damaged component without knowing it's damaged, and this could cause other components to fail.

Preventing ESD

Even though it is impossible to stop ESD, you can minimize its effects. If you feel that you are at any risk of causing ESD, please do not continue with the repair until you are certain that you are in a controlled environment. The following is a list of precautions to take before attempting to repair a piece of computer equipment. This information is also valid for repairs of any type of electrical equipment that may put you at risk of causing ESD.

- Don't wear clothes that contain synthetic materials. These clothes can transfer ESD charges from your skin when they rub against it.

- Use an ESD wrist strap *properly* to prevent ESD damage. Make sure it is securely connected to you *and* to an earth ground so that stray charges can be drained away.

- If you have no other means to remain grounded, go ahead and plug the computer into the wall outlet, keep the computer turned off, *and keep one hand on the frame of the computer while you're working on any parts that are still attached to the computer.* Obviously, this can cramp your abilities to perform the work the way you're used to working, so consider this a good reason to go out and buy an antistatic wrist strip. The frame of the computer is wired to the power supply's ground circuit. As long as you keep your hand on the frame, both you and the computer are at the same electrical potential, and no ESD transfers will take place.

WARNING   If you are planning to use the method mentioned above of plugging in the computer to stay grounded, make sure that there is no active current flowing through the computer. To do this, turn off the computer and check the output of the power supply with a voltmeter.

- Keep electronic devices in their antistatic bags until they are ready for installation. The bags keep static electricity on the outside.

- Keep humidity levels between 50% and 70%.

- If adapter cards need removal, place some insulating material between the board and anything that could short.

The best protection against the effects of ESD is an *ESD workstation.* A good ESD protective workstation consists of a rubber mat and ESD wrist strap. An ESD wrist strap contains a resistor that provides protection in case the wire meets a charged object. An ESD mat has a special rubberized surface that conducts static electricity away from the component being worked on.

Finally, a few words of wisdom: "A clean work environment is a happy work environment." Keep the work area free of dust and other contaminants that might conduct static electricity. Figure 3.1 is an example of what a good ESD-preventive environment includes.

FIGURE 3.1: The ESD-free environment

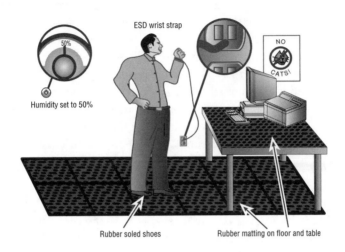

ESD wrist strap

50%

Humidity set to 50%

NO CATS!

Rubber soled shoes

Rubber matting on floor and table

WARNING   If you are working on high-voltage components, like monitors, DO NOT use an ESD strap! The strap provides such an easy path to ground it can actually do more harm than good.

Exam Essentials

Several test questions deal with the issue of ESD damage. This is logical and good, because a computer technician is supposed to be in the business of fixing hardware problems, not creating them.

Understand the general cause of ESD.   ESD is caused by the transfer of static electricity from one charged item (perhaps a person) to another item that is sensitive to the charge.

Understand the specific causes of ESD.   Walking on a carpet, shifting in a chair, wearing synthetic clothing, and even low humidity can generate static electricity and result in ESD.

Know what problems ESD can cause. ESD can damage computer chips by suddenly destroying them or by causing cumulative damage which eventually causes the chip to fail.

Know what precautions to take to prevent ESD. Some precautions you can take include wearing an antistatic wrist wrap, using rubber mats or rubber-soled shoes, and maintaining a 50% to 70% humidity level.

Key Terms and Concepts

Conductive material: Material such as metal that provides a minimal resistance to the flow of electrons.

Conductor: Any material having free electrons that allows electricity to flow.

Electrostatic discharge: Abbreviated ESD. Occurs when two objects of dissimilar charge come in contact with one another and exchange electrons in order to standardize the electrostatic charge between the two objects.

Insulative material: Material such as rubber that impedes the flow of electrons.

Static electricity: A result of the build-up of electrons on a surface.

Sample Questions

1. The effects of ESD are what?

A. Similar to the effects of EMI

B. Reversible

C. Irreversible

D. Always immediately noticeable

Answer: C. Chips damaged by ESD cannot be repaired. They must be replaced when damaged.

2. You should wear an ESD wrist-grounding strap when doing what?

   A. Working on a CRT

   B. Installing an internal modem

   C. Cleaning a mouse

   D. Rebooting the computer

   Answer: B. Any time you are working inside the computer, you should wear an ESD strap.

3. Low humidity has which of the following effects?

   A. It makes ESD less likely to occur.

   B. It makes ESD more likely to occur.

   C. It has no effect on ESD.

   D. It reduces the probability of direct damage from ESD.

   Answer: B. Low humidity, common in the winter, causes the buildup of static electricity.

CHAPTER

4

Motherboard/
Processors/Memory

A+ Core Module Exam Objectives Covered in This Chapter:

▶ Distinguish between the popular CPU chips in terms of their basic characteristics. *(pages 161 – 174)*

▶ Identify the categories of RAM (Random Access Memory) terminology, their locations, and physical characteristics. *(pages 175 – 183)*

▶ Identify the most popular type of motherboards, their components, and their architecture (for example, bus structures and power supplies). *(pages 184 – 204)*

▶ Identify the purpose of CMOS (Complementary Metal-Oxide Semiconductor), what it contains and how to change its basic parameters. *(pages 204 – 210)*

This chapter provides a description of the "guts" of a PC. The motherboard, processor, and RAM are the features that determine a PC's essential capabilities. PC technicians must know the limitations of a system so they can understand how best to work within those limitations—or whether to escape them through an upgrade. From a technician's perspective, this is not one of the typical day-to-day decisions, but it is one of the most critical.

The exam emphasizes the subjects presented here. Questions pertaining to RAM and motherboard components are especially prominent on the test.

Distinguish between the popular CPU chips in terms of their basic characteristics.

This chapter details the various characteristics of the central processing unit (CPU) and describes the line of Intel processors, which have dominated the market since the release of the IBM PC in 1981.

A technician rarely does hands-on work with the CPU. Processors are not highly configurable, and they don't fail very often (unless they overheat). Even if they do fail, it may be advantageous to buy a new computer rather than repair the old one. For these reasons, the all-important CPU has a scaled-down emphasis on the test. However, you will encounter several processor-related questions, so you need to be prepared.

Critical Information

The CPU directs the activity of all processes that take place inside the computer, and to a large extent also determines the speed at which those activities take place. This section explains the generic processor and also details the most popular processors and their specific differences.

Performance Issues of the CPU

Several factors affect the performance of a processor. Among them are availability of a math coprocessor, clock speed, internal cache memory, and the supporting circuitry.

Math Coprocessor

The math coprocessor is used to add on to the processor's number-crunching speed. It does not, however, increase the speed of simple additions and subtractions. What it does is increase the speed of calculations that involve floating decimal point operations (like calculations for algebra and statistics). Since the introduction of the 486, the math coprocessor has been built into the processor. CPU models that preceded the 486 can have a math coprocessor added as an option.

Clock Speed

The clock speed is the frequency with which a processor executes instructions. This frequency is measured in millions of cycles per second, or megahertz (MHz). There is actually a clock of sorts within the CPU. This clock signal is generated by a quartz crystal, which vibrates as electricity passes through it, thereby generating a steady pulse to every component synchronized with the signal. A system cycle is generated by this pulse (called a clock "tick"), which sends a signal through the processor telling it to perform another operation. To transfer data to and from memory, an 8086 computer needed four cycles plus "wait states." Wait states allow the processor to wait for the slower speed RAM that was used in 8086-based computers. Generally speaking, the higher the MHz value, the faster the PC will be.

Internal Cache

An internal cache memory is a storage area for frequently used data and instructions. It requires a small amount of physical RAM that can keep up with the processor. It then uses this RAM for storage. The processor contains an internal cache controller that integrates the cache with the CPU. The controller stores frequently accessed RAM locations to provide faster execution of data and instructions. Therefore, a larger cache leads to the perception of a faster CPU.

The Bus

Processor communication with the rest of the system components relies on the supporting circuitry. The underlying circuitry of the system board is called the bus. The bus allows all devices to communicate with each other, and is composed of several components, including the external bus, the data bus, and the address bus.

The External Bus (System Bus)   The external bus is also referred to as the system bus or expansion bus. The expansion bus is a bus system that allows the processor to talk to another device. It is known as an external bus system because it is outside of the processor. The devices are connected through expansion cards and slots.

The Data Bus   The data bus is used to send and receive data. The wider the bus, the more data it will transmit at one time (and, therefore, the faster the bus).

NOTE   The data bus and address bus are independent of each other, but for better performance larger data buses require larger address buses. The data bus width indicates how much data the chip can carry at one time, and the size of the address bus indicates how much memory a chip can handle.

Data in a computer is transferred digitally. A single wire carries 5 volts to indicate a 1 data bit or carries 0 volts to indicate a 0 data bit. Remember, computers use the binary system to transmit information. The greater number of wires allows more bits to be transmitted at the same time. For example, a 16-bit data bus width has sixteen wires to transmit data, and a 32-bit data chip can transmit twice the amount of data as a 16-bit chip. A good comparison would be to the highway system. A single lane for traffic allows only one car through at a time whereas two lanes allow twice the amount of traffic to pass through at one time.

Be careful not to assume that data flows the same within the processor as it does outside of the processor. Some Intel processors have an internal data bus that is greater than the external data bus. The 8088 and 80386SX are good examples of this. They are designed with an internal bus that has twice the width of the external bus.

NOTE The bus is covered in more detail later in this chapter.

The Address Bus The address bus also contains a set of wires to carry information in and out of the processor, but the information the address bus sends is used to describe memory locations (addresses). This location is used for data being sent or retrieved. The address bus carries each bit of information, relative to a digit in the address, along each wire. The larger the address bus, the more memory address locations it can support. The more memory address locations a processor can address, the more RAM a processor can use.

Another analogy relates the address bus to the address of a house or its house number. If the house numbers for a street are limited to two numbers, then the street is limited to only 100 addresses (00 to 99). For an address bus that communicates in binary language, a limit of two digits would give four addresses (00, 01, 10, and 11). Thus, the larger the address bus, the more combinations of 0 and 1 would be permitted to pass through at one time. Take a look at Table 4.1. A 286 processor has a 24-bit address bus width. Using binary theory, this translates to a little over 16 million locations, which means it allows access to as much as 16MB of RAM. Using similar calculations, a 386DX with a 32-bit address bus will allow access to as much as 4GB of RAM.

NOTE The best way to determine which CPU your computer is using is to open the case and view the numbers stamped on the CPU. Another way to determine your computer's CPU is to watch closely as your computer boots up; you should see a notation describing your processor. If you are using MS-DOS, you can also run Microsoft Diagnostics to view the processor type (that is, unless your computer has a Pentium, in which case it will report a very fast 486).

TABLE 4.1: The Intel Family of Processors

Chip	Year Added	Data Bus Width (in bits)	Address Bus Width (in bits)	Speed (in MHz)	Transistors	Other Specifications
8080	1974	8	8	2	6,000	Used only in appliances
8086	1978	16	20	5–10	29,000	Internal bus ran at 8 bits
8088	1979	8	20	4.77	29,000	29,000 transistors
80286	1982	16	24	8–12	134,000	First to use PGA
386DX	1985	32	32	16–33	275,000	
386SX	1988	32	24	16–20	275,000	
486DX	1989	32	32	25–50	1.2 million	8KB of level 1 cache

T A B L E 4.1: The Intel Family of Processors *(cont.)*

Chip	Year Added	Data Bus Width (in bits)	Address Bus Width (in bits)	Speed (in MHz)	Transistors	Other Specifications
486SX	1991	32	32	16–33	1.185 million	Math coprocessor disabled
487SX	1991			16–33		Math coprocessor for 486SX computers
486DX2	1991	32	32	33–66	2.0 million	
486DX4	1992	32	32	75–100	2.5 million	
Pentium	1993	32	32	60–166	3.3 million	Superscalar
Pentium Pro	1995	64	32	150–200	5.5 million	Dynamic execution
Pentium Pro II	1997	64	64	233–400	7.5 million	32KB of level 1 cache, dynamic execution, and MMX technology

Intel Processors

The Intel family of processors started with the 8080, which found only limited use in the computer industry. After this came the 8086 and the 8088, which were rectangular in shape and used a DIP (dual inline package) array for their CPUs. The 8086 used a 16-bit external bus and a 16-bit data bus, and originally ran at 4.77MHz with 29,000 transistors. The 8088, released in 1978, was a similar chip that followed the 8086. However, it was a slower chip than the 8086 because Intel designed it with a smaller (8-bit) external bus. It was made this way to maintain compatibility with 8-bit motherboards that were on the market at the time. The 8088 was used primarily in the IBM PC.

Intel redesigned and improved the chip in stages. Typically, improved versions of the processor included more transistors, a faster clock speed, wider external and internal data buses, and a larger cache. Some of the improved processors did not include a wider external bus. This was to maintain backward compatibility with other processors that do not support a wider bus.

Unique features of the x86 processors that followed the 8086 and 8088 are described here.

80286

The 80286 was the first to implement the PGA (pin grid array) package. It ran from 6MHz to 20MHz, and, like the 8086, had an external bus and a data bus that were 16 bits wide. Its 24-bit address bus could handle 16MB of RAM.

80386

The 386 came in two versions, both of which ran at clock speeds of 16–33MHz. The 386DX used both a 32-bit data bus and a 32-bit address bus. The 32-bit address bus allowed it to have up to 4GB of RAM. The other version of the processor, called the 386SX, had a 32-bit data bus and a 24-bit address bus.

80486

Like the 386, the 486 came in two versions, both of which included an 8K on-chip cache. The 486DX had an internal math coprocessor. The other 486 chip, the 486SX, did not.

Some 486DX chips use a technology known as *clock doubling*. This worked by allowing a chip to run at the bus's rated speed externally, but running the processor's *internal* clock at twice the speed of the bus. For example, Intel designed a chip that ran at 33MHz externally and 66MHz internally. This chip was known as the 486DX2. Intel also designed a chip with a tripled internal clock called a DX4.

The Pentium and Pentium Pro

The Pentium processor uses a 32-bit data path, 32-bit address bus, and 16-bit on-chip cache, and comes in speeds from 60MHz to 166MHz. It is basically a combination of two 486DX chips in one, larger chip. The benefit to this two-chip-in-one architecture is that each chip can execute instructions independently of the other. This is a form of *parallel processing* that Intel calls *superscalar*. Pentiums require special motherboards, because they run significantly hotter than previous processors.

After the initial introduction of the Pentium came the Pentium Pro, designed to meet the needs of today's server. It runs at speeds around 200MHz, in a 32-bit operating system environment using "dynamic execution." Dynamic execution performs out-of-order guesses to execute program codes.

Pentium II and beyond

Speeds for the Pentium II range from 233MHz to 400MHz. The unique thing about this processor is that it uses a single-edge connector (SEC) to attach to the motherboard instead of the standard PGA package. The processor is on a card that can be easily replaced. Simply shut off the computer, pull out the old processor card, and insert a new one.

Pentium Overdrive Chips and MMX Technology

Intel's 486 Overdrive processors were designed for 486 users who wanted to give their machines Pentium performance without having to pay the price for a full Pentium chip. Installing an overdrive chip is simply a matter of replacing the existing CPU with the Overdrive CPU. However, the socket must be designed for the extra pins in the Overdrive chip.

Once installed, the Overdrive chip runs at approximately two and a half times the motherboard's bus speed. For example, if you have a motherboard with a bus speed of 33MHz, the Overdrive processor will run at approximately 83MHz. Unfortunately, Overdrive processors are only 32-bit, whereas Pentiums are completely 64-bit. The Overdrive runs at least as hot as a conventional Pentium, so you have to make sure the system's ventilation can withstand the additional heat.

MMX is the latest advance in processor technology, and can increase the speed of multimedia applications by up to 60%. This new Pentium processor has three new features:

- It includes 57 new instructions for better video, audio, and graphic capabilities.

- It features *single-instruction, multiple-data (SIMD)* technology. Other Intel processors issue one instruction to one data item at a time. SIMD enables the CPU to avoid this repetition by issuing one instruction simultaneously to multiple data items.

- Its cache has been doubled to 32KB.

NOTE For more information on the new MMX technology, check out Intel's Web site, HTTP://www.intel.com.

Intel "Clones"

Cyrix, Advanced Micro Devices (AMD), and IBM are some of Intel's rival chip-makers. AMD processors include the 5x86, K5, and K6. Cyrix/IBM produced a 5x86 and a 6x86 processor. Because these CPUs are designed for compatibility with systems built around the x86 and Pentium processors, their features are similar to the Intel chips. The 5x86 processors compare to the 80486, whereas the K5, K6, and 6x86 are similar to Pentiums.

RISC Processors

Reduced Instruction Set Code (RISC) is the name for a type of processor that supports a limited set of instructions but can work very quickly, up to three instructions per cycle. It is also very small and produces very little heat, so it is an ideal choice for portables. The PowerPC, developed by Motorola, IBM, and Apple, and Digital Equipment Corporation's Alpha processor are based on the RISC technology. Their chips run between 225MHz to 500MHz. Another manufacturer, Silicon Graphics, developed its own processor based on the RISC processor and called it the MIPS.

Although RISC-based processors can find instructions faster, they cannot run applications written for Intel processors—they can only run applications and operating systems written for RISC.

CPU Sockets and Cooling Systems

When you open the case of your computer, it is not difficult to find the CPU. It is usually the largest chip on the motherboard, and may be fixed to a plastic socket assembly. A modern CPU may be hidden by a *heat sink* and a fan, as well. The chip requires a heat sink on top of the processor to absorb and ventilate the heat. (Pentium processors typically generate heat to the tune of 185° Fahrenheit!) A heat sink is shown in Figure 4.1.

FIGURE 4.1: A heat sink

A heat sink is made out of heat-conducting metal and will conduct heat away from the CPU. This heat is dissipated as air passes between its fins.

TIP It is advisable to use a passive heat sink on 486DX4 and later processors, unless you have an AT motherboard design; in this case, a heat sink/fan assembly should be used to provide additional cooling.

The CPU comes in a PLCC (plastic leadless chip carrier) or a PGA package. PGA has been the most popular CPU package since the 80286. As described in Chapter 1, this package is square and has two square sets of pins beneath it.

CPUs are mounted in plastic sockets on the motherboard. There are nine standard socket types, which are detailed in Table 4.2. If you plan to upgrade your CPU, make sure your upgrade will fit your socket type. The major difference between sockets is the number of pin holes; the pin arrangement determines which processor fits into the socket.

T A B L E 4.2: CPU Socket Characteristics

Socket	Pins	Voltage	Processor	Upgrade
0	168	3.3	486DX	486DX2/4
1	169	3.3	486DX, 486SX	486DX2/4
2	238	3.3	486DX, 486SX, 486DX2	486DX2/4, Pentium
3	237	3.3 or 5	486DX, 486SX, 486DX2/4	486DX2/4, Pentium
4	273	5	60/66MHz Pentium	Pentium
5	320	3.3	Other Pentium	Pentium
6	235	3.3	486DX4	Pentium
7	321	3.3	Other Pentium	Pentium
8	387	3.3	Pentium Pro	Pentium Pro

Socket 7 chips are the most prevalent today. The major exception is the Pentium II processor, which uses a single-edge connector (SEC) interface instead of a socket. Contained on a small circuit board, the Pentium II plugs into the SEC just like an expansion card.

Sockets will be either ZIF (zero-insertion force) or LIF (low-insertion force) sockets. ZIF sockets are easily recognized by the retaining bar that holds the chip in place. Type "0" sockets are usually LIF sockets.

SEE ALSO For instructions on upgrading the CPU, see Chapter 1, "Installation, Configuration, and Upgrading."

Exam Essentials

Although CPU features are not emphasized on the test, there will be several questions about them.

Know the physical features of the CPU. Physical features include the packaging (e.g., PGA or PLCC), pins, and socket types (ZIF or LIF), and their important distinctions.

Know what voltages are required by the CPU. The 40486 and most Pentiums run at 3.3 VDc. The older 60/66MHz Pentiums run at 5 VDc.

Understand the distinct characteristics of the CPU. The characteristics of the processor include clock speed, math coprocessor, internal cache, and bus. See the Critical Information section for a detailed explanation of these characteristics.

Know the names and basic features of each Intel processor. You should know the bus speed for each processor, the amount of memory it can address, whether it has an internal cache, and its clock speed.

Know the names and characteristics of the Intel "clones." Some of the available clones include the 5x86, 6x86, K5, and K6 processors. The 5x86 is similar to an 80486 processor, and the other chips are similar to Pentiums.

Key Terms and Concepts

80286: A 16-bit microprocessor from Intel.

80386: A 32-bit microprocessor from Intel.

80486DX: A 32-bit microprocessor from Intel that included a built-in cache and a coprocessor.

Address bus: The electronic channel, usually from 20 to 32 separate lines (wires) wide, used to transmit the signals that specify locations in memory.

Clock speed: Also known as clock rate. The internal speed of a computer or processor, normally expressed in MHz.

Clone: Hardware that is identical in function to an original, usually used to refer to a PC that functions in the same way as an IBM PC, or to a processor that functions in the same way as an Intel processor.

Data bus: Bus used to send data to and receive data from the microprocessor.

External bus: An external component connected through expansion cards and slots that allows the processor to "talk" to other devices.

Parallel processing: A computing method using several processors, all working on different aspects of the same program at the same time, that can achieve very high speeds.

Pentium: A 32-bit microprocessor from Intel with a built-in cache, coprocessor, and superscalar design.

RISC: Acronym for Reduced Instruction Set Code. A type of processor that supports a limited set of instructions, but carries them out at high speed.

Superscalar: A microprocessor architecture that contains more than one execution unit, or pipeline, allowing the processor to execute more than one instruction per clock cycle.

Wait state: A clock cycle during which no instructions are executed because the processor is waiting for data from a device or from memory.

Sample Questions

1. A 66MHz Pentium processor uses how many volts?

   A. 12

   B. 5

   C. 2.5

   D. 7

   Answer: B

2. An 80486 has what type of internal bus?

   A. Superscalar

   B. 32-bit

   C. 64-bit

   D. 16-bit

   Answer: B

3. The data bus in a PC determines what?

   A. The amount of addressable memory

   B. The speed of peripheral communication

   C. The socket type

   D. The amount of data the CPU can work with at one time

   Answer: D. The data bus describes the number of data lines (wires) internal to the CPU. The CPU can process each line simultaneously.

Identify the categories of RAM (Random Access Memory) terminology, their locations, and physical characteristics.

Along with the processor and the hard disk, memory is one of the three most important components in a computer. The word "memory" most often refers to random-access memory or RAM. RAM is the "holding tank" for all data currently available to the processor and to other peripherals. The main event that takes place every time you turn on your computer is the loading of the operating system from your hard disk into RAM memory. This critical event allows a computer to operate at very high speed. In addition to the operating system, programs located in ROMs on circuit boards (such as the BIOS on the motherboard) will also be copied into RAM.

Upgrading RAM memory is one of the basic skills a PC technician must have, and is usually the most effective means of improving system performance. Questions pertaining to memory are prevalent on the test.

Critical Information

Physically, memory is a collection of integrated circuits (ICs) that store data and program information as patterns of 1s and 0s (ons and offs) in the chip. Most memory chips require constant power (also called a constant *refresh*) to maintain those patterns of 1s and 0s. If power is lost, all those tiny switches revert back to the off position, effectively erasing the data from memory. Some memory types, however, do not require refresh. The different types of memory are detailed here.

Types of RAM

There are as many types of RAM as there are IC types. These types include SRAM, DRAM, EDO RAM, VRAM, and WRAM.

SRAM

One type of memory is known as static random-access memory (SRAM). It is called "static" because the information doesn't need a constant update (refresh). SRAM stores information as patterns of transistor ons and offs to represent binary digits. This type of memory is physically bulky and somewhat limited in its storage capacity; it can generally store only 256 kilobits per IC.

Although the original PC and XT, as well as some notebook computer systems, use SRAM chips for their main memory, its most common use is for cache memory. The reason for this is speed: SRAM is very fast, with access times of 15 to 30 nanoseconds.

DRAM

Dynamic random-access memory (DRAM) was an improvement over the expensive and bulky SRAM. DRAM uses a different approach to storing the 1s and 0s. Instead of transistors, DRAM stores information as charges in very small capacitors. If a charge exists in a capacitor, it's interpreted as a 1. The absence of a charge will be interpreted as a 0.

Because DRAM uses capacitors instead of switches, it needs to use a constant refresh signal to keep the information in memory. DRAM requires more power than SRAM for refresh signals, and therefore is mostly found in desktop computers.

DRAM technology allows several memory units, called *cells*, to be packed at a very high density. Therefore, these chips can hold very large amounts of information. Most PCs today use DRAM.

Access time for DRAM is 80 nanoseconds or more, slower than SRAM, and two or three times faster than ROM.

EDO RAM

In the last couple of years, a new type of static RAM called extended data out RAM (EDO RAM) has become popular. This new type of RAM increases performance by eliminating memory wait states. It's usually a bit more expensive than regular DRAM, which it's designed to replace, but it will increase performance about 10% over DRAM.

Video RAM

Video memory (also called video RAM or VRAM) is used to store image data for processing by the video adapter. The more video memory an adapter has, the greater the resolution and color depth it can display. Also, more VRAM allows for faster screen updates. The graphics-laden Web sites and programs in use today make faster screen updates very important.

Windows RAM (WRAM)

Window RAM (WRAM) is a specialized memory for Windows accelerator cards. Developed by Samsung, it works similarly to video RAM, except that WRAM is much faster. While information is being read from one set of WRAM addresses to draw the screen, other information can be written to another set of addresses. This is faster than normal VRAM because in VRAM all addresses can only be either read from or written to. This ability of WRAM to be read from or written to simultaneously is called *dual-ported* memory.

Memory Chip Package Types

The memory chips themselves come in many different types of packages. The ones most frequently encountered are discussed in the following sections.

Dual Inline Package (DIP)

The first type of memory chip package is dual inline package (DIP) memory (Figure 4.2). Older computers such as the IBM AT arranged these small RAM chips like rows of caskets in a small memory "graveyard." There are typically eight memory chips in one of these rows.

F I G U R E 4.2: A DIP memory chip

Back in 1984 (before the 386 arrived in 1985), every time a person wanted to add memory to a computer they had to go to a computer or electronics store and buy a *tube* of RAM. These tubes typically contained eight to sixteen of these chips. The markings on the chips indicated their speed and size. A marking of AB256-80 means a 256-kilobit chip that has an access time of 80ns. The size was commonly given in bits or kilobits (Kb). If the chips you put in were 256Kb chips and you put in eight chips, you would have added 256 kilobytes (256KB) of RAM.

These chips were used with computers based on the 8086, 8088, and 80286 processors. The problem with the 286 processor and memory was that the processor was faster then the memory. The memory would get overrun with requests from the processor, causing serious performance problems. To solve this problem, manufacturers introduced *wait states* into their RAM. A wait state causes the processor to wait one or more clock cycles, allowing the RAM to catch up. A wait state of zero means that the processor and the memory are equally matched in speed.

Single Inline Memory Module (SIMM)

The next type of RAM packaging that is commonly seen in computers is called the single inline memory module (SIMM). SIMMs were developed because DIPs took up too much "real estate" on the logic board. Someone got the idea to put several of the DIP chips on a small circuit board and then make that board easily removable. A couple of versions (there are many configurations) are shown in Figure 4.3.

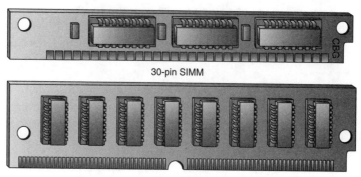

30-pin SIMM

72-pin SIMM

The first SIMMs had nine small DIP chips on them and took up less room than before, because four of them could be installed in the same space as one row of the older DIP memory chips. In order to accomplish this, the SIMMs are installed very close to each other at approximately a 45° angle.

Dual Inline Memory Module (DIMM)

The final type of memory package is known as a DIMM, or dual inline memory module. DIMMs are dual-sided memory chips that hold twice as many chips as a SIMM. (And, except for the fact that they have chips on both sides, they look just like SIMMs.) Generally, the DIMMs you'll run into will have either 72 or 168 pins. Some DIMMs are 32-bit, but more and more are 64-bit and only have to be installed one at a time in Pentium-class computers.

Memory Banks

Recall that processors have 8-bit, 16-bit, 32-bit, or 64-bit buses. The size of the bus determines how many bits of data a computer can process simultaneously. This also affects the arrangement of *memory banks* in a PC. A memory bank is built into the motherboard, and is designed to allow your computer to access memory efficiently.

A memory bank may consist of a number of DIPs or one or two SIMMs. In order for the PC to handle data efficiently, memory must be arranged in banks that equal the width of its bus. Therefore, an 8088 processor with an 8-bit bus will usually have eight 1-bit memory chips. (An extra 1-bit chip for *parity* is also present, which is explained shortly.)

A 16-bit computer uses memory banks with a total of 16 bits, and a 32-bit computer uses memory banks with a total of 32 bits. Knowing this will help to ascertain what type of SIMM you may want to use to upgrade your system. There are two types of SIMMs, described here:

- 30-pin SIMMs, which use 8 bits for data (plus a parity bit)
- 72-pin SIMMs, which usually use 32 data bits for data (plus four parity bits)

This becomes important when upgrading, because you need to add memory in complete banks. For example, if you have a 32-bit 386, you must add 30-pin SIMMs in sets of four (4 x 8 = 32), so that the data width remains compatible.

Parity

Parity is a simple form of error checking used in computers and telecommunications. In the RAM memory of most PCs, one parity bit is used for every 8-bit block in the data path. The parity bit is generated by a *comparator* chip and the result is stored in the parity chip.

Parity works by adding an additional bit to a binary number and using it to indicate any changes in that number during transmission. There are two types of parity: even and odd.

Even parity works by counting the number of 1s in a binary number and, if the number of 1s is odd, adding an additional 1 to guarantee that the total number of 1s is an even number. Using a modem as an example, consider the following transmission: 11101011. This data has an even number of 1s, so the sending computer would assign a 0 to the parity bit. On the other hand, the number 01101101 has five 1s, and so would have a 1 in the parity bit position to make the total number of 1s even. If, in the case of the second number, the receiving computer had checked the parity position after transmission and had found a 0 instead, it would have asked the sending computer to resend the last bit.

Odd parity works in a similar manner. But, instead of guaranteeing that the total number of ones is even, it guarantees that the total number is an odd number.

Parity works fine for detecting single-bit errors (where one bit has changed its value during transmission). But if the transmission is extremely garbled, two bits might be switched at the same time. If that were the case, the value for parity would still be valid; as a consequence, the sender would not be asked to retransmit. That's why transmissions that really need to be reliable often use another method of error checking called *checksumming*. In a checksum, a small program processes binary data (one byte at a time), and stores the results in a database file. This file is compared to the actual data for errors.

SEE ALSO   For more information on checksumming, see *A+ Core Module Study Guide, 2nd ed.* by David Groth (Sybex, 1998).

Exam Essentials

Know the different names for types of RAM memory.   These types include static RAM (SRAM), dynamic RAM (DRAM), extended data out RAM (EDO RAM), video RAM (VRAM), and Windows RAM (WRAM).

Understand the uses of the different types of RAM.   SRAM is used primarily for cache memory; DRAM and EDO RAM are used for primary RAM memory; VRAM and WRAM are used to speed up graphics.

Understand the characteristics of the different types of RAM.
SRAM is non-volatile and very fast memory. DRAM and EDO RAM
are not as fast as SRAM and require a refresh signal to maintain their
contents. WRAM is similar to VRAM, but is faster because it can
read and write information simultaneously.

Know the type of packaging for RAM memory. SIMMs are small
circuit boards containing memory chips on one side; DIMMs are like
SIMMs, but contain memory chips on both sides. DIPs are memory
chips either soldered onto the motherboard or contained in the
SIMM/DIMM circuit board modules.

Understand the different types of SIMM packages. SIMMs
come in 72-pin and 30-pin versions. The 72-pin SIMMs are usually
32-bit. 30-pin SIMMs are 8-bit.

Understand the significance of a memory bank. A memory bank
is a portion of physical memory with a data path equivalent to the
bus-width of the CPU, plus extra bits for parity.

Understand parity. Parity is a form of error-checking used in the
RAM memory of a PC, which requires the use of one parity bit for
every 8-bit portion of the data path.

Key Terms and Concepts

DRAM: Acronym for dynamic random-access memory. A
common type of computer memory that needs to be refreshed
every millisecond in order to retain its charge.

Dual inline package: Abbreviated DIP. A standard housing constructed of hard plastic commonly used to hold an integrated circuit.

EDO RAM: Acronym for extended data out RAM. A type of fast
RAM that eliminates wait states.

Parity: A simple form of error-checking that uses an extra, or
redundant, bit to detect errors.

Refresh: In memory systems, to recharge dynamic RAM so that
it continues to hold its contents.

SRAM: Acronym for static random-access memory. A type of computer memory that retains its contents as long as power is supplied.

Sample Questions

1. Which of the following has the fastest access time?

  A. EDO RAM

  B. DRAM

  C. ROM

  D. DIP

Answer: **A.** EDO RAM will improve your access time by at least 10% compared to DRAM.

2. When adding 72-pin SIMMs in a 64-bit system, you should add how many SIMMs?

  A. 1

  B. 2

  C. 3

  D. 4

Answer: **B.** 72-pin SIMMs use 32 data bits plus 4 parity bits. You must add memory in 64-bit banks in this case, which equal two 72-pin SIMMs.

3. One memory bank on a 32-bit system using parity may contain how many parity bits?

  A. 1

  B. 2

  C. 4

  D. 16

Answer: **C.** A parity bit is needed for each 8-bit group, so a total of four parity bits are required.

Identify the most popular type of motherboards, their components, and their architecture (for example, bus structures and power supplies).

The motherboard is the primary circuit board in a PC, and is significant because the CPU, RAM memory, BIOS, and expansion cards are all contained in the motherboard. Motherboards vary in design and bus configuration. The bus configuration is of particular importance, because most peripherals are dependent upon the bus for their interaction with the CPU. Open the case of a PC and you'll be sure to find an expansion bus containing at least a few of the following devices: display adapter, sound card, disk controller, network card, mouse card, or internal modem. It is this plug-in, modular approach that gives the PC its versatility and allows PC technicians to add and remove important parts, even lacking an expert's knowledge of electrical components.

The designers of the exam expect you to be familiar with many components of the motherboard, and they test accordingly.

Critical Information

There are two major types of system boards: integrated and non-integrated. Non-integrated system boards have each major assembly installed in the computer as an expansion card. Integrated system boards are called that because most of the circuitry that would otherwise be installed as an expansion card is integrated into the motherboard circuitry. Most system boards in a PC are of the non-integrated type. The non-integrated boards also come in two major forms: AT and ATX.

AT Motherboard

The AT system boards are either a "full" AT (older) configuration, or the "baby" AT configuration. The baby AT configuration is a compressed version of the full AT, although both feature a processor, memory slots, and expansion slots in line with one another (see Figure 4.4).

FIGURE 4.4: A "baby" AT motherboard

ATX Motherboard

The ATX design has the processor and memory slots at right angles to the expansion cards (see Figure 4.5). A processor in an ATX will run cooler because the airflow generated by the power supply fan will pass over it and cool it down. An ATX motherboard also has more space for full-length expansion slots.

F I G U R E 4.5: An ATX motherboard

Motherboard Components

In addition to the AT/ATX design of the board, which determines the location of the CPU, a few other tips may help in locating components on the motherboard:

- The expansion bus consists of long narrow slots, either empty or containing expansion cards. There are many bus technologies, which are detailed in the next section of this chapter.

- SIMM slots are arranged in several tightly-packed rows. The location of the slots is determined largely by the form of the motherboard (AT or ATX).

- The BIOS ROM is one of the largest DIP chips on the board, and is usually located just forward of the adapter slots.

- The math coprocessor chip is almost as large as the CPU.

- The CMOS battery, if present, will be a small cylindrical battery or a round battery.

- The power supply connectors are almost always located near the expansion slots at the back of the motherboard.

- The external cache (L2 cache), if present, will consist of several rows of smaller DIPs.

Expansion Bus

The expansion bus allows the computer to be upgraded using a modular approach. One way to upgrade the computer is to plug specially made circuit boards into the connectors (also known as expansion slots) on the expansion bus. The devices on these circuit boards are then able to communicate with the CPU and are semi-permanently part of the computer.

The expansion slots are made up of several tiny copper finger slots, the row of very narrow channels that grab the fingers on the expansion circuit boards. These finger slots connect to copper pathways on the motherboard. Each set of pathways has a specific function. One set of pathways provides the voltages needed to power the expansion card (+5, +12, and ground). Another set of pathways makes up the data bus, transmitting data back to the processor. Yet another set makes up the address bus, allowing the device to be addressed through a set of I/O addresses. Finally, there are other lines for different functions like interrupts, DMA channels, and clock signals.

SEE ALSO   For more information on I/O addresses, interrupts, and DMA channels, see Chapter 1.

The CPU clock differs from the bus clock. The former dictates how fast the CPU can run; the latter indicates how fast the bus can transmit information. The speed of the clock is measured in how fast it "ticks," and is given in millions of cycles per second, or megahertz (MHz). The bus or the CPU can only perform an operation on the occurrence of a tick signal.

The CPU clock and the bus clock were originally tied together. However, when CPU clocks began to outpace bus clock speeds, the two clocks were disassociated so as not to limit the speed of the CPU.

NOTE   An advanced bus feature called *bus mastering* allows a device to take control of the bus from the CPU, and read from or write information directly to another device. This feature can greatly improve performance of the device and is an improvement over DMA. Some buses can use several bus mastering devices.

The 8-Bit Expansion Bus

The 8-bit bus is characterized by having a maximum bus clock speed of 4.77 (approximately 5) MHz, eight interrupts (of which six could be used by expansion devices), four DMA channels, and one large connector with 62 tiny finger slots (channels) along the sides. See Figure 4.6.

F I G U R E 4.6: The 8-bit bus connector

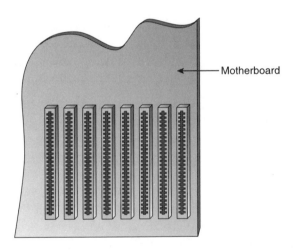

Motherboard

It is very rare to find an 8-bit bus in today's computers. If there are any, there's usually just one: an 8-bit slot for a single 8-bit expansion card (Figure 4.7). The expansion cards for this size bus are easily identifiable, as they have only one connector. The card is usually packed with resistors and other large electronics components.

F I G U R E 4.7: An 8-bit bus expansion card

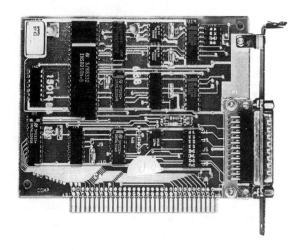

The 8-bit bus died out about the same time that the 8-bit processors fell by the wayside. It wasn't efficient to try to shoehorn 32 bits or more into a bus that can only accept 8 bits at a time. Also, since most processors run quite a bit faster than 4.77MHz, retaining the 8-bit bus would have crippled the overall speed of the newer systems.

The Industry Standard Architecture (ISA) Bus

The ISA bus is easily identifiable by the presence of the small bus connector behind the 8-bit connector, as shown in Figure 4.8. This additional connector adds several signal lines to make the bus a full 16-bit bus. The other connector is a regular 8-bit bus connector. The ISA bus has eight more interrupts than the 8-bit bus and four additional DMA channels. Also, this bus can operate at nearly twice the speed of the older, 8-bit bus (ISA can run at 8MHz, and "Turbo" models can run as fast as 10MHz reliably). Finally, this bus can use one bus-mastering device, if necessary.

F I G U R E 4.8: An ISA bus connector

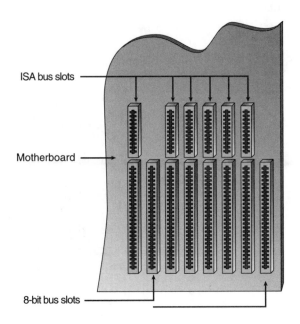

ISA expansion cards use a connector similar to the 8-bit bus, but with the additional connector for the 16-bit data and address lines (Figure 4.9).

F I G U R E 4.9: An ISA bus expansion card

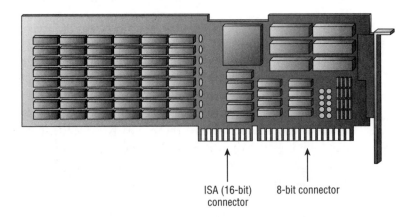

NOTE One interesting thing about the ISA bus is that it is backward-compatible with the older, 8-bit bus. ISA bus slots are basically 8-bit slots with the extra signal lines required to make them 16-bit on a second connector. Expansion cards made for the PC's 8-bit bus can be inserted into ISA slots and they will function properly. There is one exception, however. Some 8-bit cards have a "skirt" extending below the bus slot. This skirt will not allow the 8-bit card to be inserted all the way into the ISA slot. It is for this reason that you will sometimes have 8-bit slots mixed in with ISA slots on the some motherboard.

Configuring expansion cards for use in ISA buses is a little less complex than configuring 8-bit buses, mainly because there are more choices available for interrupts and DMA channels.

The Micro Channel Architecture (MCA) Bus

MCA, though a proprietary IBM bus, was a major step forward in bus design. First of all, it was available in either 16-bit or 32-bit versions. Second, it could have multiple bus mastering devices installed. Third, the bus clock speed is slightly faster (10MHz instead of 8MHz). And finally, it offered the ability to change configurations with software rather than jumpers and DIP switches.

The MCA bus connector is a high-density connector that looks similar to an ISA bus connector. However, the MCA bus connector has almost twice as many connectors in a smaller area and is segmented to provide for 16-bit, 32-bit, and video extension segments.

There are two easy ways to identify an MCA bus card. The first is by the connectors on the card (see Figure 4.10). It looks like no other expansion card. The connectors on the card are spaced very close together. The second is the labeling on the card. When you take an MCA card out of the package, you will notice that on the top of the card are two *blue* handles, some of which display the IBM logo.

F I G U R E 4.10: An MCA bus expansion card

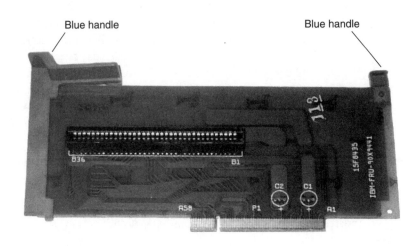

The Extended ISA (EISA) Bus

There were several new, desirable features introduced with EISA. It took the best of MCA's features and added to them. EISA has a 32-bit data path. Additionally, it has more I/O addresses, software setup capability for expansion cards, and no need for interrupts or DMA channels, and it allows for multiple bus mastering devices. However, despite all these advances it still used the 8MHz clock speed of ISA (to ensure backward compatibility with ISA cards).

The bus connector slots (Figure 4.11) have both 16-bit and 32-bit finger slots. The 16-bit finger slots are staggered every other finger slot with the 32-bit finger slots. Also, the 16-bit finger slots are located towards the top of the connector and the 32-bit finger slots are buried deep within the connector. The reason for all this staggering, burying, and arranging is that when you insert a 16-bit card, it will only go in halfway and make contact with the top (16-bit) connectors. But an EISA card (Figure 4.12), because of its longer fingers, will seat all the way into an EISA slot and make full contact with the deeper, 32-bit finger slots.

FIGURE 4.11: An EISA bus connector

FIGURE 4.12: An EISA bus expansion card

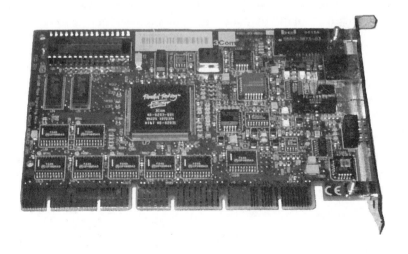

VESA Local Bus (VL Bus)

Memory and cache cards use a type of *local bus* called a "processor direct slot." The local bus is a bus that runs at the same speed as the processor. In addition to the memory and cache cards, one of the first components to be put on the local bus was the video circuitry, which also benefitted from high-speed communications.

The VESA local bus, also known as the VLB or the VL bus, is the first local bus standard for expansion cards. It is a 32-bit addition to the ISA bus, and is therefore backward-compatible with ISA. VLB has the same limitations as ISA. Configuration is still done through jumpers and DIP switches, instead of special bus configuration programs. It has been called the "big ISA" bus, because that's what it is: a 32-bit version of ISA.

The identification of a VL bus slot is very easy, if you know what to look for. First of all, VESA designed this slot to be an extension of ISA. A VL bus slot is a regular ISA slot, with the 32-bit local bus connector added to the ISA bus connector as a third bus connector (Figure 4.13). This connector is a high-density connector that has all of its lines running directly to the processor.

The VL bus expansion card is also easily identifiable. The card is slightly longer than an ISA card, and has one extra connector (the 32-bit local connector). Figure 4.14 shows two typical VL bus expansion cards. These cards are typically used for video cards (as previously mentioned), SCSI host bus adapters, and multimedia expansion cards (sound cards, hard drive and CD-ROM controllers, and video input devices) because of the amount of throughput such devices need. Typically, you'll find no more than three VL bus connectors on a motherboard (mixed with other bus types). Any more than three and the processor wouldn't be able to keep up with the bus transfers.

F I G U R E 4.13: A VL bus connector

VL-Bus connectors

simm slots   8-bit connectors   ISA (8-bit plus 16-bit)   VESA (8-bit plus 16-bit
                                   connectors   plus local-bus)
                                                              connectors

F I G U R E 4.14: VL bus expansion cards. Top: A video card. Bottom: An IDE hard-drive controller.

NOTE Because of the three-VL-bus-slot limitation, most vendors will mix VL bus slots and ISA slots (or EISA slots) on the motherboard. This approach gives the computer owner more choices for expansion.

Peripheral Component Interconnect (PCI) Bus

PCI has many benefits over other bus types. First of all, it supports both 64-bit and 32-bit data paths, so it can keep up with both 486- and Pentium-based systems. In addition, it is processor-independent. The bus communicates with a special "bridge circuit" that communicates with both the CPU and the bus. This has the benefit of making the bus an almost universal one. PCI buses can be found in PCs, Mac OS-based computers, and RISC computers. The same expansion card will work for all of them; you just need a different configuration program for each.

Another advantage to PCI over other buses is a higher clock speed. PCI (in its current revision) can run up to 33MHz. Also, the bus can support multiple bus-mastering expansion cards. These two features give PCI a maximum bus throughput of up to 265Mbps (with 64-bit cards).

The PCI bus also uses a chipset that works with PCI, ISA, and EISA. It is possible to have a PC that contains all these buses on the same motherboard. Also, the PCI cards are mostly Plug-and-Play. The cards will automatically configure themselves for IRQ, DMA, and I/O port addresses.

NOTE In some systems today that are combination PCI and ISA, each PCI slot will be located right next to an ISA slot. When you put a card in that PCI slot, you disable the ISA slot and vice versa. Only one card will fit in a combination slot at a time.

Identification of PCI bus slots is very simple. The finger slots in the bus (Figure 4.15) are very tightly packed together. This connector is usually white and contains two sections. There are two versions of the PCI bus that are found in today's systems. The versions are differentiated by the voltages that they use. One uses +5 VDc to power the expansion cards, the other uses +3.3 VDc. When you look at the connectors for these buses, the only difference you'll see is the different placement of the *blocker* (called a "key") in each connector, so that a +3.3VDc card can't be plugged into a +5.5VDc bus slot and vice-versa. A PCI expansion card is shown in Figure 4.16.

F I G U R E 4.15: PCI bus connectors

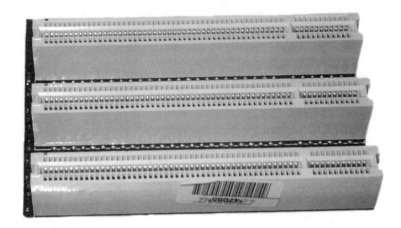

F I G U R E 4.16: A PCI expansion card

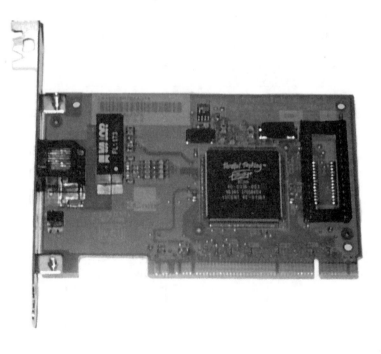

PCMCIA (PC Card Bus)

The tongue-twister *PCMCIA* stands for Personal Computer Memory Card International Association. The bus was originally designed as a way of expanding the memory in a small, handheld computer. The PCMCIA was organized to provide a standard way of expanding portable computers. The PCMCIA bus has been recently renamed to *PC card* to make it easier to pronounce. The PC card bus uses a small expansion card (about the size of a credit card). While it is primarily used in portable computers, there are PC card bus adapters for desktop PCs. It was designed to be a universal expansion bus that could accommodate any device.

The first release of the PCMCIA standard (PCMCIA 1.0, the same used in that original handheld computer) only defined the bus to be used for memory expansion. The second release (PCMCIA 2.0) is the most common and is in use throughout the computer industry; it has remained relatively unchanged. PCMCIA 2.0 was designed to be backward-compatible with version 1.0 so that 1.0 memory cards can be used in the 2.0 specification.

Most PC cards are 16-bit, but 32-bit cards are just beginning to hit the market. PC cards are limited in the following respect: they support only one IRQ, which creates a problem if you need to install two devices in a PC card bus and both devices require interrupts. 16-bit PC cards also do not support bus mastering or DMA. However, because of its flexibility, it has quickly become a very popular bus for all types of computers (not just laptops).

There are three major types of PC cards (and slots) in use today. Each has different uses and physical characteristics (see Figure 4.17). Coincidentally, they are called Type I, Type II, and Type III:

- Type I cards are 3.3mm thick and are most commonly used for memory cards.

- Type II cards are 5mm thick and are mostly used for modems and LAN adapters. This is the most common PC card type found today, and most systems have at least two Type II slots.

- The Type III slot is 10.5mm thick. Its most common application is for the PC card hard disks. Developers have been slowly introducing these devices to the market.

FIGURE 4.17: PC card types by thickness

A Summary of Bus Types

A Summary of Bus Types

To round out this section (and to make it easier to jog your memory when you're reviewing for the exam), here is a summary of some of the important points concerning bus types and their specifications (see Table 4.3).

TABLE 4.3: Summary of Bus Types

Bus Type	Bus Width (bits)	Maximum Speed (MHz)	Uses Bus Mastering?	Configuration
8-bit	8	4.77	N	Jumpers/DIP Switches
ISA	16	8 (10 for turbo)	N	Jumpers/DIP Switches (some cards are software configurable)
MCA	16 or 32	10	Y	Software—"Reference Disk"
EISA	32	8	Y	Software—"EISA Configuration Disk"
VL bus	32	Processor Speed	Y	Same as ISA

T A B L E 4.3: Summary of Bus Types *(cont.)*

Bus Type	Bus Width (bits)	Maximum Speed (MHz)	Uses Bus Mastering?	Configuration
PCI	64	Processor Speed	Y	Software—"Plug and Play"
PC card	16	33	N	Software—"PC Card & Socket Services"

Exam Essentials

Several questions on the test pertain to the information presented in this objective. You may be shown a visual representation of a motherboard and asked to name components based on their size, shape, and location in the picture.

Know the two major types of motherboards and how they are different. The two major motherboard designs are AT and ATX. In the AT design, the processor and memory are in a direct line with the expansion slots. The ATX design moved the CPU and RAM to a position at a right angle to the expansion cards.

Know what components are found on the motherboard and how to recognize them. The CPU, RAM, expansion slots, external cache, CMOS chip, battery, power supply connectors, and clock chip are some of the components located on the motherboard. See the Critical Information section for specific locations.

Know the names of the different expansion buses. The expansion buses include the following: 8-bit bus, ISA, MCA, EISA, VESA bus, PCI, and PCMCIA.

Know the features of each bus type. Each bus type may have a different data width ranging from 8 bits to 64 bits. Bus speeds vary from 4.77MHz to processor speed. Some buses can use bus mastering. See the Critical Information section for more specific details.

Know what types of boards can fit into the different buses. 8-bit boards can be used in ISA slots. ISA boards can be used in EISA and VESA slots. The other types of boards have unique slot designs and cannot be exchanged.

Understand the significance of the local bus. The local bus is designed to circumvent the 8MHz limitation of the ISA bus. Local buses are designed for devices requiring high-speed communication, such as the PCI and VESA bus, which run at a speed equal to the processor.

Know what types of cards are typically used in the different buses. Video adapters usually are designed for the local bus (PCI and VESA), as are some network cards. Other expansion cards, which may not require high-speed communication, are usually designed for the ISA or EISA bus.

Key Terms and Concepts

8-bit bus: A type of expansion bus that was used with the original IBM PC. It transmits data 8 bits at a time.

16-bit bus: A type of expansion bus that transmits data 16 bits at a time. The ISA bus is an example of a 16-bit bus.

32-bit bus: A type of expansion bus that transmits data 32 bits at a time. The EISA and VESA buses are examples of 32-bit buses.

AT: A type of motherboard in which the processors and memory are in line with the expansion slots.

ATX: A type of motherboard in which the processors and memory are at a right angle to the expansion slots.

Bus mastering: A technique that allows certain advanced bus architectures to delegate control of data transfers between the CPU and associated peripheral devices to an add-in board.

ISA: Acronym for Industry Standard Architecture. A 16-bit bus design first used in the IBM PC/AT computer with a bus speed of 8MHz.

Local bus: A PC specification that allows peripherals to exchange data at the same speed as the processor.

MCA: Acronym for Micro Channel Architecture. A 32-bit proprietary expansion bus introduced for the IBM PS/2 computer.

PCMCIA: Acronym for Personal Computer Memory Card International Association. A group that developed a standard for credit-card-sized plug-in adapters originally for use in portable computers.

VESA: Acronym for Video Electronics Standards Association. This group devised a local bus standard for expansion cards.

Sample Questions

1. 8-bit boards fit into what type of slot?

   A. ISA

   B. MCA

   C. PCI

   D. PCMCIA

   Answer: A. The ISA bus followed the 8-bit bus and was designed to maintain backward compatibility.

2. The external cache in a PC resembles what?

   A. A smaller CPU

   B. A row of ICs

   C. SIMMs

   D. An expansion board

   Answer: B. An external cache usually comprises several rows of chips on the motherboard.

3. The BIOS software is found inside what on the motherboard?

    A. The CMOS battery

    B. A ROM

    C. The CPU

    D. A cache slot

Answer: B. The BIOS is contained in a ROM on the motherboard.

Identify the purpose of CMOS (Complementary Metal-Oxide Semiconductor), what it contains and how to change its basic parameters.

A PC contains many complementary metal-oxide semiconductor (CMOS) chips, which are a common type of IC. However, a CMOS chip is different from *the* CMOS chip. The CMOS chip is a unique memory chip on the motherboard that contains the BIOS hardware configuration settings. Like most forms of programmable memory, the CMOS chip is *volatile*; this means it is bound to forget its programmed settings when the power is turned off. To prevent this from happening, a small battery supplies continual power to the chip.

The CMOS chip stores configuration information such as the hard drive type or geometry, which disk to search first for the boot information, etc. This objective describes some of these configurable features and how to change them. Several questions on the exam will relate to CMOS configuration.

Critical Information

The CMOS setup program can usually be entered by pressing a key combination during startup. This combination varies from computer to computer, depending on the manufacturer. Some setup programs are also entered by running a setup program from a floppy disk.

Here are the common user-configurable settings that can be changed in the CMOS setup program:

- **Hard disk drive type.** Setting the drive type involves entering a drive number from 1 to 47 (for older drives), or setting a user-definable drive by entering the drive geometry into the program.

SEE ALSO For detailed information on entering hard disk drive information for a user-definable drive, see the Chapter 1 objective "...installing and configuring IDE/EIDE devices."

- **Display type.** The type of display will be monochrome, CGA, or EGA/VGA.

- **Floppy drive type.** Parameters for the floppy drive include physical disk size, capacity (720KB, 1.2MB, 1.44MB, etc.), and status (installed/not installed). A second floppy drive can also be configured.

- **Boot sequence.** These settings will determine whether the A: drive (floppy drive) or the C: drive (hard disk) will be checked first at startup when the BIOS looks for the boot files.

- **LPT port configuration.** This allows you to record whether the parallel port is unidirectional (standard), bidirectional (required for Zip and Jaz drives), or enhanced (EPP or ECP). It also allows you to select the IRQ and I/O address for the port, or to disable it.

- **Serial port configuration.** This setting allows you to select the port (COM 1, 2, 3, or 4) and its corresponding IRQ and I/O address. It also allows you to disable/enable the serial ports.

- **Shadow RAM.** The BIOS can be copied into RAM at startup to allow the CPU access to this information. However, this fills a 64KB block of upper memory. The BIOS may allow you the option of disabling the shadow RAM to optimize your conventional memory.

- **Date and time**

TIP During the system boot, the computer checks what the hardware settings are in the CMOS versus what is actually installed in the computer. If they are different, the BIOS will issue a warning and usually bring you right to the CMOS setup screen.

Other features may be found in the CMOS setup program depending on your specific machinery. Some examples include the following:

- **Bus.** You can use this setting to adjust your bus speeds. You may want to increase your ISA bus from 8MHz to 12MHz.

- **Memory.** You can use these settings to adjust the speed of your memory if you have installed unusually fast memory. It also allows you to select EDO RAM instead of normal DRAM, and to configure parity/non-parity.

- **Password.** To prevent unauthorized users from booting the computer, you may want to set up a BIOS password. Be aware, however, that if you forget the password, you will not be able to start the machine. The only way to bypass this is to disconnect the battery and wait for the CMOS chip to lose its power. (Unfortunately, some machines have soldered batteries!)

- **Power.** These settings can be used for power management. You can instruct the computer to shut itself down after a fixed amount of time.

WARNING Changing some of these settings, such as memory speed and bus speed, could render your system nonfunctional or damage the components. It is best to leave these settings alone, unless you are sure you know how to restore the computer to its default settings.

In addition to the battery-powered type of CMOS, there are also non-volatile EEPROM and NVRAM CMOS chips. These chips do not require battery power. Unlike other types of ROM, the programming in these chips can be altered using the computer. NVRAM stands for nonvolatile RAM, and is a type of flash RAM used on the newest machines.

Necessary Procedures

The following procedure describes how to change a setting in a typical CMOS setup program. Every program, however, is different, and some of these details may vary from PC to PC.

Changing a Setting in CMOS

1. Enter the CMOS setup program. This is accomplished by striking key combinations at startup, or running a setup program from a floppy disk. Check your documentation to find the correct key combination. Several common ones are as follows:

   - Press Del during the POST test if you have an AMI BIOS.

   - Press Ctrl+Alt+Esc during the POST test if you have an Award or Phoenix BIOS.

   - Press F1 or F10 when you see a rectangular cursor flash on the screen during startup. One of these two keys will work for a Compaq, IBM, or NEC machine.

2. Use your mouse or keyboard to negotiate through the menu-driven setup program. Click the setting you want to configure, and a list of options will appear.

3. Select the desired option.

4. Press Esc and the CMOS setup program will prompt you to save changes and exit.

5. Press Enter and reboot.

After rebooting, the computer will operate with the modified settings.

Exam Essentials

Although CMOS configuration is not greatly emphasized on the test, there will be several questions pertaining to this objective.

Know what aspects of a computer can be configured through CMOS. Hard disk drives, floppy drives, display type, ports, shadow RAM, and passwords are some of the configurable aspects of CMOS.

Know the reasons for changing the CMOS configuration. Different hardware can be enabled/disabled through CMOS, resources such as I/O addresses can be changed, passwords can be added to the BIOS for security reasons, conventional memory can be optimized through the use of shadow RAM, etc. See the Critical Information section for more details.

Know how to enter the CMOS setup program. The CMOS setup program can be entered by striking specific key combinations at startup, such as Del or Ctrl+Alt+Esc (some systems use a floppy-based setup program). Use the menu-driven program to change settings, and reboot.

Understand the difference between CMOS chips. Most CMOS chips are volatile; they require a battery in order to retain their settings when the computer is shut off. Nonvolatile CMOS chips are EEPROM or NVRAM. These chips retain their settings and do not require battery power.

Key Terms and Concepts

Bidirectional parallel port: A type of parallel port that can transmit and receive data.

CMOS: Acronym for complementary metal-oxide semiconductor. A type of integrated circuit used for processors and memory. In the PC, a special CMOS chip stores hardware parameters.

Enhanced capabilities port: Abbreviated ECP. A type of parallel port capable of high-speed bidirectional throughput.

Enhanced parallel port: Abbreviated EPP. A type of parallel port capable of high-speed throughput for printers.

NVRAM: Acronym for nonvolatile RAM. A type of memory that retains its contents when power is shut off.

Shadow RAM: A technique of copying the contents of the BIOS ROM into faster RAM when the computer boots up.

Unidirectional parallel port: The standard parallel port (SPP) in a PC, which can only transmit data one way: out of the computer. It is commonly used for printers.

Volatile memory: Any memory system that does not maintain its contents when power is lost, including DRAM and SRAM.

Sample Questions

1. In the CMOS setup program, it is possible to configure all of the following except _____. (Fill in the blank.)

   A. BIOS password.

   B. SCSI hard disk drives.

   C. Shadow RAM.

   D. display type.

Answer: B. All these feature except a SCSI disk drive can be configured in CMOS. For a SCSI drive, the "Drive Not Installed" setting should be left unchanged in CMOS.

2. If your computer searches the IDE master drive for the boot files before the floppy drive, and you want to switch the search order, you must:

   A. Enable the floppy drive.

   B. Disable the hard disk.

   C. Change the boot sequence.

   D. Change the boot sequence to C:, A:.

   Answer: C. The boot sequence must be changed to A:, C:.

CHAPTER

5

Printers

A+ Core Module Exam Objectives Covered in This Chapter:

▶ **Identify basic concepts, printer operations and printer components.** *(pages 212 – 232)*

▶ **Identify care and service techniques and common problems with primary printer types.** *(pages 232 – 252)*

▶ **Identify the types of printer connections and configurations.** *(pages 252 – 258)*

Have you ever heard of the "paperless society?" It's a dream that has never been realized (at least not yet)—but whose dream is it, anyway? It's probably rooted in the mind of the PC technician whose fitful sleep, after a long day at the office, is tormented by the echoing voices of desk-bound clerical workers, all shouting, "I CAN'T PRINT!"

This chapter is intended to provide you with some basic tools for understanding how printers work—and how to keep them working. Not incidentally, it will also help you improve your performance on the exam, for this reason: printer-related issues are heavily emphasized on the test by its designers. (They know how the priorities line up in a culture that feeds itself primarily on letters, contracts, paper money, and newsprint.)

▶ Identify basic concepts, printer operations, and printer components.

Printers are electromechanical output devices that are used to put information from the computer onto paper. They have been around since the introduction of the computer. After the display monitor, the printer is the peripheral most frequently purchased for a computer, since most people need to have paper copies of the documents they create.

This objective describes the different printer technologies, the components involved in the printing process, and how the printing process works. All these issues are emphasized on the test.

Critical Information

The three major types of printer technologies are impact, bubble-jet, and laser.

Impact Printers

The most basic category of printers is known as *impact printers*. Impact printers, as their name suggests, use some form of impact and an inked ribbon (like a typewriter) to make an imprint on the paper.

There are two major types of impact printers: daisy-wheel and dot-matrix. Each type has its own service and maintenance issues.

Daisy-Wheel Printers

The *daisy-wheel* printer contains a wheel with raised letters and symbols on each "petal" of the flower-shaped wheel (see Figure 5.1). When the printer needs to print a character, it sends a signal to the mechanism that contains the wheel. This mechanism is called the *printhead*. The printhead rotates the daisy wheel until the required character is in place. An electromechanical hammer (called a *solenoid*) then strikes the back of the "petal" containing the character. The character pushes up against an inked ribbon, which ultimately strikes the paper and makes the impression of the requested character.

Daisy-wheel printers were one of the earliest types of impact printer developed. The first designs could print only two to four characters per second (cps). They are very noisy printers, but they are inexpensive and can print on multipart forms (like carbonless receipts). Their quality of print is equivalent to a typewriter, which resulted in the *letter quality* (LQ) designation for this type of printer.

FIGURE 5.1: A daisy-wheel printer mechanism

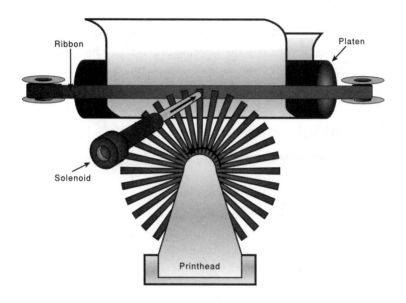

Dot-Matrix Printers

The other common type of impact printer is the *dot-matrix* printer. These printers work in a manner similar to daisy-wheel printers, except that instead of a spinning, character-imprinted wheel, the printhead contains a row of "pins" (short, sturdy stalks of hard wire). These pins are triggered in patterns that form letters and numbers as the printhead moves across the paper (see Figure 5.2).

The pins in the printhead are wrapped with coils of wire to create a solenoid. The pins are held in the rest position by a combination of a small magnet and a spring. When a particular pin is triggered by the printer controller, the printer controller sends a signal to the printhead, which energizes the wire around the appropriate print pin. This turns the print wire into an electromagnet, which repels the print pin, forcing it against the ink ribbon, making a dot on the paper. It's the arrangement of the dots in columns and rows that makes the letters and numbers we see on the page.

FIGURE 5.2: Formation of images in a dot-matrix printer

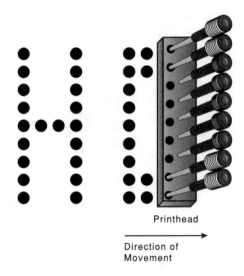

Printhead

Direction of
Movement

Dot-matrix printers have relatively poor image quality, which in early models was rated as *draft quality*. Later versions of the printer crammed more pins into the printhead (17 or 24 instead of 9), improving the output to *near letter quality* (NLQ) print. Dot-matrix printers can attain very high speeds (even up to 500 characters per second!) and, as impact printers, they can also print on multipart forms.

Bubble-Jet Printers

The next category of printer technology, bubble-jet, is one of the most popular in use today. This category of printers is actually an advanced form of an older technology known as ink-jet printers. Both types of printers spray ink on the page, but ink-jet printers use a reservoir of ink, a pump, and an ink nozzle to accomplish this. These printers are messy, noisy, and inefficient. Bubble-jet printers work much more efficiently.

Bubble-jet printers are very basic printers with very few moving parts. All bubble-jet printers work in a similar fashion.

Bubble-jet printers contain a special part called an ink cartridge (see Figure 5.3). This part contains the printhead and ink supply, and it must be replaced when the ink supply runs out.

F I G U R E 5.3: A typical ink cartridge

Inside this ink cartridge are several small chambers. At the top of each chamber is a metal plate and tube leading to the ink supply. At the bottom of each chamber is a small pinhole. These pinholes are used to spray ink on the page to form characters and images as patterns of dots (similar to the way a dot-matrix printer works, but with much higher resolution).

When a particular chamber needs to spray ink, an electric signal gets sent to the heating element, energizing it. The elements heat up quickly, causing the ink to vaporize. Because of the expanding ink vapor, the ink gets pushed out of the pinhole and forms a bubble of ink. As the vapor expands, the bubble eventually gets large enough to break off into a droplet. The rest of the ink is pulled back into the chamber due to surface tension of the ink. When another drop needs to be sprayed, the process begins again.

Laser Printers (Page Printers)

Laser printers are referred to as page printers because they receive their print job instructions one page at a time (rather than receiving instructions one line at a time). The two major types of page printers are those that use the electrophotographic (EP) print process and those that use the Hewlett-Packard (HP) print process. Both work in basically the same way, with slight differences.

Electrophotographic (EP) Laser Printer Operation

Electrophotographic technology uses a combination of electrostatic charges, laser light, and a black powdery substance called *toner.* Printers that use this technology are called EP Process laser printers, or just *laser printers.* Every laser printer technology has its foundations in the EP printer process.

Basic Components Any printer that uses the EP process contains eight standard field replaceable unit (FRU) assemblies. These assemblies are described below.

The Toner Cartridge

The EP toner cartridge (Figure 5.4), as its name suggests, holds the toner. Toner is a black, carbon substance that is sensitive to electrical charges. The toner cartridge also contains the EP print drum, the charge corona wire, and the cleaning blade. The EP print drum is coated with a photosensitive material that can hold a static charge when not exposed to light. The charge corona wire (also called the *main corona*) charges the drum, and the cleaning blade scrapes "used" toner off the drum to keep it clean.

NOTE In most laser printers, "toner cartridge" means an EP toner cartridge that contains toner and a photosensitive drum in one plastic case. In some laser printers, however, the toner and photosensitive drum can be replaced separately, instead of as a single unit.

The Laser Scanning Assembly

The laser scanning assembly houses the laser mechanism, which shines on particular areas of the photosensitive print drum as it turns. The electrical charge in these areas is reduced, allowing toner to become attached to the drum.

FIGURE 5.4: An EP toner cartridge

SIDE VIEW

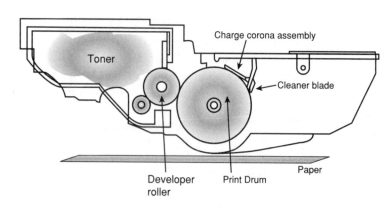

High-Voltage Power Supply (HVPS)

The high-voltage power supply converts house AC current (120 volts, 60 Hertz) into higher voltages used to energize both the charge corona wire and transfer corona wire.

DC Power Supply (DCPS)

The DC power supply converts house current into three voltages: +5 VDc and –5 VDc for the formatter board, and +24 VDc for the paper transport motors. This component also runs the fan that cools the internal components of the printer.

Paper Transport Assembly

The paper transport assembly is responsible for moving the paper through the printer. It consists of a motor and several rubberized rollers that perform two distinct functions.

- The *feed roller* or *paper pickup roller* (Figure 5.5) picks up a single sheet of paper from the paper tray.

- The *registration rollers* (also shown in Figure 5.5) synchronize the paper movement with the image formation process in the EP cartridge. These rollers don't feed the paper past the EP cartridge until the cartridge is ready for it.

F I G U R E 5.5: Paper transport rollers

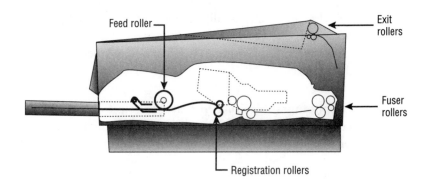

The Transfer Corona Assembly

The transfer corona assembly consists of either a wire or roller located beneath the EP printer cartridge, and is charged with a high-voltage electrical charge. This assembly charges the paper, which pulls the toner from the photosensitive drum. The roller mechanism is capable of higher speeds than the wire and is more common in today's printers.

A *static-charge eliminator strip* drains away the charge imparted to the paper by the corona and prevents paper from jamming the printer.

Fusing Assembly

The fusing assembly or *fuser* applies pressure and heat to fuse the plastic toner particles to the paper. It is made up of three main parts: a halogen heating lamp, a Teflon-coated aluminum fusing roller, and a rubberized pressure roller. Before the fusing process begins, the halogen lamp heats the fusing roller to about 350°F.

Formatter Board

The formatter board is a circuit board that formats the information from a computer into a page's worth of line-by-line commands for the laser scanner. The formatter board is the printer's controller card; it sends commands to each of the components telling them to "wake up" and start the EP print process.

This circuit board is usually mounted underneath the printer. The board has connectors for each of the types of interfaces, and cables to each assembly. It contains RAM and ROM memory on upgradeable SIMMs.

Electrophotographic Print Process The electrophotographic print process is the process an EP laser printer uses to form images on paper. It consists of six major steps, listed in chronological order:

1. charging
2. exposing
3. developing
4. transferring
5. fusing
6. cleaning

Before any of these steps can begin, however, the controller must sense that the printer is ready to start printing (toner cartridge installed, fuser warmed to operating temperature, and all covers in place). Printing cannot take place until the printer is ready. Before you read the detailed printing process description that follows, carefully look at the diagram provided in Figure 5.6.

FIGURE 5.6: The EP print process (simplified)

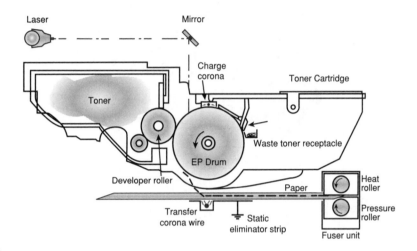

Step 1: Charging

The first step in the EP process is the *charging* step (Figure 5.7). In this step, the charge corona wire within the EP toner cartridge (above the photosensitive drum) gets a high voltage from the HVPS. It uses this high voltage to apply a strong, uniform negative charge (–600 VDc) to the surface of the drum.

Step 2: Exposing

The next step in the EP process is the *exposure* step. In this step, the laser is turned on and "scans" the drum from side to side, flashing on and off according to the bits of information the printer controller sends it while communicating the individual bits of the image. The photosensitive drum's charge is severely reduced in those areas touched by the laser, from –600 VDc to a slight negative charge (around –100 VDc). As the drum rotates, a pattern of exposed areas is formed, representing the images to be printed. Figure 5.8 shows this process.

FIGURE 5.7: The charging step of the EP process

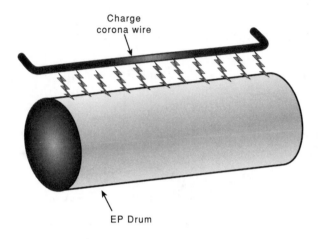

FIGURE 5.8: The exposure step of the EP process

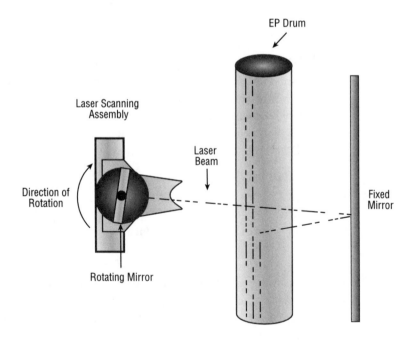

At this point, the controller sends a signal to the pickup roller to feed a piece of paper into the printer, where it stops at the registration rollers.

Step 3: Developing

Now that the surface of the drum holds an electrical representation of the image being printed, its discrete electrical charges must be converted into something that can be transferred to a piece of paper. The EP process step that accomplishes this is the *developing* step (Figure 5.9). In this step, toner is transferred to the areas that were exposed in the exposure step.

F I G U R E 5.9: The developing step of the EP process

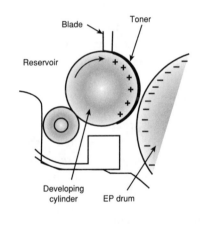

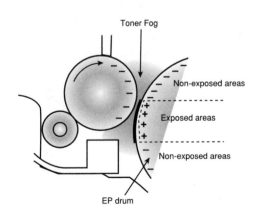

There is a metallic roller called the *developing roller* inside an EP cartridge that acquires a –600 VDc charge (called a *bias voltage*) from the HVPS. The toner sticks to this roller because there is a magnet located inside the roller and because of the electrostatic charges between the toner and the developing roller. As the developing roller rotates towards the photosensitive drum, the toner acquires the charge of the roller (–600 VDc). When the toner comes between the developing roller and the photosensitive drum, the toner is attracted to the areas that have been exposed by the laser (because these areas have a lesser charge, of –100 VDc). The toner also is repelled from the unexposed areas (because they are at the same –600 VDc charge, and like charges repel). This toner transfer results in a "fog" of toner forming between the EP drum and the developing roller.

The photosensitive drum now has toner stuck to it where the laser has written. The drum continues to rotate until the developed image is ready to be transferred to paper in the next step, the transfer step.

Step 4: Transfer

At this point in the EP process, the developed image is rotating into position. The controller notifies the registration rollers that the paper should be fed through. The registration rollers then move the paper underneath the drum and the process of transferring the image can begin, with the *transfer* step.

The controller sends a signal to the transfer corona assembly and tells it to turn on. The corona wire/roller then acquires a strong positive charge (+600 VDc) and applies that charge to the paper. The paper, thus charged, pulls the toner from the drum at the line of contact between the roller and the paper, because the paper and toner have opposite charges. Once the registration rollers move the paper past the corona wire, the static-eliminator strip removes all charge from that portion of the paper. Figure 5.10 details this step. If the strip didn't bleed this charge away, the paper would attract itself to the toner cartridge and cause a paper jam.

FIGURE 5.10: The transfer step of the EP process

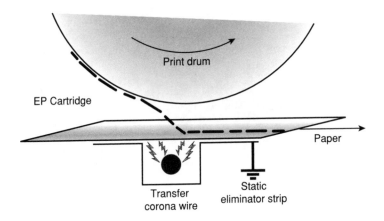

The toner is now held in place by weak electrostatic charges and gravity. It will not stay there, however, unless it is made permanent, which is the reason for the next step, the fusing step.

Step 5: Fusing

In the next step, the *fusing* step, the toner image is made permanent. The registration rollers push the paper towards the fuser. Once the fuser grabs the paper, the registration rollers push for only a short time more. The fuser is now in control of moving the paper.

As the paper passes through the fuser, the 350°F fuser roller melts the polyester resin of the toner and the rubberized pressure roller presses it permanently into the paper (Figure 5.11). The paper continues on through the fuser and eventually exits the printer.

Once the paper completely exits the fuser, it trips a sensor that tells the printer to finish the EP process with the next step, the cleaning step.

FIGURE 5.11: The fusing step of the EP process

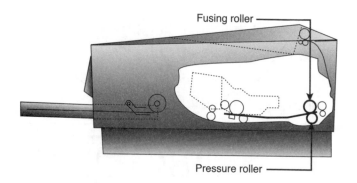

Fusing roller

Pressure roller

Step 6: Cleaning

Now that the image has been transferred to paper and permanently fixed to the page, the printer needs to clean up after itself. In the final step—the *cleaning* step— a rubber blade inside the EP cartridge scrapes any untransferred toner into a used toner receptacle inside the EP cartridge, and a fluorescent lamp discharges any remaining charge on the photosensitive drum. (As mentioned earlier, the drum, being photosensitive, loses its charge when exposed to light.) This step is illustrated in Figure 5.12.

FIGURE 5.12: The cleaning step of the EP process

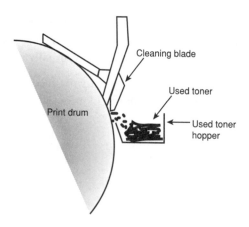

Cleaning blade

Used toner

Print drum

Used toner hopper

The EP cartridge is constantly cleaning the drum. It may take more than one rotation of the photosensitive drum to make an image on the paper. The cleaning step keeps the drum fresh for each use. If you didn't clean the drum, you would see "ghosts" of previous pages printed along with your image.

NOTE The actual amount of toner removed in the cleaning process is quite small. The cartridge will run out of toner before the used toner receptacle fills up.

At this point, the printer can print another page and the EP process can begin again.

HP LaserJet Operation

The largest manufacturer of laser printers is Hewlett-Packard. These printers are based on the EP print process, so the two types share most of the same basic components. There are some differences, however, both in the components and in the process.

Basic Components   HP LaserJets differ from EP laser printers in the following areas:

- method of charging the toner
- type of toner cartridge

NOTE Apple LaserWriters and HP LaserJets use the same print engine, so some of the parts (including the toner cartridges) are interchangeable. For example, an Apple LaserWriter II uses the same toner cartridge as an HP LaserJet II. The HP cartridges are slightly cheaper than Apple-brand cartridges. Also, the fusers and some of the rollers (pickup and registration) are the same and can be interchanged, if necessary. Be careful, though, as not *every* component of these two types of printers is interchangeable. The controller boards, for instance, are completely different.

- use of light-emitting diodes (LEDs) to erase the photosensitive drum during the cleaning stage of the HP process

- different polarities on the high voltages

HP Print Process Just as HP LaserJet components are very similar to EP laser printer components, the HP print process is similar to the EP print process. The six printing steps that follow emphasize the different terms used in HP technology, as well as differences in the process itself.

1. *Conditioning.* This step is equivalent to the charging phase of the EP printing process. The surface of the photosensitive drum in the toner cartridge is charged by the HVPS with a uniform negative charge to its surface by a charge roller.

2. *Writing.* This step is equivalent to the exposing phase of the EP printing process. During this phase, the laser scans the surface of the drum, discharging selected areas to ground (0 VDc, or zero charge). The pattern formed by the laser represents the image that is being printed.

3. *Developing.* Toner is transferred from the developing roller to areas of the photosensitive drum that the laser has passed over.

4. *Transferring.* A strong positive charged is applied to the back of the paper by a roller. This charge is strong enough to pull the toner from the print drum and transfer it to the paper. Usually, HP LaserJets use a *transfer roller* to apply this charge.

5. *Fusing.* The fuser roller heats the paper and toner and the pressure roller presses the toner into the paper.

6. *Cleaning.* Toner residue from the previous print image is removed by a cleaning blade and stored in the toner cartridge's waste toner receptacle. A set of LEDs totally exposes the drum, and the process begins again.

Exam Essentials

Printers and the printing process are covered in great detail on the test. The following Exam Essentials reflect this.

Know the different types of printers. Impact printers include daisy-wheel and dot-matrix printers. Bubble-jet printers and ink-jet printers use an ink cartridge to release ink. Laser printers are usually classified as EP or HP.

Know how each printer type functions. Daisy-wheel printers function like typewriters. Dot-matrix printers use a printhead composed of numerous metal pins. Bubble-jet printers use a cartridge to release vaporized ink; the ink is heated by small metal plates within the chambers of the ink cartridge. Laser printers draw an image by laser, fill the image with toner, and transfer the image to paper.

Know the replaceable parts in a laser printer. Field replaceable units in a laser printer include the toner cartridge, high-voltage power supply, DC power supply, paper transport assembly, transfer corona assembly, fusing assembly, and formatter board (a circuit board). The formatter board includes upgradeable RAM and ROM.

Know the terminology and chronology for the different phases in the EP printing process. The steps in the EP printing process are: charging, exposing, developing, transferring, fusing, and cleaning.

Understand what occurs during each phase of the EP printing process. For specific information on the EP printing process, see the Critical Information section.

Know the terminology and chronology for the different phases in the HP printing process. The steps in the EP printing process are: conditioning, writing, developing, transferring, fusing, and cleaning.

Understand what occurs during each phase of the HP printing process. The HP printing process is similar to the EP printing process. See the Critical Information section for more information.

Key Terms and Concepts

Bubble-jet: A printer technology that uses vaporized ink to create an image. The ink is vaporized by a heating element that is energized by an electric signal.

Charge corona: A roller or wire used to apply a charge to the print drum in a laser printer. Also called the main corona.

Daisy-wheel: An impact printer technology that uses a plastic or metal print mechanism with a different character on the end of each spoke of a wheel.

DCPS: Acronym for DC power supply. The power supply in a laser printer used to run the paper transport motors, formatter board, and fan.

Dot-matrix An impact printer technology that uses columns of small pins and an inked ribbon to create patterns of dots that form characters.

Formatter board: A type of circuit board that takes information from a computer and turns it into commands for the various components in a printer.

Fuser: Device on an EP printer that uses two rollers to heat toner particles and melt them onto paper.

HVPS: Acronym for high-voltage power supply. The power supply in a laser printer used to charge both of the corona wires.

Impact printer: Type of printer that works by striking through an inked ribbon onto paper.

Print drum: A photosensitive cylinder in a laser printer that retains a charge when not exposed to light.

Transfer corona: A charged wire or roller in a laser printer used to attract toner onto paper from the print drum.

Sample Questions

1. The fluorescent lamp in a laser printer does what?

    A. Discharges the print drum

    B. Charges the print drum

    C. Attracts toner from the drum onto the paper

    D. Attracts toner to the print drum

    Answer: A. The lamp effectively erases the charge on the print drum.

2. A dot-matrix printer uses what to form the print image?

    A. An ink cartridge

    B. A daisy wheel

    C. A halogen lamp

    D. Pins

    Answer: D. A dot-matrix printer is a type of impact printer that uses a printhead consisting of 9, 17, or 24 pins.

3. In laser printer terminology, what happens in the "developing" phase?

    A. The laser shines on the print drum.

    B. The corona charges the print drum.

    C. Toner attaches to the print drum.

    D. Toner melts into an image on the paper.

    Answer: C. Toner is attracted to areas on the print drum that have been exposed to the laser during the "exposing" phase.

4. Which event takes place after the initial "conditioning" phase of a laser printer?

    A. Charging

    B. Writing

    C. Developing

    D. Transfering

Answer: B. In HP terminology, the "writing" phase is second. This corresponds to the "exposing" phase in the EP process.

Identify care and service techniques and common problems with primary printer types.

Much of the information you'll learn in this section (particularly concerning laser printers) is derived from the mechanical printer processes that you studied in the preceding objective. Knowing how something works is often the key to repairing it.

This information will help you remedy the "I can't print!" syndrome typical in many offices. The service and repair of printers is an important subject on the exam, and you will be tested on it.

Critical Information

Each type of printer has unique care and service requirements as well as unique problems. For this reason, information in this section is arranged by printer type.

Dot-Matrix Printer Problems

Dot-matrix printers are relatively simple devices and have only a few problems: low print quality, paper jams, and (uncommonly) problems with the stepper motor.

Low Print Quality

Problems with print quality are easy to identify. When the printed page comes out of the printer, the characters are too light or have dots missing from them. Table 5.1 details some of the most common print quality problems, their causes, and their solutions.

TABLE 5.1: Common Dot-Matrix Print-Quality Problems

Characteristics	Cause	Solution
Consistently faded or light characters	Worn-out print ribbon	Replace ribbon with a new, vendor-recommended ribbon.
Print lines that go from dark to light, light to dark as the printhead moves across the page	Print ribbon advance gear slipping	Replace ribbon advance gear or mechanism.
A small, blank line running through a line of print (consistently)	Printhead pin stuck inside the printhead	Replace the printhead.
A small, blank line running through a line of print (intermittently)	A loose, broken, or shorting printhead cable	Secure or replace the printhead cable.
A small, dark line running through a line of print	Printhead pin stuck in the "out" position	Replace the printhead. (Pushing the pin in may damage the printhead.)
Printer makes printing noise, but no print appears on page	Worn, missing, or improperly installed ribbon cartridge	Replace ribbon cartridge correctly.
Printer prints "garbage"	Cable partially unhooked, wrong driver selected, or bad printer control board (PCB)	Hook up cable correctly, select correct driver, or replace PCB (respectively).

Paper Jams

A paper jam happens when something prevents the paper from advancing through the printer evenly, usually resulting in the audible sound of crinkling paper. Obstructed paper paths are often difficult to find. Usually you must disassemble the printer to find the bit of crumpled-up paper or other foreign substance that's blocking the paper path. A very common obstruction is a piece of the "perf"—the perforated sides of tractor-fed paper—that has torn off and become lodged in the paper path. It may be necessary to remove the platen roller and feed mechanism to get at the obstruction. If you need to clean the paper path, use a dry cloth.

TIP   Peel-off labels can be especially troublesome when they jam in a dot-matrix printer. DO NOT roll the feed roller backwards (except in small increments) to re-align the sheet. This can result in labels getting stuck beneath the platen, which can't be removed without taking apart the paper feed assembly. If a label is misaligned, try realigning the whole sheet of labels *slowly* using the feed roller, with the power off.

Stepper Motor Problems

A *stepper motor* is a motor that can move in very small increments. Printers use stepper motors to move the printhead back and forth as well as to advance the paper (these are called the *carriage motor* and *main motor*, respectively). These motors are very sensitive to stray voltage, and become damaged when they are forced in any direction while the power is on. Common causes for a damaged motor include:

- movement of the printhead (usually with the intention of installing a printer ribbon)

- movement of the paper feed roller (with the intention to align paper)

A damaged stepper motor is easy to detect. Damage to the stepper motor will cause it to lose precision and move farther with each "step." Lines of print will be unevenly spaced if the main motor is damaged (which is the more likely to happen). Characters will be "scrunched" together if the carriage motor goes bad. In fact, if the motor is bad enough, it won't move at all in any direction. It may even make high-pitched squealing noises. If any of these symptoms show themselves, it's time to replace one of these motors.

Stepper motors are usually expensive to replace. They are about half the cost of a new printer! Damage to them is very easy to avoid: simply make sure you turn off the power if you must move anything that affects the motor.

TIP   If you're buying a new dot-matrix printer, consider an Okidata. With nothing but a flat blade screwdriver and your hands, you can completely disassemble an Okidata dot-matrix printer in less than ten minutes. Replacing parts on them is just as easy. All parts snap into place, including the covers!

Bubble-Jet Printers

Bubble-jet printers are very popular, and are the most commonly sold printers for home use. Here's a look at some of the usual service issues with bubble-jet printers.

Print Quality

The majority of bubble-jet printer problems are quality problems. Ninety-nine percent of these can be traced to a faulty ink cartridge. With most bubble-jet printers, the ink cartridge contains the print-head and the ink. The ink will dry out in the small nozzles of the cartridge, blocking them if they are not used at least once a week.

An example of a dried nozzle is when you have thin, blank lines present in every line of text on the page. This indicates that at least one of the pinhole-sized ink nozzles has dried out. Replacing the ink cartridge solves this problem easily.

WARNING Some people will try to save a buck by refilling their ink cartridge when they need to replace it. If you are one of them, STOP! Almost all ink cartridges are designed *not* to be refilled. They are designed to be used once and thrown away! By refilling them, you make a hole in them, and ink can leak out and the printer will need to be cleaned. Also, the ink will probably be of the wrong type, and print quality can suffer. Finally, a refilled cartridge may void the printer's warranty.

If an ink cartridge becomes damaged it can result in the smearing of characters. Again, the solution is to replace the ink cartridge.

One final print quality problem does not directly involve the ink cartridge. If the print goes from dark to light quickly, then prints nothing, it may indicate a broken or malfunctioning *priming pump*. This is a small suction pump inside the printer that "primes" the ink cartridge before each print cycle. If you experience this problem, replace the pump.

TIP If the problem of the ink going from dark to light quickly and then disappearing ever happens to you, and you really need to print a couple of pages, try this: take the ink cartridge out of the printer, squirt some window cleaner on a paper towel, and gently tap the printhead against the wet paper towel. The force of the tap plus the solvents in the window cleaner should dislodge any dried ink, and the ink will flow freely again.

Paper Jams

Paper jams in bubble-jet printers are likely to be caused by either a worn pickup roller or the wrong type of paper.

The pickup roller usually has one or two D-shaped rollers mounted on a rotating shaft. When the shaft rotates, one corner of the "D" rubs against the paper, pushing it into the printer. When the roller gets worn, it gets smooth and doesn't exert enough friction against the paper to push it into the printer.

If the paper used in the printer is too smooth, it causes the same problem. Pickup rollers use friction, and smooth paper doesn't offer much friction. If the paper is too rough, on the other hand, it acts like sandpaper on the rollers, wearing them smooth. Check the documentation to see what kind of paper to use with the printer.

Laser Printers

Service problems for laser printers are the most complex, but they are also easily identifiable and have specific fixes. Most of the problems can be diagnosed with knowledge of the inner workings of the printer and a little common sense.

Paper Jams

Laser printers today run at copier speeds. Because of this, their most common problem is paper jams. Paper can get jammed in a printer for several reasons. First of all, feed jams happen when the paper feed rollers get worn (similar to feed jams in bubble-jet printers). The solution to this problem is easy: replace the worn rollers.

TIP   If your paper feed jams are caused by worn pickup rollers, there is something you can do to get your printer working while you're waiting for the replacement pickup rollers. Scuff the feed roller(s) with a Scotch-Brite® pot-scrubber pad (or something similar) to roughen up the feed rollers. This trick only works once. After that, the rollers aren't thick enough to touch the paper.

Another cause of feed jams is related to the drive of the pickup roller. The drive gear (or clutch) may be broken or have teeth missing. Again, the solution is to replace it. To determine if the problem is a broken gear or worn rollers, print a test page, but leave the paper tray out. Look into the paper feed opening with a flashlight and see if the paper pickup rollers are turning evenly and don't "skip." If they turn evenly, the problem is more than likely worn rollers.

Worn exit rollers can also cause paper jams. These rollers guide the paper out of the printer into the paper-receiving tray. If they are worn or damaged, the paper may "catch" on its way out of the printer. These types of jams are characterized by a paper jam that occurs just as the paper is getting to the exit rollers. If the paper jams, open the rear door and see where the paper is. If the paper is very close to the exit roller, the exit rollers are probably the problem.

The solution is to replace all the exit rollers. You should replace all of them at the same time, since others may also be failing. Besides, they're cheap.

Paper jams can actually be caused by the paper absorbing moisture from the air. If your printer consistently tries to feed multiple pages into the printer, the paper isn't dry enough. If you live in an area with high humidity, this could be a problem. The best solution is to keep the paper wrapped until it's needed. Also, keep the humidity around 50% or lower (but above 25% if you can, in order to avoid problems with electrostatic discharge).

Finally, there is a metal, grounded strip called the static eliminator strip inside the printer that drains the corona charge out of the paper before it exits. If that strip is missing, broken, or damaged, the charge will remain on the paper and may cause it to stick to the EP cartridge, causing a jam. If the paper jams after reaching the corona assembly, this may be the cause. (Refer to Figure 5.6 earlier in this chapter for the locations of these internal components.)

Blank Pages

There's nothing more annoying than printing a ten-page contract and receiving ten pages of blank paper from the printer. Blank pages are a somewhat common occurrence in laser printers. Somehow, the toner isn't being put on the paper. There are three major causes of blank pages:

- the toner cartridge
- the transfer corona assembly
- the high-voltage power supply (HVPS)

Toner Cartridge   The toner cartridge is, predictably, the source of most quality problems, since it contains most of the image-formation pieces for printers. A blank page will come out of the printer if there is no toner in the toner cartridge. That sounds simple, but some people think these things will last forever. It's very easy to check: just open the printer, remove the toner cartridge, and shake it. You will be able to hear if there's toner inside the cartridge. If it's empty, replace it.

TIP   If you think the toner cartridge is dry, and need to print a few more jobs, shake it gently and put it back in the printer; the last remains of toner will settle at the bottom of the cartridge, and may allow you to complete a few more print jobs.

Another problem that crops up is caused by the use of refilled or reconditioned toner cartridges. During the recycling process, these cartridges may get filled with the wrong kind of toner (for example, one with an incorrect charge). This may cause toner to be repelled from the EP drum instead of attracted to it. Thus, there's no toner on the page because there was no toner on the EP drum to begin with. The solution, once again, is to replace the toner cartridge with the type recommended by the manufacturer.

A third problem related to toner cartridges happens when someone installs a new toner cartridge and forgets to remove the sealing tape that is present to keep the toner in the cartridge during shipping. The solution to this problem is easy and obvious; just remove the toner cartridge from the printer, remove the sealing tape, and reinstall the cartridge.

Transfer Corona Assembly   The second cause of the "blank page" problem is a damaged or missing corona wire. If there is a lost or damaged wire, the developed image won't transfer from the EP drum to the paper. Thus, no image appears on the printout. To determine if this is causing your problem, do the first half of the self-test (described later in this section). If there is an image on the drum, but not on the paper, you will know that the corona assembly isn't doing its job.

To check if the corona assembly is causing the problem, open the cover and examine the wire (or roller, if your printer uses one). The corona wire is hard to see, so you may need a flashlight. You will know if it's broken or missing just by looking—it will either be in pieces or not there at all. If it's not broken or missing, the problem may be related to the HVPS.

The corona wire (or roller) is a relatively inexpensive part and can be easily replaced with the removal of two screws and some patience.

High-Voltage Power Supply (HVPS)   The HVPS supplies high-voltage, low-current power to both the charge and transfer corona assemblies in laser printers. If the HVPS is broken, neither assembly will work properly. If the half self-test shows an image on the drum but none on the paper, and the corona assembly is present and not damaged, then the HVPS is at fault.

All Black Pages

At least as annoying as all blank pages is all black pages. This happens when the charging unit (the charge corona wire or charge corona roller) in the toner cartridge malfunctions and fails to place a charge on the EP drum. Because the drum is grounded, it has no charge. Anything with a charge (like toner) will stick to it. As the drum rotates, all the toner will be transferred to the page and a black page is formed.

This problem wastes quite a bit of toner, but can be fixed easily. The solution (again) is to replace the toner cartridge with a known, good, manufacturer-recommended one. If that doesn't solve the problem, then the HVPS is at fault (it's not providing the high voltage that the charge corona needs to function).

Repetitive Small Marks or Defects

Repetitive marks occur frequently in heavily used (as well as older) laser printers. They may be caused by toner spilled inside the printer. They can also be caused by a crack or chip in the EP drum, which mainly occurs in recycled cartridges. These cracks can accumulate toner. In both cases, some of the toner will get stuck onto one of the rollers. Once this happens, every time the roller rotates and touches a piece of paper, it will leave toner smudges spaced a roller circumference apart.

The solution is relatively simple: clean or replace the offending roller. To help you figure out which roller is causing the problem, the service manuals contain a chart like the one in Figure 5.13. To use the chart, place the printed page next to the chart. Align the first occurrence of the smudge with the top arrow. The next smudge will line up with one of the other arrows. The arrow it lines up with tells which roller is causing the problem.

FIGURE 5.13: Laser printer roller circumference chart

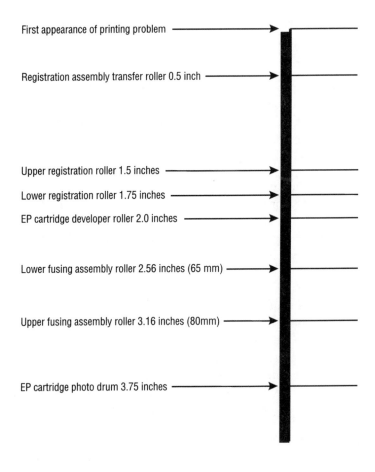

NOTE Remember that the chart in Figure 5.13 is only an example. Your printer may have different size rollers (and thus need a different chart). Check your printer's service documentation for a chart like this.

Vertical Black Lines on Page

A groove or scratch in the EP drum can cause the problem of vertical black lines running down all or part of the page. Since a scratch is "lower" than the surface, it doesn't receive as much of a charge (if any) as the other areas. The result is that toner will stick to it as though it were discharged. Since the groove may go around the circumference of the drum, the line may go all the way down the page.

Another possible cause of vertical black lines is a dirty charge corona wire. A dirty charge corona will prevent a sufficient charge from being placed on the EP drum. Since the EP drum will have a charge of almost zero, toner will stick to the areas that correspond to the dirty areas on the charge corona.

The solution to the first problem is, as always, to replace the toner cartridge (or EP drum if your printer uses a separate EP drum and toner). You can also solve the second problem with a new toner cartridge, but that would be an extreme solution. It's easier to clean the charge corona with the brush supplied with the cartridge.

Vertical White Line on Page

Vertical white lines running down all or part of the page are relatively common problems on older printers, especially ones that don't see much maintenance. They are caused by some foreign matter (more than likely toner) caught on the transfer corona wire. The dirty spots keep the toner from being transmitted to the paper at those locations, with the result that streaks form as the paper progresses past the transfer corona wire. The solution is to clean the wire.

To clean it, remove the toner cartridge. Then wipe it clean using the brush supplied with the cartgridge. Another method of cleaning the transfer corona wire is to wipe the wire clean with a Q-tip® and alcohol. Although this method is slow, it is effective, because the trough containing the transfer corona wire is covered by a thin web of material that can inhibit use of the brush. Clean one section of the wire at a time by inserting the Q-tip® between the web filaments.

Image Smudging

If you can pick up a sheet from a laser printer, run your thumb across it, and have the image come off on your thumb, you have a fuser problem. The fuser isn't heating the toner and fusing it into the paper. This could be caused by a number of things—but all of them would be taken care of with a fuser replacement. For example, if the halogen light inside the heating roller has burned out, that would cause the problem. The solution is to replace the fuser. The fuser can be replaced with a rebuilt unit, if you prefer. Rebuilt fusers are almost as good as new fusers, and some even come with guarantees. Plus, they cost less.

TIP The whole fuser assembly may not need to be replaced. Components can be ordered from parts suppliers and the fuser can be rebuilt by you. For example, if the fuser has a bad lamp, you can order a lamp and replace it in the assembly.

A similar problem is when there are small areas of smudging that repeat themselves down the page. Dents or "cold spots" in the fuser heat roller cause this problem. The only solution is to replace either the fuser assembly or the heat roller.

"Ghosting"

"Ghosting" is what you have when you can see light images of previously printed pages on the current page. This is caused by one of two things: bad erasure lamps or a broken cleaning blade. If the erasure lamps are bad, the previous electrostatic discharges aren't completely wiped away. When the EP drum rotates towards the developing roller, some toner will stick to the slightly discharged areas. A broken cleaning blade, on the other hand, causes old toner to build up on the EP drum and consequently present itself in the next printed image.

Replacing the toner cartridge solves the second problem. Solving the first problem involves replacing the erasure lamps in the printer. Since the toner cartridge is the least expensive cure, you should try that first. Usually, replacing the toner cartridge will solve the problem. If it doesn't, you will then have to replace the erasure lamps.

Printer Prints Pages of Garbage

This has happened to everyone at least once. You try to print a one-page letter and ten pages of what looks to be garbage come out of the printer. This problem can be traced to one of two different sources: the printer driver software or the formatter board.

Printer Driver The correct printer driver needs to be installed for the printer you have. For example, if you have an HP LaserJet III, then that is the driver you need to install. Once the driver has been installed, it must be configured for the correct page description language: PCL (Printer Control Language) or PostScript. Most HP LaserJet printers use PCL (but can be configured for PostScript). Determine what page description your printer has been configured for and set the printer driver to the same setting. If this is not done, you will get garbage out of the printer.

TIP Most printers that have LCD displays will indicate that they are in PostScript mode with a "PS" or "PostScript" somewhere in the display.

If the problem is the wrong driver setting, the "garbage" that the printer prints will look like English. That is, the words will be readable, but they won't make any sense.

Formatter Board Another cause of garbage printouts is a bad formatter board. This circuit board takes the information that the printer receives from the computer and turns it into commands for the various components in the printer. Usually problems with the formatter board produce wavy lines of print or random patterns of dots on the page.

It's relatively easy to replace the formatter board in a laser printer. This board is usually installed underneath the printer and can be removed by loosening two screws and pulling the board out. Typically, replacing the formatter board also replaces the printer interface, another possible source of garbage printouts.

HP LaserJet Testing

Most printers come with built-in diagnostics tests. The tests described here are for the popular HP LaserJet laser printers, but the information can be applied to other types of laser printers as well.

Self-Tests   When you troubleshoot laser printers, there are four tests you can perform on the printer to narrow down which assembly is causing the problem. The four tests are the *engine self-test*, the *half self-test*, the *secret self-test*, and the *control panel self-test*.

1. **Engine self-test:** The engine self-test tests the print engine of the LaserJet, bypassing the formatter board. This test will cause the printer to print a single page with vertical lines running its length. If an engine self-test can be performed, you will know that the laser print engine can print successfully. To perform an engine self-test, you must press the printer's self-test button, which is hidden behind a small cover on the side of the printer (see Figure 5.14). The location of the button varies from printer to printer, so you may have to refer to the printer manual. Using a pencil or probe, press the button and the print engine will start printing the test page.

2. **Half self-test:** A print engine half self-test is performed the same as the self-test, but you interrupt it halfway through the print cycle by opening the cover. This is useful in determining what component of the print process is causing the printer to malfunction. If you stop the print process and find part of a developed image on the EP drum and part transferred to the paper, you know that the pickup rollers, registration rollers, laser scanner, charging roller, EP drum, and transfer roller are all working correctly. You can stop the half self-test at various points in the print process to determine the source of a malfunction.

FIGURE 5.14: Print engine self-test button location (location may vary on different printers)

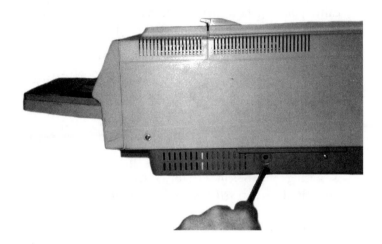

3. **Secret self-test:** This test generates an advanced test print with gray scales, horizontal lines, and vertical lines that can be used for comparison purposes. You need to keep an original print made when the printer was "healthy" in order to make the comparison.

To activate this test you must first put the printer into service mode. To accomplish this, turn the printer on while simultaneously holding down the On Line, Continue, and Enter buttons. When the screen comes up blank, release the keys and press, in order, Continue, then Enter. The printer will perform an internal self-test, then display "00 READY."

At this point you are ready to initiate the rest of the secret self-test by taking the printer off-line and pressing the Test button on the front panel and holding it until you see the "04 Self Test" message. When you see this message, release the Test button. This will cause the printer to print one self-test page. (If you want a continuous printout, then instead of releasing the Test button at the "04 Self Test" message, keep holding the Test button down until the message "05 Self Test" is displayed. The printer will print continuous self-test pages until you power off the printer or hit On Line, or until the printer runs out of paper.)

4. **Control panel self-test:** This test is invoked by pressing the "Test Page" control panel button. If it is successful, this means the entire printer is working properly. The only possibilities for problems would be outside the printer (e.g., interface, cable, or software problems).

Error Codes In addition to the self-tests, you have another tool for troubleshooting HP laser printers. Error codes are a way for the LaserJet to tell the user (and a service technician) what's wrong. Table 5.2 details some of the more common codes displayed on an HP LaserJet.

TABLE 5.2: HP LaserJet Error Messages

Message	Description
00 Ready	The printer is in standby mode and ready to print.
02 Warming Up	The fuser is being warmed up before the 00 Ready state.
05 Self-Test	Full self-test has been initiated from the front panel.
11 Paper Out	The paper tray sensor is reporting that there is no paper in the paper tray. Printer will not print as long as this error exists.
13 Paper Jam	A piece of paper is caught in the paper path. To fix, open the cover and clear the jam (including all pieces of the jam). Close the cover to resume printing. Printer will not print as long as this error exists.
14 No EP Cart	There is no EP cartridge (toner cartridge) installed in the printer. Printer will not print as long as this error exists.
15 Engine Test	An engine self-test is in progress.
16 Toner Low	The toner cartridge is almost out of toner. Replacement will be necessary soon.
50 Service	A fuser error has occurred. Most commonly caused by fuser lamp failure. To solve, power off the printer and replace the fuser. Printer will not print as long as this error exists.

T A B L E 5.2: HP LaserJet Error Messages *(continued)*

Message	Description
51 Error	Laser scanning assembly problem. Test and replace, if necessary. Printer will not print as long as this error exists.
52 Error	The scanner motor in the laser scanning assembly is malfunctioning. Test and replace as per service manual. Printer will not print as long as this error exists.
55 Error	Communication problem between formatter and DC controller. Test and replace as per service manual. Printer will not print as long as this error exists.

Troubleshooting Tips for HP LaserJet Printers

There is a set of troubleshooting steps that are usually used by printer technicians to help them solve HP LaserJet printing problems.

1. **Is the exhaust fan operational?** This is the first component to receive power when the printer is turned on. If you can feel air coming out of the exhaust fan, this confirms that AC voltage is present and power is turned on, that +5 VDc and +24 VDc are being generated by the DC power supply (DCPS), and that the DC controller is functional. If there is no power to the printer (no lights, fan not operating), the DCPS is at fault. Replacement involves removing all printer covers and removing four screws. You can purchase new DCPS modules, but it is usually cheaper to replace it with a rebuilt unit.

TIP If you are into electronics, you can probably rebuild the DCPS yourself simply and cheaply. Usually it's the main rectifier that fails in these units; it can easily be replaced if you know what you're doing.

---

2. **Do the control panel LEDs work?** Lights indicate that the formatter board can communicate with the control panel. If the LEDs do not light, it could mean that the formatter board is bad, the control panel is bad, or the wires connecting the two are broken or shorting out.

3. **Does the main motor rotate at power-up?** Turn the power off. Remove the covers from the side of the printer. Turn the printer back on and carefully watch and listen for main motor rotation. If you see and hear the main motor rotating, this indicates that the toner cartridge is installed, all photosensors are functional, all motors are functional, and the printer can move paper (assuming there are no obstructions).

4. **Does the fuser heat lamp light up after the main motor finishes its rotation?** You will need to have the covers removed to notice. The heat lamp should light after the main motor rotation and stay lit until the control panel says "00 Ready."

5. **Can the printer perform an engine self-test?** If this test print is successful, the engine can be ruled out as a source of the problem.

6. **Can the printer perform a control panel self-test?** If the control panel self-test is successful, check for interface-, cable-, or software-related problems.

Exam Essentials

The exam will focus on specific mechanical details of the various printer types. Some of those questions will pertain to the service-related issues described in this objective.

Know how to recognize and fix problems in dot-matrix printers. Various print quality problems in dot-matrix printers are caused by a bad ribbon cartridge or printhead. Paper jams are often caused by a "perf" caught in the paper path.

Know how to recognize and fix problems in bubble-jet printers. Ink cartridges in bubble-jet and ink-jet printers frequently clog and need to be replaced, especially if they are unused for a week or more. The "priming pump" is another component that is prone to failure and may need to be replaced.

Know the common problems of laser printers.   Malfunctioning laser printers may print blank pages, black pages, black vertical lines, repetitive marks, white vertical lines, smudged images, and "ghosted" images. They also print garbage if they have the wrong driver or a malfunctioning formatter board.

Understand what causes most of the problems in a laser printer. A bad toner cartridge, dirty or broken corona wires, worn rollers, a bad HVPS or DCPS, a bad fuser, the wrong driver, and a bad formatter board are the most common reasons for a problem in a laser printer. See the Critical Information section for more specific information.

Know how to fix the problems in a laser printer. Most of the problems in a laser printer involve field replaceable units. These units must be cleaned, if possible, or replaced.

Know the purpose of the HP self-tests. The HP engine self-tests can diagnose whether the printing mechanism is malfunctioning. The half self-test is used to troubleshoot individual printer components. The control panel self-test indicates whether a problem is internal or external to the printer. The secret self-test produces an advanced test print that can be used for comparison purposes.

Understand the troubleshooting steps for the HP LaserJet printers. The steps for troubleshooting HP LaserJet printers are, in order: check the exhaust fan, control panel LEDs, main motor, and fuser heat lamp. Then perform the engine self-test. Finally, perform the control panel self-test. See the Critical Information section for more information.

Key Terms and Concepts

Carriage motor: The motor in a dot-matrix printer that moves the printhead back and forth.

Ghosting: A problem in which light images of previously printed pages show up on the current printed page.

PCL: Acronym for Printer Control Language. A page description language used by HP printers.

PostScript: A page description language developed by Adobe systems, used when printing high-quality text and graphics.

Priming pump: A component in a bubble-jet printer that uses a suction cup to prepare the ink cartridge for printing.

Stepper motor: A motor capable of moving in very small increments.

Sample Questions

1. What is one cause of "ghosting"?

   A. A dirty transfer corona wire

   B. A broken charge corona wire

   C. A bad static eliminator strip

   D. A bent cleaning blade

   Answer: D. A bent cleaning blade may result in leftover toner on the print drum, which can result in unwanted images from previous print jobs.

2. Use what item(s) to clean the charge corona wire?

   A. Soap and water

   B. Light detergent

   C. A brush

   D. A lint-free cloth

   Answer: C. Laser printers are often equipped with a brush intended to clean the corona wires.

3. You should replace the toner cartridge in which of the following situations:

   A. Streaks on the print drum

   B. Worn exit rollers

C. Worn registration rollers

D. Small toner smudges on the prints

Answer: A. The print drum is contained in the same housing as the toner in a laser printer.

Identify the types of printer connections and configurations.

Printer connections and configurations are called the printer *interface*. The interface is the collection of hardware and software that allows the printer to communicate with a computer. Hardware provides the physical connection, while printer configuration takes place through interface software. Several questions on the test pertain to the printer interface.

Critical Information

There are several components to an interface, including its *connection type* (serial, parallel, or network) as well as the interface software. Each aspect must be matched on both the printer and the computer. For example, an HP LaserJet 4L only has a parallel port. Therefore, you must use a parallel cable as well as the correct software for the platform being used (i.e., an HP LaserJet 4L driver).

Printers have at least one built-in connection; some printers have several, in order to make them more flexible in a multiplatform environment. If a printer has several interfaces, it can usually switch between them "on the fly" so that several computers can print at the same time.

Connection Type

"Connection type" refers to the hardware technology involved in getting the printed information from the computer to the printer. There are three major types: serial, parallel, and network.

Serial

When computers send data serially, they send it one bit at a time, one after another. The bits "stand in line" like people at a movie theater, waiting to get in. As with modems, the communication parameters (baud, parity, start and stop bits) must match on both entities (the computer and printer) before communication can take place. The printer cable will use a female DB connector to attach to the physical port on the back of a PC. This port is designated by the operating system as one of the four serial ports (COM1 through COM4) that it supports.

Parallel

When a printer uses parallel communication, it is receiving data eight bits at a time over eight separate wires (one for each bit). Parallel communication is the most popular way of communicating from computer to printer, mainly because it's faster than serial.

A parallel cable consists of a male DB-25 connector that connects to the computer and a male 36-pin Centronics connector that connects to the printer. Most of the cables are shorter than 10 feet long. The physical port to which the printer cable is attached is designated as one of the three parallel ports (LPT1 through LPT3) that the PC supports.

WARNING   Keep parallel printer cable lengths to less than 10 feet. Some people try to run printer cables more than 50 feet. After 10 feet, communications can become unreliable due to crosstalk.

Network

Some of the newer printers have a special interface that allows them to be hooked directly to a network. These printers have a *network interface card* (*NIC*) and ROM-based software that allow them to communicate with networks, servers, and workstations.

The type of network interface used on the printer depends on the type of network the printer is being attached to. For example, if you're using a token-ring network, the printer should have a token-ring interface.

Interface Software

Computers and printers can't talk to each other by themselves. They need interface software to translate software commands into commands that the printer can understand.

There are two factors to consider with interface software: the *page description language* and the *driver software*. The page description language determines how efficient the printer will be at converting the information to be printed into signals the printer can understand. The driver software understands and controls the printer. It is very important that you use the correct interface software for the printer you are using. If you use either the wrong page description language or the wrong driver software, the printer will print garbage, or possibly nothing at all.

Page Description Languages

A page description language (or PDL) works just like its name suggests. A page description language describes the whole page being printed. The controller in the printer interprets these commands and turns them into laser pulses (or pinstrikes).

NOTE The most basic page description language is no page description language. The computer sends all the instructions that the printer needs in a serial stream, like so: Position 1, print nothing; Position 2, strike pins 1 and 3; Position 3, print nothing. This type of description language is used for most dot-matrix printers, but is not efficient for laser printers.

The first page description language was PostScript. Developed by Adobe, it was first used in the Apple LaserWriter printer. It made printing graphics fast and simple. PostScript works like this: The PostScript printer driver "describes" the page in terms of "draw" and "position" commands. The page is divided into a very fine grid (as fine as the resolution of the printer). To print a square, a communication like the following might take place:

```
POSITION 1,42%DRAW10%POSITION 1,64%DRAW10% . . .
```

These commands tell the printer to draw a line on the page from line 42 to line 64 (vertically). In other words, a page description language tells the printer to draw a line on the page, gives it the starting and ending points, and that's that. Rather than send the printer the location of each and every dot in the line and an instruction at each and every location to print that location's individual dot, PostScript can get the line drawn with fewer than five instructions. As you can see, PostScript uses more or less English commands. The commands are interpreted by the processor on the printer's controller and converted into the print control signals.

Another page description language is the Printer Control Language or PCL. Currently in revision 5 (PCL 5), it was developed by Hewlett-Packard for their LaserJet series of printers as a competitor to Post-Script. PCL works in much the same manner as PostScript, except PCL is found mainly in Hewlett-Packard printers (including their DeskJet bubble-jet printers). Other manufacturers also use PCL, however. In fact, some printers support both page description languages and will automatically switch between them.

The main advantage to page description languages is that they remove some of the processing from the computer to the printer. With text-only documents, they don't offer much benefit. However, with documents that have a lot of graphics, or that use numerous fonts, page description languages make the processing of those print jobs happen much faster. This makes them an ideal choice for laser printers. Other printers, such as the previously mentioned DeskJet bubble-jet and some dot-matrix printers, can use them as well.

Printer Driver Software

The *driver software* controls how the printer processes the print job. When you install a printer driver for the printer you are using, it allows the computer to print to that printer correctly (assuming you have the correct interface configured between the computer and printer).

When you need to print, you select the printer driver for your printer from a preconfigured list. The driver you select has been configured for the type, brand, and model of printer as well as the computer port it is hooked to. You can also select which paper tray the printer should use, as well as any other features the printer has (if applicable). Also, each printer driver is configured to use a particular page description language.

WARNING If the wrong printer driver is selected, the computer will send commands in the wrong language. If that occurs, the printer will print several pages full of garbage (even if only one page of information was sent). This "garbage" isn't garbage at all, but in fact the printer page description language commands printed literally as text instead of being interpreted as control commands.

Exam Essentials

You will encounter a few exam questions covering printer connections and configurations. Serial, parallel, and network printers are the most heavily covered topics from this objective.

Know the features of a serial printer. A serial printer receives data one bit at a time through a serial port connection on the PC, and requires the setting of communication parameters such as baud rate, parity, start and stop bits, etc.

Know the features of a parallel printer. A parallel printer receives data eight bits at a time through a parallel port connection on the PC, and usually uses a cable with a DB-25 connector on one end (attached to the PC) and a Centronics connector on the other (attached to the printer).

Know the features of a network printer. These printers use a network interface card (NIC) and ROM-based software to communicate with networks, servers, and workstations.

Understand page description languages. PostScript and PCL are two major types of page description languages (PDLs). These printer languages describe a whole page at a time rather than print a continuous stream of lines, characters, or dots. PDL is a fast system and is most useful for printing graphics.

Understand the function and purpose of printer driver software. Printer driver software controls how the printer processes print jobs. The correct software driver must be selected on the PC (based on printer brand, name, and model number) or printing will be impaired.

Key Terms and Concepts

Network printer: A printer that can be accessed over a network rather than by a printer cable connection.

Parallel printer: A printer that receives data eight bits at a time through the parallel interface on a PC.

Printer driver: A small program (device driver) that allows a computer to communicate with and control a printer.

Serial printer: A printer that receives data one bit at a time through the serial interface on a PC.

Sample Questions

1. A parallel port may be named:

   A. COM1

   B. COM2

C. LPT1

D. NIC

Answer: C. LPT1 through LPT3 may be used by a parallel port.

2. What is PostScript?

   A. A page description language

   B. A printer driver

   C. A PCL

   D. A type of HP printer

   Answer: A

CHAPTER

6

Portable Systems

A+ Core Module Exam Objectives Covered in This Chapter:

▶ **Identify the unique components of portable systems and their unique problems.** *(pages 260 – 268)*

If miniaturization trends continue, it won't be long before the power of a mainframe computer will be contained in a wristwatch or other piece of jewelry. To that end, many people have embraced the current crop of portable systems. In the PC world, a *portable system* is any computer that contains all the functionality of a desktop computer, but is significantly smaller and lighter.

Many of the computers available on the market are portable systems, and for this reason the subject of portable systems is covered on the exam.

Identify the unique components of portable systems and their unique problems.

This objective covers the unique features of the two major portable systems: laptops and portable digital assistants. Only a few questions on the test pertain to these unique features, but the information is important. As a PC technician, you will meet individuals or company personnel (often management) who use portable systems. If they need help, they'll ask you; the rather obvious advantage, then, in learning the information presented here is that it will help you do the job you're being paid for.

Critical Information

Laptop computers are the most common type of portable computer. They contain a built-in keyboard, pointing device, and LCD screen in a clamshell design. They are also called "notebook" computers because they resemble large notebooks.

A more recent type of portable computer is the palmtop computer (also known as a Personal Digital Assistant or PDA). These PDAs are basically small digital notepads that use a pen-like stylus and hand-writing interpretation software to perform operations. The Apple Newton and 3Com Pilot are two examples of PDAs.

One type of PDA is known as a handheld PC (HPC). These are basically "shrunken" laptops. The HPCs run an operating system from (who else?) Microsoft known as Windows CE. Windows CE is basically Windows 95 reduced to fit into the limited RAM of the HPC. Instead of using a mouse to point to the icons and menus in Windows CE, the HPCs use the PDA stylus.

Portable Computer Components

Because portable computers are unique in size and weight, their components (or the features of their components) are unique as well. These components include batteries, AC adapters, LCDs, docking stations, and expansion cards.

Batteries

There are many different sizes and shapes of batteries, but most of them are either nickel-cadmium (NiCad) or nickel metal hydride (NiMH). Both of them perform equally well as batteries, but NiCad batteries can only be recharged a finite number of times. After a time, they develop a "memory," which progressively shortens their charge duration. To correct this problem, the battery must be recharged on a special "deep charging" machine. NiMH batteries don't normally develop a memory and can be recharged many times. The problem with NiMH batteries is that they're a little more expensive.

The newest type of battery available for portable systems is the lithium ion (LiOn) battery. This battery is expensive, and can only be recharged about 300 times, but it has become popular quickly because it runs longer than NiCad and NiMH batteries.

TIP Before using your battery for the first time, you should *condition* it. This involves charging it overnight, then discharging and recharging it three times in succession. This will significantly increase the life of the battery.

Because of the importance of battery power in a portable system, most laptops are equipped with power management features, such as sleep mode, which blanks out the monitor. Sleep mode is engaged when the computer is idle for a few minutes.

NOTE Some of the palmtop computers can use either NiCad or NiMH batteries, but some vendors, including Hewlett-Packard, took a simpler approach: they designed it to use standard AA batteries. AA batteries, however, do not retain a charge as long as the other batteries.

AC Adapter

Most notebook computers are also able to run on AC power (instead of using their batteries) with a special adapter called an AC adapter that converts AC power into DC power. These can be integrated into the notebook (as on some Compaq notebooks) or as a separate "brick" with a cord that plugs into the back of the laptop.

Docking Stations

Also unique to portable computers is the *docking station*. When attached (or "docked") to the station, a portable computer can function as a desktop computer. The docking station usually contains interfaces and expansion ports and bays that the laptop can only use when it is docked. Access to a large monitor and full-size keyboard through a docking station is also a plus.

Liquid Crystal Displays

Because portable computers have a limited power source when running on batteries, liquid crystal display (LCD) technology is used for its display system. An LCD display consumes much less power than a standard CRT monitor.

There are two types of LCD displays used in portable computers: active-matrix screen and passive-matrix screen. Both types use some kind of lighting behind the LCD panel to make the screen easier to view.

Active Matrix   An active-matrix screen works in a similar manner to the LCD watch. The screen is made up of several individual LCD pixels. A transistor behind each pixel, when switched on, activates two electrodes, which align the crystals and turn the pixel dark. This type of display is very crisp and easy to look at.

The major disadvantage of an active-matrix screen is that it can't operate on a battery for more than two hours.

Passive Matrix   Within the passive-matrix screen, there are two rows of transistors: one at the top, another at the side. When the computer's video circuit wants to turn a particular pixel on (turn it black), it sends a signal to the X and Y coordinate transistors for that pixel, thus turning them on. This then causes voltage lines from each axis to intersect at the desired coordinates, turning the desired pixel black. Figure 6.1 illustrates this concept.

Passive-matrix screens do not respond quickly to rapid changes. The on-screen mouse pointer, for example, disappears during mouse movement and reappears when movement slows down. This effect is known as "submarining." The viewing angle is more narrow and the colors are weaker in passive-matrix technology. However, they have two advantages over active-matrix screens: they are cheaper and they do not consume as much power.

Expansion Cards and the PCMCIA bus

Most expansion cards in portable computers are called *PC cards* and use the PCMCIA bus, which was specially designed for portable systems. (The major exception to this is memory cards, which often use a proprietary bus. If this is your situation, you must purchase additional memory from the manufacturer.)

F I G U R E 6.1: A passive-matrix display

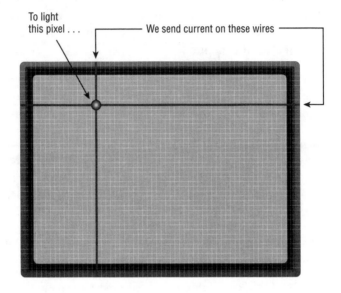

PC Card Types   Three major types of PC cards (and slots) are currently in use:

- Type I cards are 3.3mm thick and are most commonly used for PCMCIA memory cards.

- Type II cards are 5mm thick and are mostly used for modems and LAN adapters. Most systems have at least two Type II slots.

- The Type III slot is 10.5mm thick and is commonly used for PC card hard disks.

SEE ALSO   For more information on the PCMCIA bus, see Chapter 4, "Motherboard/Processors/Memory."

PC cards support only one IRQ, which creates a problem if you need to install two devices in a PC card bus and both devices need interrupts. PC cards also do not support bus mastering or DMA.

A PC card requires special software called Socket Services and Card Services.

Socket Services   Socket Services software is a BIOS-level interface to the PCMCIA bus slot. Socket Services replaces the BIOS as the interface between the CPU and a PC card—this is significant because it allows the PC card to be installed or removed while the computer is running ("hot swapped"). This software can detect when a card has been inserted and what type of card it is.

Card Services   Card Services software is the second component of the PC card architecture. This software is the interface between the application and Socket Services. It tells the applications which interrupts and I/O ports the card is using. Applications that need to access the PC card don't access the hardware directly. Instead, they tell Card Services they need access to a particular feature and Card Services gets the appropriate feature from the PC card. Card Services also allows a portion of the PC card's ROM to be copied "on the fly" into the CPU's available memory addresses. As with Socket Services, this feature makes hot swapping possible.

Necessary Procedures

This section details the procedure for installing a PC card, which differs in a few points from the standard procedure for installing other expansion cards.

Installing a PC Card

1. Install Card Services and Socket Services on the computer.

2. Shut down the computer.

3. Install the PC card into its slot, making sure the slot matches the card. (Some portable systems will not have space to add a Type III card if a Type II card is already installed. You may have to remove the Type II card.

4. Run the software configuration program (Windows 95 will do this automatically). The program will automatically configure IRQs and I/O addresses.

WARNING Even though PC cards are designed to be hot swapped, it is recommended that you shut down your computer before changing cards (doing so reduces the likelihood of a system crash). Also, before removing a PC card, you should disable its driver. Windows 95 allows you to do this by clicking on the PC card icon in the Taskbar.

Exam Essentials

Know the major types of portable computers. The major types of portable computers are laptop (notebook) computers and PDA computers. One type of PDA computer is known as an HPC.

Know what components are unique in portable systems. The batteries, AC adapter, display system, docking station, and expansion bus are unique in portable systems.

Know the features of expansion cards that use the PCMCIA bus. The PCMCIA bus takes PC card types I, II, or III. These cards are of varying thickness and use. Socket Services and Card Services are specialized software that is required in order for PC cards to function.

Know the common problems and limitations that are specific to portable computers. Problems specific to portable computers include running out of battery power and having NiCad batteries develope "memory." Limitations include only one available IRQ, and "submarining" on passive-matrix displays.

Know the important differences between the two types of LCDs. Active-matrix displays use more battery power but provide a clearer image than passive-matrix displays.

Key Terms and Concepts

Active matrix: An LCD mechanism that uses individual transistors to control each pixel on the screen.

Card Services: Software support for PCMCIA hardware that controls use of the system interrupts, memory, and power management.

HPC: Acronym for handheld PC. A type of PDA that uses a pen-like stylus instead of a mouse with Windows CE, a streamlined version of the Windows operating system.

Laptop: A small portable computer with a flat screen and keyboard that fold together. Also called a notebook computer.

PC card: An expansion card that fits into a PCMCIA bus slot.

PDA: Acronym for Personal Digital Assistant. A pocket-sized computer that uses a pen-like stylus and handwriting interpretation software.

Passive matrix: An LCD mechanism that uses two rows of transistors to control all pixels on the screen.

Socket Services: Software support for PCMCIA hardware that controls the hardware interface.

Sample Questions

1. To reduce power consumption, a laptop computer may contain:

A. A VGA display

B. A SuperVGA display

C. Socket services

D. An LCD

Answer: D. An LCD does not consume as much power as the CRT technology used with VGA and SVGA.

2. If your portable computer has slots for two Type II cards, and you try to install an internal modem and a LAN card, the problem you are most likely to have is:

   A. Insufficient space for a Type II card

   B. Insufficient space for a Type III card

   C. Lack of battery power

   D. An interrupt conflict

   Answer: D. The modem and the LAN card both require an IRQ, but only one is available on a portable computer.

CHAPTER

7

Basic Networking

A+ Core Module Exam Objectives Covered in This Chapter:

▶ **Identify basic networking concepts, including how a network works.** *(pages 270 – 292)*

▶ **Identify procedures for swapping and configuring network interface cards.** *(pages 292 – 296)*

▶ **Identify the ramifications of repairs on the network.** *(pages 297 – 300)*

The stand-alone personal computers developed in the 1970s were of limited interest to large companies, which often needed to share information between offices, sometimes over great distances. This was not possible on a stand-alone personal computer. Networks were developed to overcome these and other limitations.

This chapter focuses on the basic concepts surrounding how a network works, including the way it sends information and what it uses to send information. Also included is material on adding network interface cards and on issues related to network repair. Several questions on the test are network-related.

▶ Identify basic networking concepts, including how a network works.

The sprawling computer systems and printers present in almost every business office today did not exist a few short decades ago. In those days the clickety-clack of typewriters predominated (like the roaring of tyrannosaurs in the Jurassic age) and people had never heard of e-mail. E-mail is one form of communication that only became available due to the introduction and growth of *networks*.

It is important for you as a service professional to have an understanding of networks, because you are likely to confront problems related to the fact that a computer is connected to a network. Although the test does not greatly emphasize these issues, it will contain some network-related questions.

Critical Information

To address the limitations of the stand-alone computer, *networks* were born. Networks link two or more computers together to communicate and share resources (such as printers, applications, and files). Their success was a revelation to the computer industry as well as businesses. A network is classified as either a *local area network* (*LAN*) or a *wide area network* (*WAN*).

LANs and WANs

LANs consist of computers linked together for the purpose of sharing resources within a closed environment. The first simple LANs were constructed a lot like Figure 7.1. They were limited to about 30 users, and the first software programs that ran on a LAN were not capable of permitting more than one user at a time to use a program (this constraint was a known as *file locking*).

FIGURE 7.1: A simple LAN

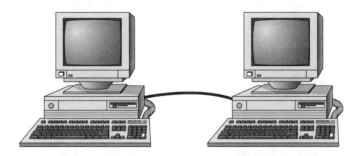

Whereas LANs are limited to single buildings, WANs are able to span buildings, states, countries, and even continents. Figure 7.2 gives an example of a simple WAN.

FIGURE 7.2: A simple WAN

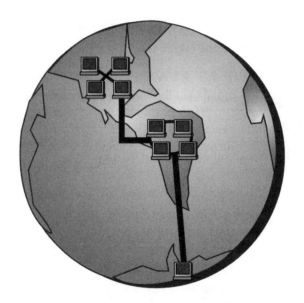

A new type of network is the *metropolitan area network* (or *MAN*). Developed for resource sharing, these networks are larger than LANs and may range in size from a small group of buildings to a city-sized arrangement. A MAN network uses high-speed digital connections such as fiber-optic cable, and is owned by a consortium of users or a network provider.

Primary Network Components

Putting together a network is not as simple as it was with the first PC networks. You can no longer consider two computers cabled together a fully functional network. Today, networks consist of three primary components:

- servers

- workstations or clients

- resources

Servers

Servers are a core component of the network, providing a link to the resources necessary to perform any task. Servers offer networks the capability of centralizing the control of resources, and can thus reduce administrative difficulties. They can be used to balance the load on the computers and can thus increase speed and performance. They can also offer the departmentalizing of files for improved reliability. That way, if one server goes down, not all of the files are lost.

Servers that provide files to the users on the network are called *file servers*. Likewise, servers that host printing services for users are called *print servers*. Novell's intraNetWare is known for its File and Print Sharing servers. *Application servers*, also very common, host programs such as Microsoft Exchange, SMS, SNA, SQL, and IIS. These and other network applications provide a wide range of services that includes mail, Internet, database management, remote access, inventory, network installation, diagnostics, etc. One server may fulfill several of these roles.

Another distinction used in categorizing servers is whether they are *dedicated* or *non-dedicated*. The former is used exclusively in its server capacity and offers improved network performance. The latter serves a dual role as a server and a workstation and offers flexibility.

A server may run a network operating system (NOS) to control the communication with resources and the flow of data across the network. Some of the more popular network operating systems at this time include Unix, Novell's intraNetWare, and Microsoft's Windows NT Server.

Workstations or Client Computers

Workstations are the computers on which the users on a network do their work, performing activities such as word processing, database design, graphic design, e-mail, and other office or personal tasks. Workstations are basically nothing more than your everyday computer, except that they are connected to a network that offers additional resources. Workstations can range from a diskless computer system to a desktop system. In network terms, workstations are also known as *client computers*. As clients, they are allowed to communicate with the servers in the network in order to use the network's resources.

Some of the advantages to network participation for a workstation may include the ability to:

- store data externally (on a server)
- share information with other users
- use programs that are normally too large for the workstation

Network Resources

A *resource* (as far as the network is concerned) is any item that can be used on a network. Network resources include a broad range of items; the most important of these are printers, files, applications, and disk storage space. With the exception of printers, network resources will be contained on a server.

The sharing of these resources can reduce costs dramatically for almost any business.

NOTE The sharing of applications over a network must be by special arrangement with the application vendor, who may wish to set the price of the application according to the number of users who will be using it. The arrangement allowing multiple users to use a single installation of an application is called a *site license*.

Network Resource Access

Generally, resources are accessed on a network through one of two resource access models: *peer-to-peer* or *server-based*.

Peer-to-Peer Networks

In a peer-to-peer or *workgroup* network, the computers act as both workstations and servers. An example of a peer-to-peer resource model is shown in Figure 7.3.

F I G U R E 7.3: The peer-to-peer resource model

Peer-to-peer networks are great for small, simple, and inexpensive networks. In fact, this model can be set up very quickly, with little extra hardware required. Windows 95 is a popular operating system that supports a peer-to-peer resource model.

There is no centralized administration or control in the peer-to-peer resource model. This lack of centralized control can make it difficult to manage network resources and workstations; for the same reason, it's not very secure. Moreover, since each computer is acting as both a workstation and a server, locating the resources may not be easy. The person who is in charge of a resource may have moved it without anyone's knowledge.

Peer-to-peer resource models are generally considered the right choice for small companies. If the company grows, moving to a server-based network will be a natural transition.

Server-Based Resource Model

The server-based model is better than the peer-to-peer model for large networks (25 users or more) that need a more secure environment and centralized control. Server-based networks use a central dedicated server. All administrative functions and resource allocation are performed from this point. This makes it easier to share resources, perform backups, and support an almost unlimited number of users. It also offers better security. However, this model does need more hardware than is used by the typical workstation/server computer in a peer-to-peer model. Additionally, it requires specialized software (the NOS) to manage the server's role in the environment. An example of a server-based resource model is shown in Figure 7.4.

FIGURE 7.4: The server-based resource model

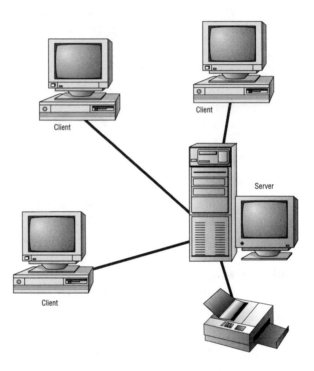

Server-based networks offer the flexibility to add more resources and clients almost indefinitely into the future. Hardware and licensing costs may be more, but, with the centralized administration, managing resources becomes less time-consuming.

Network Topologies

A *topology* is a way of "laying out" the network. Each topology differs by its cost, ease of installation, fault tolerance (how it handles problems like cable breaks), and ease of reconfiguration (as when adding a new workstation to the existing network).

There are five primary topologies, each of which has its advantages and disadvantages:

Bus

The bus topology consists of a single cable that runs to every work-station, as in Figure 7.5. Although the bus uses the least amount of cabling and is therefore the least expensive and simplest of the net-works to install, adding a workstation to a bus network is difficult. If you want to add another workstation, you'll have to completely reroute the cable. Ethernet cabling (covered later in this chapter) can use a bus topology.

FIGURE 7.5: The bus topology

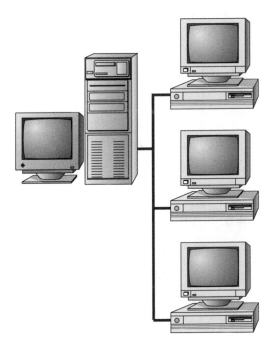

Star

In the star topology, each network device branches off from a central device called a *hub*. The hub is placed in a central location in the office (for example, a utility closet). Because each workstation has a separate connection to the hub, expanding the network is very easy. Also, if any workstation goes down, it will not affect the rest of the network. The star network, however, is more expensive due to the cost of the hub (large star topologies may require several hubs) and extra cabling. Some types of Ethernet and ARCNet use a physical star topology. Figure 7.6 gives an example of the organization of the star network.

FIGURE 7.6: The star topology

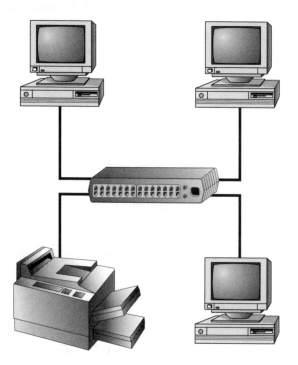

Ring

In this type of network, each computer connects to two other computers, joining them in a circle creating a unidirectional path where messages move from workstation to workstation. Each entity participating in the ring reads a message, then regenerates it and hands it to its neighbor. While providing efficient data transfer, this model is expensive and difficult to reconfigure. IBM's Token Ring technology is a *logical* ring topology. Physically, a logical ring topology may be structured as another network form, but functionally (the way it handles data) it acts like ring topology. See Figure 7.7 for an example of a ring topology.

FIGURE 7.7: The ring topology

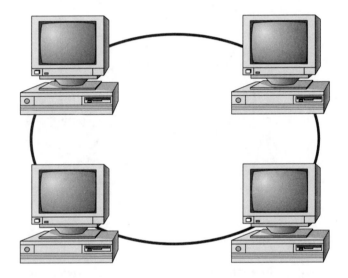

Mesh

In this type of network, each device is connected to every other device (Figure 7.8). Although it is highly fault tolerant, it is not used in LANs because of the complex cabling. It is, however, used to connect multiple sites across WAN and MAN links.

Hybrid

The hybrid topology is simply a mix of the other topologies. Most networks today are actually hybrid. Table 7.1 summarizes the advantages and disadvantages of each type of network topology.

FIGURE 7.8: The mesh topology

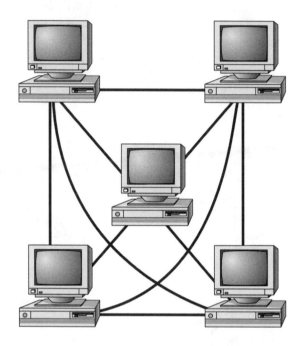

TABLE 7.1: Topologies—Advantages and Disadvantages

Topology	Advantages	Disadvantages
Bus	Cheap; easy to install	Difficult to reconfigure; break in bus disables entire network
Star	Cheap; easy to install; easy to reconfigure; fault-tolerant	More expensive than bus
Ring	Efficient; easy to install	Reconfiguration difficult; very expensive

TABLE 7.1: Topologies—Advantages and Disadvantages *(cont.)*

Topology	Advantages	Disadvantages
Mesh	Simplest data communication; most fault-tolerant	Extremely expensive; very complex to install and reconfigure
Hybrid	Gives combination of best features of each topology used	Complex (less so than mesh, however)

Network Communications

Network communications take place using protocols. A *protocol* is a set of rules that govern communications. Protocols detail what "language" the computers are speaking when they talk over a network. If two computers are going to communicate, they both must be using the same protocol. 802.3 CSMA/CD and 802.5 Token Ring, developed by the IEEE (Institute of Electrical and Electronics Engineers), are the two predominant standards for network protocols.

IEEE 802.3 CSMA/CD

The 802.3 CSMA/CD model defines a bus topology network that uses a 50-ohm baseband coaxial cable and carries transmissions at 10Mbps. This standard groups data bits into *frames* and uses the Carrier Sense Multiple Access with Collision Detection (CSMA/CD) cable access method to put data on the cable.

CSMA/CD specifies that every computer can transmit at any time. As sometimes happens when two machines transmit at the same time, a "collision" takes place and no data can be transmitted for either machine. The machines then back off for a random amount of time and try to transmit again. This process repeats until transmission takes place successfully. The CSMA/CD technology is also called *contention* technology.

The only major downside to 802.3 is that with large networks (more than 100 computers on the same cable), the number of collisions increases to the point where there are more collisions than transmissions taking place.

IEEE 802.5 Token Ring

The IEEE 802.5 standard specifies a physical star, logical ring topology that uses a token-passing technology to put the data on the cable.

In *token passing*, a special chunk of data called a *token* circulates through the ring from computer to computer. Any computer that has data to transmit must wait for the token before sending anything. The main advantage of the token-passing access method over contention (the 802.3 model) is that it eliminates collisions.

IBM developed this technology for their mainframe and minicomputer networks. IBM's name for it was Token Ring. The name stuck, and any network using this type of technology is called a Token Ring network.

Network Architectures

Network architectures define the structure of the network, including hardware, software, and layout. The architectures are differentiated by the hardware and software required to maintain optimum performance levels. Two of the major architectures in use today are Ethernet and Token Ring.

Ethernet

The original definition of the 802.3 model included a bus topology using a baseband coaxial cable. From this model came the first Ethernet architecture.

Ethernet has several specifications, each one including speed, communication method, and cable. The original Ethernet was given a designation of 10Base5. The "10" in Ethernet 10Base5 stands for the 10Mbps transmission rate. "Base" stands for the baseband communications used. Finally, the "5" stands for the maximum distance of 500 meters to carry transmissions. This method of identification soon caught on, and as vendors changed the specifications of the Ethernet architecture, they followed the same naming convention. The most common Ethernet specifications are shown in Table 7.2.

T A B L E 7.2: Common Ethernet Specifications

Specification	Throughput	Max. Length	Wiring
10Base5 (Thicknet)	10Mbps	500 m	coaxial cable
10Base2 (Thinnet)	10Mbps	200 m	thin coaxial cable
10BaseT	10Mbps	100 m	twisted-pair
100BaseT	100Mbps	100 m	twisted-pair

Token Ring

Token Ring networks are exactly like the IEEE 802.5 specification because the specification is based on IBM's Token Ring technology. Token Ring uses a physical star, logical ring topology. All workstations are cabled to a central device, called a *multistation access unit* or *MAU*. The ring is created within the MAU by connecting every port together with special circuitry in the MAU. Token Ring can use shielded or unshielded cable and can transmit data at either 4Mbps or 16Mbps.

Network Media

The physical material on which network data is transferred from one point to another is the *medium*. There are two parts to the medium: the cabling and the network interface card (NIC). The type of cabling determines the type of NIC that must be used.

Cabling

The cabling you choose must support both the architecture and the topology of the network. There are four main types of cabling methods: twisted-pair cable, coaxial cable, fiber-optic cable, and wireless.

Twisted-Pair   Twisted-pair is one of the most popular methods of cabling because of its flexibility and low cost. It consists of several pairs of wire twisted around each other within an insulated jacket, as shown in Figure 7.9. Twisted-pair is most often found in 10BaseT Ethernet networks (hence the "T"), although other systems can use it.

F I G U R E 7.9: Twisted-pair cable

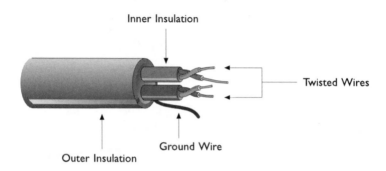

Twisted-pair cabling is usually divided into two types: unshielded twisted-pair (UTP) and shielded twisted-pair (STP). UTP is simply twisted-pair cabling that is unshielded. STP is the same as UTP except that STP has a braided foil shield around the twisted wires (to decrease electrical interference).

UTP comes in different grades to offer different levels of protection against electrical interference.

- Category 1 is for voice-only transmissions, and is in most phone systems today. It uses two twisted pairs of wires and an RJ-11 connector.

- Category 2-5 is able to transmit data at speeds of 4 to 100 Mbps (the higher the category, the higher the speed). It uses four twisted pairs of wires and an RJ-45 connector.

Each of these five levels has a maximum transmission distance of 100 meters.

Coaxial The next choice of cable for most LANs would be coaxial cable. The cable consists of a copper wire surrounded by insulation and a copper or foil shield, as shown in Figure 7.10. It is very similar to the cable used to connect cable television.

Coaxial cable is often called "Thinnet" or "Cheapernet." It comes in many thicknesses and types and is most commonly used for Ethernet 10Base2 cabling. It uses BNC-T and AUI connectors.

FIGURE 7.10: Coaxial cable

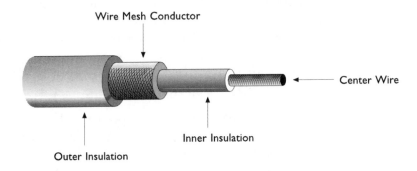

Fiber-Optic Fiber-optic cable consists of a thin, flexible glass fiber surrounded by a rubberized outer coating (see Figure 7.11). It provides transmission speeds from 100Mbps up to 1Gbps and a maximum distance of several miles. Because it uses pulses of light instead of electric voltages to transmit data, it is completely immune from electrical interference.

FIGURE 7.11: Fiber-optic cable

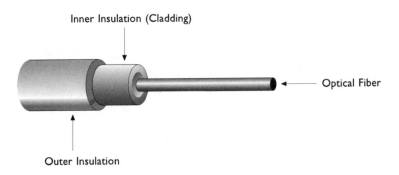

Fiber-optic cable has not become a standard in networks, however, because of its high installation cost. Networks that need extremely fast transmission rates or transmissions over long distances, or that have had problems with electrical interference in the past, often use fiber-optic cabling.

Wireless Networks   One of the most fascinating cabling technologies today—and, actually, it's one that doesn't really *use* cable—is wireless. Wireless networks offer the ability to extend a LAN without the use of traditional cabling methods. Wireless transmissions are made through the air by infrared light, laser light, narrow-band radio, microwave, or spread-spectrum radio.

Wireless LANs are becoming increasingly popular as businesses are becoming more mobile and less centralized. You can see them most often in environments where standard cabling methods are not possible or wanted. However, they are still not as fast or efficient as standard cabling methods. Also, they are more susceptible than standard cabling methods to eavesdropping and interference.

The Network Interface Card (NIC)

It takes several components to make a workstation into a client. You must install a *network interface card* (NIC), a special expansion card that allows the PC to talk on a network. You must connect the workstation to a cabling system that connects to another computer (or several other computers). And you must install some special software, called *client software*, that allows the workstation to talk to the servers. Once all this has been accomplished, the workstation will be "on the network."

SEE ALSO   For more information on NICs, see the next section of this chapter, "Identify procedures for swapping and configuring network interface cards."

Connectivity Devices

Connectivity devices allow communications to exceed the limits imposed by cabling technology on network size, thus enabling your computers to talk to other computers in the next building, the next city, or the next country.

There are several categories of connectivity devices, including the following:

- repeaters
- hubs
- bridges
- routers

These connectivity devices have made it possible to extend the physical dimensions of the network to almost unlimited distances.

Repeaters

Repeaters are very simple devices. They allow a cabling system to extend beyond its maximum allowed length by amplifying the network voltages so they travel farther. Repeaters are nothing more than amplifiers, and, as such, are very inexpensive. Along with the network signal, they also amplify noise; if you use enough repeaters, this can result in a drowned-out signal.

Hubs

Hubs are devices used to link several computers together. They are most often used in 10BaseT Ethernet networks. They are also very simple devices. In fact, they are just multiport repeaters. They repeat any signal that comes in on one port and copy it to the other ports (a process that is also called *broadcasting*).

There are two types of hubs: *active* and *passive*. Passive hubs simply connect all ports together electrically and are usually not powered. Active hubs use electronics to amplify and clean up the signal before it is broadcast to the other ports.

Bridges

Bridges are used to divide network segments. Bridges keep traffic on one side from crossing to the other. For this reason, they are most often used to reduce traffic and increase network performance.

Bridges are not able to distinguish one protocol from another. If a bridge is unaware of a destination address, it will forward a data packet to all network segments. Unlike repeaters, bridges *can* filter out noise.

The main disadvantage to bridges is that they can't connect dissimilar network types or perform intelligent path selection. For that function, you would need a router.

Routers

Routers connect multiple network types and determine the best path for sending data. They can route packets across multiple networks and use routing tables to store network addresses to determine the best destination.

The advantage of using a router rather than a bridge is that routers can determine the best path that data can take to get to its destination. Like bridges, they can segment large networks and can filter out noise. However, they are slower than bridges because they analyze every packet, causing packet-forwarding delays. They are also more expensive.

At least two routers are normally used to form a WAN or MAN (by connecting one LAN to another).

Brouters

A *brouter* is a combination of a bridge and a router. It is used to connect dissimilar network segments and to route only one specific protocol. The other protocols are bridged (forwarded) instead of being dropped. Brouters are used when only one protocol needs to be routed or where a router is not cost-effective (such as in a branch office).

Gateways

Gateways connect dissimilar network environments and architectures. They convert data and repackage it to meet the requirements of the destination address. This makes gateways slower than other connectivity devices, and costly. An example of a gateway would be the NT Gateway Service for NetWare, which, when running on a Windows NT Server, can connect a Microsoft Windows NT network with a Novell NetWare network.

Exam Essentials

Relatively few test questions are about networks; however, those that *are* on the test vary widely in subject matter, so the list here is fairly extensive.

Understand the function and purpose of a network.   A network is a group of computers connected by a communications channel for purposes that include rapid exchange of information; sharing of files, printers, applications, and other resources; and the backing up of user data.

Understand the difference between a LAN and a WAN.   All the devices within a LAN are located in close physical proximity. A WAN or MAN may be a collection of LANs or a network that transcends the physical limits of a typical LAN.

Understand the purpose of a workstation, a network resource, and a server.   A workstation is a computer on which a user performs work activities. A resource refers to any item that can be used on a network (which is usually contained on a server). A server refers to a computer that provides network resources and/or manages and controls network communication.

Understand the difference between a server-based and a peer-to-peer network.   Server-based networks use a centralized server or servers to provide network administrative functions and resource sharing. They offer better security and more centralized control than a peer-to-peer network. In a peer-to-peer network, any computer can function as both a workstation and a server.

Know the five network topologies and how they differ. The five network topologies are bus, star, ring, mesh, and hybrid. See the Critical Information section for their differences.

Know the features of the major network architectures. Ethernet is an architecture based on the IEEE 802.3 CSMA/CD standard, the most common version of which is 10BaseT, with 10Mbps throughput and a maximum cable length of 100 meters. Token Ring is an IBM architecture that uses a ring topology. It transmits data at either 4Mbps or 16Mbps.

Know the different types of cabling media. Twisted-pair, coaxial, fiber-optic, and wireless are some of the primary types of network cabling. For detailed information, see the Critical Information section.

Understand the types and purposes of the connectivity devices. Repeaters, hubs, bridges, and routers are four of the common connectivity devices. These devices serve different purposes, which include extending the physical cable limits of a network and reducing network traffic.

Key Terms and Concepts

Coaxial: A high-capacity cable used in networking. It contains an inner copper conductor surrounded by plastic insulation, and an outer braided copper or foil shield.

Ethernet: A type of network architecture that adheres to the IEEE 802.3 CSMA/CD standard.

Fiber optics: A transmission technology that sends pulses of light along specially manufactured optical fibers.

LAN: Acronym for local area network. A group of computers and associated peripherals connected by a communications channel capable of sharing files and other resources between several users.

NIC: Acronym for network interface card. The PC expansion board that plugs into a personal computer or server and works with the network operating system to control the flow of information over the network.

Server: In networking, any computer that makes access to files, printing, communications, or other services available to users of the network.

Token ring: A LAN with a ring structure that uses token passing to regulate traffic on the network and avoid collisions.

Topology: A way of laying out a network. It can describe either the physical or logical layout.

Twisted pair: A type of cable that comprises two insulated wires twisted together at six twists per inch.

WAN: A network that expands LANs to include networks outside of the local environment and also to distribute resources across distances.

Sample Questions

1. 10BaseT Ethernet networks use what type of wiring?

   A. Fiber-optic

   B. Twisted-pair

   C. Coaxial

   D. IEEE 802.3

   Answer: B. 10Base2 networks use coaxial cables, but 10BaseT use twisted-pair.

2. An advantage of a peer-to-peer network over a server-based network is:

   A. Centralized control

   B. Better security

C. Less complexity

D. E-mail

Answer: C. Peer-to-peer networks are easier to set up and are relatively inexpensive. Server-based networks offer far better security and more centralized control.

Identify procedures for swapping and configuring network interface cards.

The network interface card provides the physical interface between computer and cabling. It prepares data, sends data, and controls the flow of data. It can also receive and translate data into bytes for the CPU to understand.

Because it's the PC technician's job to add workstations to the office network, this objective describes different NIC features, and explains how to install and configure these expansion cards. However, only a few test questions deal with the information presented in this objective.

Critical Information

The NIC translates the data from the computer into signals that can flow easily along the cable. It does this by translating digital signals to electrical signals (or in the case of fiber-optic NICs, to optical signals).

The first step in adding a PC to a network is to install the NIC into its expansion bus. This gives it a physical port to which the network cables can be attached. Next, you must install client software in order to enable network communication.

For successful network communication, the cards must agree on several things, such as size of data frames, speed of data transmission, etc. If the cards cannot agree, the sending of data does not occur.

Card Types

In order to successfully send data on the network, you need to make sure the network cards are of the same type (e.g., all Ethernet, all Token Ring, all ARCNet) and they are connected to the same piece of cable. If you use cards of different types (e.g., one Ethernet and one Token Ring), neither of them will be able to communicate with the other.

Card Features

Unlike other expansion cards, NICs also have a unique hardware address, called a media access control (MAC) address. If two cards have the same MAC address, neither one of them will be able to communicate. For this reason, the IEEE has established a standard for hardware addresses; they assign blocks of these addresses to NIC manufacturers, who then hardwire the addresses into the cards.

When choosing a NIC, use one that fits the bus type of your PC. If you have more than one type of bus in your PC (for example, a combination ISA/PCI), use a NIC that fits into the fastest type (the PCI in this case). This is especially important in servers, as the NIC can very quickly become a bottleneck if this guideline isn't followed.

SEE ALSO   To refresh your memory about the bus architectures mentioned in this discussion, refer back to Chapter 4, "Motherboard/ Processors/Memory."

Several other ways to optimize network performance through a network card include these optional features:

- DMA channels
- shared memory adapter
- bus mastering

If the network card can use DMA channels, then data can move directly from the card's buffer to the computer's memory, bypassing the CPU. A shared memory adapter is a NIC that has its own RAM.

This feature allows transfers to and from the computer to happen much more quickly, increasing the performance of the NIC. Shared system memory allows the NIC to use a section of the computer's RAM to process data. Bus mastering lets the card take temporary control of the computer's bus to bypass the CPU and move data directly to RAM. This is more expensive, but can improve performance by 20 to 70 percent. However, EISA and MCA cards are the only ones that support bus mastering.

Configuration and Installation

Configuring a NIC is similar to configuring any other type of expansion card. The NIC usually needs a unique IRQ channel and I/O address, and possibly a DMA channel.

In order for the computer to use the network interface card, you must also install the necessary device drivers. For the computer to be able to access network servers, you will need to install the client software.

SEE ALSO For more information on configuring a new expansion card, see the Chapter 1 objective, "Identify available IRQs, DMAs, and I/O addresses and procedures for configuring them for device installation."

Necessary Procedures

The procedure for installing and configuring a network interface card is similar to that for most expansion cards.

1. If it is a new card rather than a replacement, you must determine available resources (IRQs, DMA channels, I/O addresses) and then configure those resources.

2. Shut off the power, use ESD precautions, and remove the case.

3. Align the connector on the bottom of the card with the connector on the motherboard, and insert the card into its connector. You should feel a slight amount of resistance. Applying even pressure, push the card firmly into place. Stop pushing when all of the card's connectors are making contact with the "fingers" in the expansion slot.

4. Replace the lid and attach the network cable.

5. Install the necessary software drivers.

6. Install the network client software.

Exam Essentials

Although configuration of expansion cards in general is important on the test, there are only a few questions specific to NICs.

Know the features of a NIC.   NICs feature a MAC address, and some use DMA channels and/or a shared memory adapter. Bus mastering is supported by EISA and MCA cards only.

Understand which NIC features affect network performance. NIC features are more critical on network servers than on clients. The fastest bus slot (usually PCI) should be used for this expansion card for maximum network performance. NIC performance can also be improved if the card features bus mastering, a shared memory adapter, or a DMA channel.

Know what a MAC address is.   A MAC address is a unique hardware address that is hardwired into a NIC. A duplicate hardware address would cause conflicts on the network.

Know how to configure and install a NIC.   See the Necessary Procedures section for details on configuration and installation.

Key Terms and Concepts

Client software: The software that allows the computer to communicate with the network.

MAC: Acronym for media access control. A unique hardwired address on a NIC that allows communication to take place. These addresses are assigned by the IEEE.

Shared memory adapter: A type of NIC that has its own RAM, used to increase the speed at which it transfers data.

Sample Questions

1. A MAC address is:

    A. Hardwired

    B. Assigned by the EEEI

    C. Configured by the network administrator

    D. Used by Apple computers

    Answer: A. A MAC address is a fixed address. B would be correct if the order of the letters was revised to IEEE.

2. If a server in a 10BaseT network has an ISA/PCI bus, you should use what type of NIC for maximum network throughput:

    A. A card that uses DMA

    B. A PCI network card

    C. An 802.5 Token Ring card

    D. A card with bus mastering

    Answer: B. A PCI network card is the best answer. Bus mastering is good, but is only available with EISA or MCA bus slots.

Identify the ramifications of repairs on the network.

Because of the increasing reliance upon network services, it is important to know the ramifications of network problems and repairs. The topics covered in this objective are, above all, economic issues. A large corporation can lose vast amounts of money in a matter of hours due to a network failure, which may in fact stem from a very simple cause. The exam also touches on these issues, albeit briefly.

Critical Information

A device on a network in need of repair may have disastrous effects on network communications. The greater the dependence on network resources, the greater the damage will be. In addition to device failures, other events, such as poorly timed backups and power fluctuations, may also cause a communication breakdown. These breakdowns usually fall into one of two categories:

- bandwidth problems
- network interruptions

Bandwidth Problems

In networking terms, *bandwidth* is used to signify the volume of data that a hardware medium (e.g., a cable) can transmit at one time. If the utilization of bandwidth is too high, communication problems may occur. Access to network resources can slow down (or shut down completely), thereby making it difficult for users to print, access file servers, etc.

A few common causes of network slowdowns are poorly timed backups of user data (performed during working hours), the addition of new computers to the network, and the addition of new services (such as e-mail or Internet access). These problems must be dealt with directly and may require the addition of a bridge, a router, or a cable upgrade.

A *broadcast storm* is an event in which one or more network devices sends a constant stream of data, effectively creating an informational traffic jam by using up close to 100% of the bandwidth. The most common causes of a broadcast storm are:

- a bad NIC
- a downed server

In the case of a bad NIC, you must narrow down the problem to a single machine. (You can do this through software or process of elimination.) Before replacing the NIC, shut down the offending computer and restart. If the problem persists, you will need to replace the network card immediately.

In the case of a downed server, the broadcast storm may be caused by another machine attempting to communicate with the server and sending requests to it as frequently as once every millisecond. You should reboot or shut down the offending machine.

Network Interruptions

Network interruptions that can potentially disable a network may be caused by:

- downed or malfunctioning servers
- power fluctuations
- network architecture (bus topology)

Downed servers in a server-based network will be unable to provide essential services such as printing, etc. The server in a server-based network should be using a UPS (uninterruptible power supply) to prevent power fluctuations from disabling the network.

SEE ALSO   For more information on protecting computers against power problems, see Chapter 3, "Safety and Preventive Maintenance."

Networks using the bus topology are vulnerable to cable breaks, which will disable the entire network. Many hybrid networks use a bus section to join other network segments. Something as simple as a loose cable in a hub may disconnect a large number of users.

Exam Essentials

Know what circumstances can lead to bandwidth problems. Broadcast storms (caused by bad NICs or downed servers), poorly-timed network backups, changes in network services or usage-level for network services, and the addition of new workstations can lead to bandwidth problems.

Know what circumstances can lead to network interruptions. Power fluctuations and the bus topology network structure can lead to network interruptions.

Key Terms and Concepts

Bandwidth: A term commonly used to refer to the volume of data that a hardware medium can transmit at one time.

Broadcast storm: A situation in which one or more devices transmit a constant stream of data onto a network, using up close to 100% of the bandwidth.

Sample Questions

1. A broadcast storm may be caused by:

   A. Low utilization of bandwidth

   B. A power fluctuation

   C. A network backup

   D. A downed server

   Answer: D. A broadcast storm is usually caused by a bad NIC or a downed server.

2. A cable break in a network using a star topology may result in:

   A. One workstation unable to print

   B. Several workstations unable to print

   C. A disabled network

   D. No effect

   Answer: A. Star topologies are highly fault-tolerant. Each cable connects only one workstation to the hub.

CHAPTER

8

Customer Satisfaction

A+ Core Module Exam Objectives Covered in This Chapter:

▶ **Differentiate effective from ineffective behaviors as these contribute to the maintenance or achievement of customer satisfaction.** *(pages 302 – 309)*

Customer satisfaction is the result of good customer service. Most service professionals know better than to make the customer angry, and many of them already have what it takes to practice good customer service.

So why is it important to address this topic, and why is it covered on the exam? The knowledge and skills that define good customer service do not come naturally to most people; they are not inborn, but must be studied and practiced. In the service industry, the level of standards has increased to the point where competition can break a business, even though that business may be providing good service. Customers know the difference between good and excellent customer service practices, and to be competitive, so should you.

▶ # Differentiate effective from ineffective behaviors as these contribute to the maintenance or achievement of customer satisfaction.

A customer can be anyone from a coworker to a large corporation. Common sense tells us that practicing good customer service helps businesses make a profit. Customer service is also an opportunity to improve business relations through solutions.

This chapter will focus on two areas: communication and quality of service. The Customer Satisfaction section of the exam is optional, and you will not be graded on the results. However, it is important material, and by establishing your own standards for customer satisfaction, you can gain more control over personal job satisfaction.

Critical Information

Studies have shown that customers who are unhappy with the service they receive will tell eleven people; customers who are happy with the service they receive will tell only four. In other words, almost three times as many potential customers will hear about your bad service as will hear about your good service.

This fact has far-reaching implications, and has deep personal as well as economic impact. It also means you had better know your customer.

Who Is the Customer?

A customer is anyone who buys goods or services. However, a broader definition, when applied creatively by a service professional, can promote better communication and a more supportive atmosphere. Banks, for instance, started handing out suckers years ago to the children of people who do business with them. In placating bored or crying children, they treated not just the parents but the whole family as customers.

Your customer's first impression of you will be the longest lasting, so, of course, you will always want to make a good first impression. Once a bad impression is made, it is almost impossible to recover fully.

Even though customers formulate their impressions of you based on initial contact, you must be careful to withhold your impression of the customer. Why withhold it? Because a preconception formed during the initial contact is often a MISconception.

Good Communication

Before you can meet a customer's needs, you must discern those needs. How do you determine a customer's needs? You need to ask—it's as simple as that! However, even this simple aspect of a service call presents a few pitfalls. Listed below are some tips on avoiding common mistakes that hinder good communication.

- **Listen.** Active listening is much harder than you think. The customer should be allowed to finish speaking. Try not to form your response before the customer has finished speaking (that means you're not listening).

- **Paraphrase.** Once the customer has spoken, repeat back to them the information they just gave you. "Let me repeat what you just said so I can make sure that I'm understanding you correctly." Then say it back.

- **Speak slowly and calmly.** People unconsciously try to match their rate of speech with that of the person with whom they are speaking. A customer who is under pressure may speak faster and with a higher pitch, so slowing down your speech should have a calming effect. If this fails, ask them to speak more slowly.

- **Document.** When you are gathering information in person or over the telephone, indicate to the customer that you will need to write the information down. (You should not try to write as the customer is speaking; you're likely to make a mistake or miss important information.) Most tech service companies have a standard form for their personnel to fill out to help them collect complete information.

- **Ask questions.** Whenever a customer provides information in the form of a general statement, they haven't provided you with enough information. You may need to pry the facts out of them. Example:

   "My printer doesn't work!"

   "Can you give me a better idea of what exactly isn't working? For instance, is there a problem getting the printer turned on, or is it having trouble printing?"

- **Don't interrupt.** Wait for a customer to finish speaking before offering a solution or asking additional questions. NEVER interrupt someone while they are describing a problem. They could interpret that action as rude and decide that you have a "know-it-all" attitude.

- **Avoid predictive statements.** When you're asked, "What's wrong with it?" keep your theories to yourself. Otherwise, they'll be checking YOU out, and you'll have to prove you're right. To answer their question, say, "I need more information."

Quality of Service

Quality of service may be described as either bad or good. Of course, there are many other words that could be used to describe service (no doubt about that!), but these two will serve as basic models.

Providing Bad Service

Many customers will not tell you when they have received bad service. Instead, they will tell others. A service professional would not intentionally provide bad service, but often it happens unknowingly. Ascertaining precisely what a customer's expectations are can be very difficult.

For those customers who complain about your service to everybody else except you, there is a special tool you can use to turn the complaint to your advantage. It's called follow-up. One primary purpose of follow-up is to reduce the flow of negative information. Another is quality control. Yet another reason to follow up is that it indicates to the customer that they are important to you and your company.

Customer complaints will usually come as no surprise. Sometimes things don't go as smoothly as you would have liked with a customer. When this happens, whether or not you think the customer will complain, tell your supervisor or manager about it. That way, if a complaint does result, the manager or supervisor is prepared to handle the situation and can have a solution ready for the customer.

Handling Conflicts   If the customer becomes angry, stay focused on the problem and try to brainstorm with that customer for a solution the customer can agree with. Avoid using the words "you" and "I" in the conversation, because in a situation that involves anger, these words can become the verbal equivalent of pointing your finger and assigning blame.

You will also come across situations where there is just no pleasing the customer. This could be due to a conflict in personalities, and it might be time to ask another service professional to service this customer.

A skilled and educated service professional seeks a win/win solution (a solution where both the customer and the service professional win) every time. Sometimes, a little creative thought may yield a solution to a seemingly unresolvable problem.

Providing Good Service

Companies that practice good service have standards, written or unwritten, that they adhere to. These standards could be based on an industry code of ethics, certifications, company policies, corporate culture, any combination of these things, and more. The service professional who practices and provides good service understands the importance of all of the following:

- smiling, having a positive attitude

- anticipating problems that could arise

- focusing on the solution and not the problem

- using (and remembering) the customer's name

- always answering the telephone in a calm manner and friendly tone of voice (no matter what)

- leaving a business card with the customer every time

- using checklists to make certain nothing is forgotten

- respecting the customer's opinions, values, time

- bringing more parts and tools to the customer's site than what is needed

- avoiding jargon (industry terminology) that the customer won't understand

- being on time

- following up with the customer

- teaching the customer so he or she can help themselves

- keeping up to date on the latest information

- using knowledge for solutions rather than power

- never disclosing a negative opinion about your competition or another customer

- saying thank you

The whole reason to provide good customer service is to keep the customer coming back for more products and services. This does not mean you should fix their computer so that it will break down in three months and they will have to return for you to fix it again. It *does* mean you should fix it once so that that problem doesn't recur. Then, if the customer has a different problem, they won't hesitate to bring it to your company.

Customers who receive good service will call again. They may recommend you or your company, and you will eventually hear about it. Sometimes customers will write letters complimenting your work. Some will even express their appreciation with a gift. Even if you were only their hero/heroine for an hour, that is all it takes to make the job worthwhile. The more genuine your desire is to provide good service, the easier your job becomes.

Exam Essentials

As mentioned at the beginning of the chapter, the Customer Satisfaction objective is optional, and will not be figured into your score.

Know the guidelines for good communication with customers. Guidelines for good communication with customers include listening, paraphrasing, speaking slowly and clearly, documenting problems, asking questions, not interrupting, and avoiding predictive statements.

Know what to do in the event of a service problem. Following up with a customer who makes indirect complaints can defuse negative reports. Inform your supervisor if you have had problems with a customer while on a service call.

Know how to handle conflicts. Avoid "you" and "I" statements during arguments, as they imply blame. If personality clashes are unavoidable, you may have to ask another service professional to take over.

Know the indicators for good service. For a list of these indicators, see the Critical Information section. Many of the customer service questions on the test involve these good service indicators.

Key Terms and Concepts

Jargon: Nonstandard terms and phrases specific to a particular field or subject.

Paraphrasing: A technique of good communication in which you repeat back to a customer what they have just told you.

Win/win solution: A desirable solution in which both the customer and the service professional benefit.

Sample Questions

1. If you're on a service call and several of the office employees are crowding around a TV in the lunchroom watching a breaking news story, you should:

   A. Develop camaraderie by staying and watching the news with them.

   B. Make a few jokes about their work habits, then get to work.

   C. Inquire briefly as to the nature of the news, then get to work.

   D. Inform their supervisor.

Answer: C. As you're being paid for your visit, this answer best reflects your respect for their time and values. Answers A and B are inappropriate and could be offensive.

2. If you are attempting to fix a computer by replacing a bad hard disk drive and a customer asks what caused the problem, you should:

    A. Give an in-depth explanation of the hard disk drive problem, using technical terms and jargon.

    B. Tell them you're still gathering information.

    C. Tell them it's very complicated, then change the subject.

    D. Explain the problem briefly in simple terms.

    Answer: D. Avoid the use of highly technical terms and jargon when giving explanations. "B" would be a good answer only during the diagnosis phase of the repair.

Index

Note to the Reader: First level entries are in **bold**. Page numbers in **bold** indicate the principal discussion of a topic or the definition of a term. Page numbers in *italic* indicate illustrations.

M

UTP (unshielded twisted-pair) cables, 284
upgrading PROM (programmable ROM),
  87, 89
upper memory, 91, 91
upper memory blocks (UMBs), 101
user errors, 127–128

V

vertical black lines on laser printouts, 242
vertical white lines on laser printouts,
  242–243
VESA local bus (VL bus), 194–196, *195, 196,*
  200, 203
VGA monitors, 69–70, 76
video cards, 69, 71
video technologies, 69–70
volatile memory, 209
voltage
    measuring, 83, *83*
    of power supplies, 122
volts, 85
VRAM (video RAM), 177

W

wait states, 162, 174, 178
WANs (wide area networks), 272, *272,* 291
Web sites about computer recycling, *150*
white lines on laser printouts, 242–243
win/win solutions, 306, 308
Windows RAM (WRAM), 177
wireless networks, 286
workgroup networks, 274–275, *275*
workstations, 273–274
writing step in HP LaserJet printers, 228

Z

ZIF (zero-insertion force) sockets, 172

Boost Your Career with Certification

Detailed information on more than 70 computer and network certification programs, including:

- Computer hardware
- Operating systems
- Software
- Networking hardware
- Network operating systems
- Internet
- Instructor and trainer certifications

COMPUTER AND NETWORK PROFESSIONAL'S CERTIFICATION GUIDE

J. SCOTT CHRISTIANSON
AVA FAJEN

COVERS THE FULL RANGE OF COMPUTER AND NETWORKING CERTIFICATIONS

LEARN WHICH CERTIFICATIONS WILL ADVANCE YOUR CAREER

DEMONSTRATE YOUR SKILLS BY MAXIMIZING YOUR CREDENTIALS

ISBN: 0-7821-2260-4
512 pp; 5 7/8 x 8 1/4; Softcover
$19.99

Learn why to get certified, when to get certified, and how to get certified.

MCSE ELECTIVE STUDY GUIDES FROM NETWORK PRESS®

Sybex's Network Press expands the definitive study guide series for MCSE candidates.

ISBN: 0-7821-2224-8
688pp; 7¹/₂" x 9"; Hardcover
$49.99

ISBN: 0-7821-2261-2
848pp; 7¹/₂" x 9"; Hardcover
$49.99

ISBN: 0-7821-2248-5
704pp; 7¹/₂" x 9"; Hardcover
$49.99

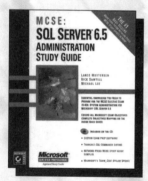

ISBN: 0-7821-2172-1
672pp; 7¹/₂" x 9"; Hardcover
$49.99

ISBN: 0-7821-2194-2
576pp; 7¹/₂" x 9"; Hardcover
$49.99

ISBN: 0-7821-1967-0
656pp; 7¹/₂" x 9"; Hardcover
$49.99

STUDY GUIDES FOR THE MICROSOFT CERTIFIED SYSTEMS ENGINEER EXAMS

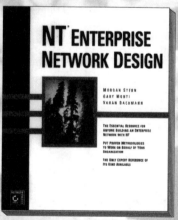

CNA AND CNE GUIDES FROM
NETWORK PRESS®

NETWORK PRESS®
SYBEX®

www.sybex.com